Europe at the Seaside

Published in association with
Institute for Corporate Culture Affairs (ICCA)

Europe at the Seaside

The Economic History of Mass Tourism in the Mediterranean

Edited by

Luciano Segreto, Carles Manera,
and
Manfred Pohl

Berghahn Books
NEW YORK • OXFORD

Published in 2009 by
Berghahn Books

www.berghahnbooks.com

Library of Congress Cataloging-in-Publication Data

Europe at the seaside : the economic history of mass tourism in the Mediterranean / edited by Luciano Segreto, Carles Manera, and Manfred Pohl.
p. cm.
Includes bibliographical references and index.
ISBN 978-1-84545-323-7 (alk. paper)
1. Tourism—Mediterranean Region—History. 2. Package tours—Mediterranean Region—History. 3. Cruise lines—Mediterranean Region—History. 4. Seaside resorts—Mediterranean Region—History. I. Segreto, Luciano. II. Manera, Carles, 1957–. III. Pohl, Manfred, 1944-.

G155.M46.E87 2009
338.4'791091822—dc22

2008053758

British Library Cataloguing in Publication Data

A catalogue record for this book is available from
the British Library.

Printed in the United States on acid-free paper

Contents

Illustrations

Tables

Figures

Foreword

The original idea for an economic history of mass tourism in the Mediterranean came from Professor Carlos Manera and Professor Luciano Segreto. The time seemed ripe for an exploration into what has become the world's biggest industry – the tourism industry. A conference was organized at the University of Mallorca with contributions from leading academics in the field of European tourism and mass travel. The results of this conference have now been collated in this volume to be published together for the first time. The book is ultimately intended to constitute the definitive guide to the academic study of tourism in this field.

The ICCA would like to thank all participating authors as well as all those who contributed toward the realization of this project – in particular, Contessa Roberts as well as Sonja Haxel, Sandra Cabboi, and Nicola McClellan. We greatly appreciate your time and commitment. We would also like to thank all those involved, both our members and our partners, who have helped or supported the publication of this book. We would especially like to thank the University of Mallorca, whose steadfast support of this project has made this publication possible.

We trust that you will find *Europe at the Seaside* a useful reference guide and welcome your feedback at n.tolhurst@cca-institute.org.

May 2009
Frankfurt am Main

ICCA Editorial Board

Introduction

The Mediterranean as a Tourist Destination

Past, Present, and Future of the First Mass Tourism Resort Area

Carles Manera, Luciano Segreto, and Manfred Pohl

The history of tourism has become an increasingly popular research topic in recent years as books on tourism and especially its importance in shaping modern societies have gained wider interest among both academics and the wider reading public. Whereas early research naturally dealt with the fascinating, but also rather elitist, eighteenth-century concept of the "Grand Tour," and those tours that followed in the nineteenth century,[1] recent studies in tourism have moved to the history of mass tourism, a phenomenon deeply rooted in the twentieth century and the "era of the masses" and democratic society. The beginnings of mass tourism can be found in the first appearance of seaside resorts in France and England, a process linked with the development of public transport systems and efficient (and cheap) railway networks, which linked the industrial towns and capitals to the beaches. Economic development and new industrial relations, as well as new types of contract for manual and white-collar workers, which included holidays, encouraged the growth of this process in the early years of the twentieth century. However, other more socio-cultural factors, such as new attitudes toward and increased interest in sport and fitness, played a decisive role in encouraging more people to use their vacations as a time to discover the seaside and to relax and enjoy the sunshine and all the other amenities of seaside resorts.[2]

Notes for this section begin on page 9.

Recent years have seen a mushrooming of research into the history of tourism conducted by social, cultural, and economic historians, sociologists, economists, and environmental scholars.[3] In 2003 the International Commission for History of Travel and Tourism was established, which has enabled the exchange of ideas on related topics by means of "H-Travel," a network for the academic discussion of the history of travel and tourism.

Most books on the history of tourism agree on the leading role of the Mediterranean area as the first mass tourism destination area. Today this region is made up of twenty-two countries, whose common characteristic is their border with the Mare Nostrum. Nevertheless, given this historical reality, surprisingly few studies have been made of the Mediterranean region as a whole as a tourist destination, although separate analyses have been made of its sun and sand destinations. This absence of general studies of an area of such crucial importance in terms of economics of tourism can perhaps be explained by the lack of statistics. The aim of this book is to fill this gap by introducing readers to the history of mass tourism in the Mediterranean region over the last fifty years. This collection of essays, originally presented in February 2003 at the Palma de Mallorca conference on The Economic History of Mass Tourism in the Mediterranean after World War II, aims to offer a better understanding of the region's general economic and social networks involved in this phenomenon over the last fifty years; to examine the most popular tourist destinations, with special attention to the north Mediterranean coast; and to highlight some of the crucial actors in the process of development, such as hotel entrepreneurs, companies developing a network of seaside resorts, travel agencies, charter companies, and so on. This project has been the result of a long-term scientific and cultural cooperation between the University of the Balearic Islands and the University of Florence, with the organizational and scientific support of the Institute for Corporate Culture Affairs (ICCA), a leading international institution, well known for its dissemination of research into business history and business culture among both the academic and business communities. The project is also grateful for the generous support of the Government of the Balearic Islands.

The Macroeconomic Image of the Mediterranean Area: A Changing Kaleidoscopic World

Few areas of the world have changed so much over the centuries as the Mediterranean. Throughout its history, its population growth has fluctuated, with an uneven distribution that has depended on the prevailing subsistence model adopted by its inhabitants at given moments in history. Nonetheless, with the passing of the centuries the population has greatly increased, leading to the creation of a strong network of cities stretching from the coast to the remotest corners in far-flung valleys and mountains. Given the Mediterranean's fragmented geography, different cultural groups have emerged.[4] For millennia, these cultures have taken advantage of the relative ease of maritime communication, leading to the creation of a common fund of cultural, religious, and symbolic elements, and shared behavior patterns in relation to the environment. Through agricultural activities and livestock farming in areas that were barely suitable for human occupation (given the lack of water resources, shallow soil prone to erosion by torrential rain, and the predominance of slow-growing vegetation), a fragile balance was maintained between man and nature that lasted for centuries. This balance is now being threatened by the unprecedented urban growth of the last four decades.

At the beginning of the 1880s, no Mediterranean city's population reached one million inhabitants. Istanbul, which was the capital of the Ottoman Empire, was closest with 875,000 inhabitants, followed by Naples (475,000), Madrid (400,000), Lisbon (300,000), Rome (275,000), and Barcelona (250,000). Just over a century later, fourteen cities in the Mediterranean have over one million inhabitants, one-third of the world's tourists come to the region (about 228 million tourists visit the Mediterranean coast annually) and, in the countries that border its shores, over 4,500 sq. km are occupied by tourist accommodation facilities and associated infrastructure. These figures highlight the incredible development that has occurred in the Mediterranean in a relatively short space of time, because the phenomenon only dates back to the tourist boom of the 1950s.[5]

Initially, cities grew by expanding into areas that adjoined the existing early twentieth-century nuclei, which had been created by industrial development. But during the post-war European reconstruction, including the increased income of the European population, the massive use of individual means of transport (which dramatically changed the population's mobility patterns), and the social organization of work (with paid holidays and increased leisure time), transformed the concept of rest into a new activity, as well as generating a different type of urban development. New coastal and inland areas were colonized as the industrial economies of Europe grew due to domestic migration. At first, this led to isolated building developments, scattered here and there, comprising separate dwellings, second homes, and tourist or hotel complexes. Over the years though, these areas have become denser, forming the tourist resorts, particularly along the coast. This process, which was first identified in the late nineteenth century in Liguria (the Riviera), in Provence, and especially in the Côte d'Azur, speeded up in the 1950s, with mass tourism initially making an appearance on the Catalan coast (the Costa Brava) and later in Greece and the Balearics (Mallorca), before extending along the Spanish Mediterranean coast, the Italian Adriatic, and finally some areas of northern Africa (Tunisia, Morocco).[6]

It is nothing new to say that the Mediterranean Basin is the world's leading tourist destinations. The figures say it all. With revenue from tourism of US$134 billion a year (28 percent of the world's tourist expenditure), a large part of the economic activity of the Mediterranean region is based on tourism services, with important repercussions: annually, tourism expenditure in these countries accounts for about 3.7 percent of the GDP (data for 2002). There can be little debate, however, about the variety of tourism. From traditional sun and sand destinations (Spain, Turkey, and Tunisia) to those with a high cultural and heritage-based (France and Italy, but above all Greece), the coastlines that are mainly visited for vacation or leisure purposes, even if other incentives are gradually gaining ground, such as health tourism or travel for professional or business purposes, thereby helping to diversify destinations and customer profiles. Europeans are the most frequent visitors (accounting for 9 out of every 10 tourists), with the Americans lagging far behind (less than 5 percent of all travelers). More recently, a boom in tourism from the Middle East and Southeast Asia has been detected, with a market share that doubled between 1987 and 2002.[7] The strength of this historic sea's tourist industry cannot be denied. Today, the Mediterranean offers a total of seven million tourist beds in accommodation centers mainly concentrated in France, Spain, and Italy (which have two out of every three beds). Despite this remarkable vigor, a number of factors seem to indicate changes for the future.

As an international tourist destination, the Mediterranean is without doubt starting to lose ground. Although the number of visitors to the Mediterranean grew from 130 million in 1987 to 228 million in 2002 (an increase of 76 percent), it is also equally true that the area's market share has been falling. In fact, over the same period of time, the global number of tourists throughout the world rose by 95 percent. In other words, although in 1987 36 percent of all recorded tourists chose the Mediterranean as a destination, this proportion had dropped to 32 percent by 2002. The most crucial variable is also of concern: tourist expenditure in the Mediterranean has remained stable, with a slight downward trend. At the same time, there has been a change in the composition of tourism issuing markets to the Mediterranean. Tourism from traditional issuing markets (Europe and America) has slowed, given the almost stagnant trend in international tourist travel, and the market share of both has fallen in comparison with new Middle Eastern and Southeast Asian markets. Within the context of rising tourist numbers – up by 95 percent – European and American visitors to the Mediterranean rose by 37 percent and 22 percent respectively, whereas visitors from the Middle East and Southeast Asia went up by 136 percent and 115 percent, respectively. This indicates the existence of potential new customers.[8]

A change can also be observed in European tourists' choice of destination. European tourists, the Mediterranean's main market, are tending to opt for different Mediterranean tourist centers from the resorts that spearheaded the process of tourism development in France, Spain, and Italy. In the span of just a few years, the number of European visitors to other countries in the Mediterranean has doubled: 23 million tourists visited other nations in 1987; by 2002 the figure had gone up to 47 million. A clear change in their choice of tourist destination is evident, as in 2002 the Mediterranean received 98 million more tourists than in 1987. France, Spain, and Italy accounted for a large part of these new customers (69 million), but they were also shared by Turkey, Greece, Egypt, and Tunisia. As a result, the three leaders experienced a slight drop in their market share, falling from 77 percent of all tourists to the Mediterranean (1987) to 74 percent (2002). These figures affect another key vector – investment – as a slower rise in the number of tourist beds in traditional destinations can be observed as opposed to a clear rise in emerging destinations. The slower growth of the three big traditional destinations (France, Spain, and Italy) has been reflected by private investment in fixed tourism assets. Throughout the Mediterranean region, there has been an increase in tourist accommodation (measured in terms of tourist beds) of 1.8 million new beds (a growth of 37 percent). However, while in France, Spain, and Italy accommodation rose by only 22 percent, in other Mediterranean countries there was an 81 percent rise.

Mass tourism is gaining in importance from a macroeconomic perspective, but its heavy environmental impact is also on the increase. In 1987, tourist expenditure accounted for 2.2 percent of the GDP, rising to 3.7 percent by 2002 (an increase of 67 percent). This aggregate figure is highly significant, but a breakdown can be even more revealing. In 1987, only seven countries in the Mediterranean had a level of tourist expenditure that accounted for over 5 percent of their respective incomes. In 2002, there were twelve countries in this position. In fact, in the case of Albania, Algeria, Bosnia-Herzegovina, Syria, and Croatia, the impact of tourist expenditure on their GDPs has risen dramatically. In contrast, France, Spain, and Italy have experienced more moderate growth. The same trend is repeated for tourism's environmental externalities, which have gradually extended along the Mediterranean coast. Between 1987 and 2002, the number of tourist stays per sq. km of land doubled. As a result, twelve Mediterranean countries now exceed the average Mediterranean figure of 158 tourist stays. This variable clearly indicates that some areas have reached their saturation point. The real estate sector and, above all, the building industry have benefited from the urgent need for new infrastructure, with relatively rapid recovery of the initial investment.[9]

Old and New Actors for a Successful Story

The macroeconomic approach does not explain everything. The tangible success of any area in the Mediterranean Basin has been the result of a series of variables and the interaction of multiple actors, such as entrepreneurs, hotel groups, international travel agencies, specialized and non specialized workers, local, regional, and national governments. The approach proposed in the chapters that follow takes into account all the possible variables to be considered in this context. The chapters include national studies on Greece (by Margarita Dritsas) and Portugal (by Benedita Câmara); individual geographic area studies, which have been the most successful in mass tourism in recent years, such as the Costa del Sol, whose development is studied by Carmelo Pellejero Martínez, and the Balearic Islands in Spain presented by Carles Manera and Jaume Garau-Taberner; contributions by Philippe Mioche on the French Riviera, and by Patrizia Battilani on Rimini, the most famous tourism area in Italy on the Adriatic coast, which are considered to be the first places to experience the arrival of the tourist industry.

Other chapters deal with individual business actors. Peter Lyth presents a study on the airline companies that started the charter system, which is so crucial for mass tourism; Ellen Furlough analyzes what is probably the most famous tourism group, the Club Méditerranée, and Hubert Bonin investigates a French group, Accor, and its traditional difficulties in shifting from the business customer sector to tourism. Family firms are the core of two other contributions, highlighting Majorcan hotel entrepreneurs (Antoni Serra) and the leading Italian group Alpitour (Luciano Segreto).

The different case studies make it clear that tourism does not differ markedly from other economic sectors. Each nation's "imprint" is quite evident and throws light on new aspects of the discussion about the differences in the history of economic development in Europe. Entrepreneurial capabilities and styles emerge as key factors in understanding – more than the success of a single country or a single area (which in part has to do with specific local geographical distribution of resources) – the long-term performance of the main actors.

The business history approach throws new light on understanding successful as well as unsuccessful stories, and the history of this sector is full of both. Travel agencies, hotel, and tourism groups reproduce, with a few differences, the national business models:[10] the large and managerial enterprise with its large bureaucratic and strong financial structure in France (where families nevertheless play an important role, interacting in a more or less informal way with financial institutions, as the recent developments in the Accor Group management structure seem to show),[11] the United Kingdom, and Germany;

the family business with its limits – but also with its extreme flexibility and creativity – in Southern Europe, especially in Italy and Greece, while in Spain the emergence of medium size or even large groups is, in some cases, one of the main characteristics even in this sector of the modernization process, which has taken place in this country in the last two decades.

For a long time, in the pioneer era, during the major upsurge of mass tourism in Europe, family firms were dominant everywhere. The tourist appreciated the modest but warm approach of the family running the hotel or the resort (whose structure was most probably very Spartan so that to speak of them as authentic resorts does not appear to be a very suitable expression). Then the tour operators, the charter flight companies, the travel agencies multiplied their efforts, following the increase in the standard of living in Western European societies. This engendered different responses in the Mediterranean area, where the entrepreneurial culture, if it existed, was different compared to the rest of Western Europe. Mass tourism and its increasing demand for better quality and cheaper prices played a crucial role in changing the mentality of the social and economic actors in this sector. Some countries or areas went directly to the core problem of the tourism structure (the hotels and resorts, the beaches, the infrastructures, etc.), trying to cope with the new demands and styles of mass tourism; others ignored these factors, and tried to multiply and diversify what they were offering outside the traditional structures, which remained more or less the same.

The Spanish case and, to some extent in more recent years, the Portuguese and the Greek, belong to the first category. A huge effort has been made in the infrastructure of these countries, under the pressure of the big international tour operators and with the use of EU regional funds.[12] This policy has also permitted the emergence of important local groups that have been able to interact with the big European tour operators. The Italian case shows different patterns. In the Peninsula the logic and the culture of family business still dominate. Few groups have emerged as national or international actors, and when they did so, they remained in a relatively secondary position in their relationships with the big names in the European sector, especially those located in Germany and in the United Kingdom. Vacations are a framework in which seaside activities are just a part (and a decreasing part at that) of the time devoted to relaxation; increasing priority is given to dance halls, night clubs, water parks and many other attractions, as well as activities like gymnastics, karaoke, and so on. The Italian beaches are less popular with foreign tourists, although they are, with some difficulty, resisting this trend in terms of the home market. Foreign tourists tend to associate Italy more and more with culture and towns of art and historical importance (Rome, Florence, Venice, etc.), reducing Italy's importance as a traditional summer destination, which can also be explained by the relatively expensive cost of spending a vacation, compared with many other destinations in the Mediterranean.[13]

Another element directly connected with the emergence of mass tourism is, in a way, its opposite: elite tourism. The diversification of the offer and the competition of more exotic places outside the Mediterranean Basin have contributed to readdressing part of the tourism structures and flows in this direction, with remarkable success in many cases. But elite tourism has partly lost its original meaning, because investment in luxury structures and resorts is not the only way to transform tourism.

Not Only Mass Tourism: The Environment Issue

The environmental question, as a crucial element for many people when they have to evaluate and compare one vacation destination with another, has contributed to a massive change in the priorities and thus the structure of the costs in the tourism industry.[14] The emergence of the environmental question in the tourism industry has reinforced the need for strict coordination between different levels of responsibility: the local and national governments, the entrepreneurial associations and pressure groups of the tourism sector, the ethics of all the actors working in this industry, and also of any person connected to an economic or an industrial activity in tourism areas. In fact, the coexistence of different sectors is partly the historical result of the economic development of the Mediterranean countries. Today it may become the basis for a more balanced growth, but also a new source of major conflicts of interest, which urgently require political decisions. Environmental and tourism policies are not at the top of the political agenda of national governments in Southern Europe. The situation is slightly better where local or regional governments have more power to intervene directly in such issues. For many years some of them appear to have been extremely interested in modernizing their tourism policies while respecting the environment. In many areas of the north basin of the Mediterranean Sea, and especially the islands, most of these institutions have worked together coherently and successfully to offer new areas of discussion with all the political, economic, and scientific actors involved in the tourism industry.

In order to counterbalance this attitude, one should also consider that in such cases it is also relatively more difficult to maintain the objectivity and independence of the local, sometimes very powerful, pressure groups, both in tourism and other sectors. In other cases, like in Sardinia, the offensive of the local government for sustainable tourism led to new taxes on luxury tourism, opening the door to a new political conflict, possibly leading to domestic tourism competition in Italy between tourist regions led by center-right or center-left regional governments.[15] Local governments, politicians at national level, opinion leaders, and even, to a certain extent, "jet-set" people, all seem to be interested in discussing the uses and abuses of mass and deluxe tourism in the Mediterranean area. Most of them do not have a clear understanding of the complex impact of tourism on those regions, nevertheless insisting on the positive role it is playing in economic development. Only a long-term perspective can ensure that decisions about tourism will not be the ephemeral result of partial approaches, dependant on the distorted use – and abuse – of economic data that in this sector are so difficult to accumulate, and very easy to manipulate. The approach to the history of mass tourism in the Mediterranean area over the last years proposed by this book might possibly offer some suggestions aimed at creating a more consensual evaluation of the vision necessary to develop a tourism policy with a good balance among mass tourism, environmental preservation, economic development, and sustainability.

Notes

1. W.K. Ritichie, *The Eighteenth Century Grand Tour* (London: Longman, 1972); C. Hibbert, *The Grand Tour* (London: Metheun, 1987); *Grand Tour: adeliges Reisen und europäische Kultur vom 14. bis zum 18. Jahrhundert*, Akten der internationalen Kolloquien in der Villa Vigoni 1999 und im Deutschen Historischen Institut Paris 2000, herausgegeben von Rainer Babel und Werner Paravicini, Ostfildern, Thorbecke, 2005; A. Brilli, *Il viaggio in Italia: storia di una grande tradizione culturale* (Bologna: il Mulino, 2006).
2. P. Battilani, *Vacanze di pochi, vacanze di tutti. L'evoluzione del turismo europeo* (Bologna: il Mulino, 2001).
3. L. Tissot, *Development of a Tourist Industry in the 19th and 20th Centuries: International Perspectives* (Alphil, Neuchâtel, 2001); J. Mak, *Tourism and the Economy: Understanding the Economics of Tourism* (Honolulu: University of Hawaii Press, 2004); D. McLaren, *Rethinking Tourism and Ecotravel,* 2nd ed. (Bloomfield, CT: Kumarian Press, 2003). McLaren's book was first published in 1998 under the title *Rethinking Travelling and Ecotourism: The Paving of Paradise and What You Can Do to Stop It.*
4. F. Braudel, *La Méditerranée et le monde méditerranéen a l'époque de Philippe 2* (Paris: Colin, 1966); D. Abufalia, *The Mediterranean in History* (Cambridge: Cambridge University Press, 2003).
5. Y. Apostolopoulos, P. Loukissas, and L. Leontidou, *Mediterranean Tourism. Facets in Socioeconomic Development and Cultural Change* (London: Routledge, 2001). For a general view of the economic growth in that area, see N. Crafts and G. Toniolo, eds., *Economic Growth in Europe since 1945* (Cambridge: Cambridge University

Press, 1996); and P. Rhode and G. Toniolo, eds., *The Global Economy in the 1990s. A Long-Run Perspective* (Cambridge: Cambridge University Press, 2006).

6. A.M. Williams and G. Shaw, eds., *Tourism and Economic Development: Western European Experiences* (London: Belhaven, 1991).
7. C.S. Aron, *Working at Play: A History of the Vacations in the United States* (New York: Oxford University Press, 1999); S. Baranowski and E. Furlough, *Being Elsewhere: Tourism, Consumer Culture, and Identity in Modern Europe and North America* (Ann Arbor: University of Michigan Press, 2001); C. Manera and J. Garau, "Il turismo di massa nel Mediterraneo (1987–2002): un'opportunità di crescita," *Economia Marche* 1 (2006).
8. J. Alegre and L. Pou, "The Determinants of Probability of Tourism Consumption: An Analysis with a Family Expenditure Survey," Departament d'Economia Aplicada Working Papers no. 39, Universitat de les Illes Balears; T. Toivonen, "Changes in the Propensity to Take Holiday Trips Abroad in EU Countries between 1985 and 1997," *Tourism Economics* 10, no. 4 (2004).
9. M.T. Sinclair and M. Stabler, *The Economics of Tourism* (London and New York: Routledge, 1997).
10. R. Whittington and M. Mayer, *The European Corporation: Strategy, Structure and Social Science* (Oxford: Oxford University Press, 2000); A. Colli, *The History of Family Business, 1850–2000* (Cambridge: Cambridge University Press, 2003); T. Clarke and J.F. Chanlat, *European Corporate Governance* (London: Routledge, 2006).
11. M. Jasor, "Succession chez Accor: une série de faux pas," *Le Monde*, 14–15 October 2005.
12. H.W. Armstrong, *EC Regional Policy*, in *The Economics of the European Community*, ed. A. M. El-Agraa (London: Harvester Wheatsheaf, 1994).
13. "Turismo senza timoniere," *Corriere Economia*, 14 February 2005.
14. At an international level, "sustainable tourism" has become one of the most discussed issues over a number of years. The high-level meetings on tourism took place at the Commission on Sustainable Development in 1999 and the Convention on Biological Diversity in 2000. See http://www.wwf.org.uk/filelibrary/pdf/wwf_tourism_backgrounder_2001.pdf, as well as the United Nations Environment Programme Production and Consumption Branch site at http://www.uneptie.org/pc/tourism/home.htm.
15. The center-left Sardinian regional government, led by the Internet entrepreneur Renato Soru (the founder of the Tiscali company), introduced a tax on luxury boats harbored in the island's ports in the spring of 2006, and reduced the number of planning permits to build new second houses along the coasts of the island by a large margin. In late summer of 2006 the center-right Veneto regional government launched a major press campaign suggesting that all the boats taxed in Sardinian harbors would not pay anything if they sailed to Veneto.

Chapter 1

Flying Visits

The Growth of British Air Package Tours, 1945–1975

Peter Lyth

> Do you remember the magic carpet of the fairy-tales? Silently, swiftly, effortlessly it floated its passengers to their destination. Perhaps you have wished for just such a magic carpet to take you to the holiday places you long to visit.... well, this booklet contains the answer ... the magnificent air fleet of BEA can carry you to the holiday country of your choice with ease, comfort and speed.
>
> – *The Best Holiday of Your Life*, British European Airways (BEA), brochure publicity, 1957

Two closely interwoven threads in the economic and social fabric of the twentieth century are the development of the international tourist industry and the growth of commercial air transport. As international tourism became the largest single industry in the world, so air travel became popular and "democratized," with the tourist replacing the businessman as the typical passenger.[1] In *economic* terms, the trend was an important part of the shift in employment and investment from manufacturing to the service sector; as a *social* change it is comparable to the effect in Britain of the railways on Victorian society. Air transport caused a revolution in the use of leisure time. Combined with rising levels of disposable income and a breakthrough in technology, it allowed workers of the cold and industrialized nations of northern Europe (and North America) to travel south, for vacations of "sun, sea and sand."

Notes for this chapter begin on page 28.

This chapter is about the leisure industry, which grew up in Europe with *mass air travel*. It focuses on Britain, the pioneer of this industry, in the three decades following the end of World War II in which Europe enjoyed unparalleled levels of economic growth, with major increase in both the *demand* and *supply* of tourist services. It argues that British air tourism to the Mediterranean took off in the 1960s because of a combination of economic, social, and technological factors influencing both demand and supply. A greater propensity to take vacations and a *proletarianization* of Britons' foreign vacation-making combined with the entry of new capital and entrepreneurs into the independent airline industry in Britain, at the right moment to exploit the jet engine's development as a successful propulsion system for commercial aircraft. By taking the British case as an example of the crucial link between technology and growth in the international tourist industry, the chapter shows that jet engines not only changed the size of the industry, but also its character: as jets made it faster, tourism became cheaper and moved down market. *Tourism became cheaper as it became faster.*

Tourist Demand in Britain

Before World War II, only a few Britons took vacations abroad. Many workers could not afford to take vacations at all and for those who could, domestic resorts by the seaside like Brighton, Blackpool, and Scarborough, or regions of natural beauty like the Yorkshire Dales, the Lake District, and the Norfolk Broads, were sufficient to provide a break of a week or two away from their places of employment.[2] This pattern changed fundamentally with the war. By 1945 many lower and middle-income Britons had traveled abroad for the first time with the armed forces, and many more had become familiar with aircraft and air transport. Their horizons had, literally, been raised. Then, in the twenty years of economic growth that followed the war, their living standards also rose. As they joined the consumer society, they began to take for granted things like cars and electrical goods, which had been regarded as luxuries only a generation before; and, not surprising, an annual vacation consisting of two weeks at a wet and windy resort on the North Sea was no longer enough. Britons wanted the sun and they wanted to travel to where warm weather was guaranteed, namely the Mediterranean.[3] The new British tourist, however, remained suspicious of travel abroad and worried about encounters with foreign officials, foreign languages, foreign culture, and foreign food. For the average working or lower-middle class Briton, "abroad" was an intimidating concept and they were not ready to follow in the footsteps of their more educated compatriots and make their own travel arrangements on Channel ferries and Continental railways. What they needed was a *Fordist* solution to their demands and they found it in the "inclusive tour," *the holiday from the assembly line.*[4]

Inclusive tours were not new – Thomas Cook had pioneered them in the 1880s. What *was* new was their combination with air transport. Not only was it very much faster than transport by train and ferry, but it had the potential to be much cheaper and, reassuringly for the uninitiated British tourist, it transported him directly to a beach resort in the duralumin cocoon of an aircraft fuselage, thus "protecting" him from the foreign and unfamiliar.[5] The opening quotation, from a 1957 British European Airways (BEA) brochure, gives a sense of this cocoon by referring to a "magic carpet." The holiday jet is a socially determined technology, a function of the behavior and psychology of a social class. The historian David Nye has shown how "the tourist gaze … is embedded in technological structures" in such a way that the modern tourist exerts his or her mastery over tourist *sites.*[6] This "embeddedness in technological structure" is also present in *transport to* a tourist destination. The new British tourist, visiting Spain for the first time in the 1960s, wanted sun, sand, and sea, and perhaps the occasional packaged "artifact of the tourist gaze" (a bullfight perhaps?).[7] But he was not interested in the cultural splendors of the Spanish hinterland; his sunny beach could just as well have been anywhere along the Mediterranean littoral.

Just as the inclusive tour and the chartered jet aircraft were key technological developments for Spanish tourism, so the resorts of the Spanish Mediterranean coastline and the Balearic Islands, was a key element in the demand structure generated by the new British tourist in the 1960s (see table 1.1).

Table 1.1 Foreign destinations of British tourists, 1951–1972 (percentage)

	1951	1955	1963	1965	1966	1967	1968	1969	1970	1971	1972
Spain /Majorca	6	10	23	22	23	25	30	34	32	35	36
Italy	14	17	19	21	19	16	12	12	13	10	11
France	40	33	28	26	21	19	16	15	16	15	16
Ireland	26	15	10	9	9	11	10	10	8	6	4
Austria	6	10	9	9	9	10	8	8	10	8	6
Switzerland	14	14	14	14	11	10	9	8	8	7	6
West Germany	3	11	12	13	13	10	10	9	11	9	8
Belgium/Lux	15	11	14	12	10	9	8	7	6	6	6
Netherlands	4	7	4	5	5	4	5	4	4	4	4
Scandinavia	2	–	3	3	4	3	3	4	3	3	3
Yugoslavia	–	–	2	3	3	3	2	3	3	4	5
Greece	–	–	2	2	1	1	2	2	2	4	5
Portugal	–	–	1	2	2	1	2	2	2	2	2
USSR/E.Europe	–	–	1	1	1	1	1	2	1	2	3
Canar./Madeira	–	–	1	1	1	1	1	2	1	2	2
EUROPE	–	–	94	93	96	94	93	93	93	93	90

Source: *The British on Holiday*, Research Department, British Tourist Authority, London, March 1973, 7.

Unlike the traditional overseas resorts in France, Italy, or Switzerland, Spain developed spontaneously as a tourist destination, based on jet aircraft, its low cost-of-living, and the active encouragement of the Franco regime. The Spanish aimed for mass, low-cost tourism and set about developing former fishing villages to cater to British and German tourists of modest means.[8] As the pioneer *high-speed* tourist destination, Spain was immensely successful and the number of foreign visitors it received rose rapidly from around 2.5 million in 1955 to 43.2 million by 1985.[9]

The general picture of British tourist demand, therefore, is of continuous and rapid growth. By 1970 about 5.7 million Britons were taking overseas vacations and spending around £460 million a year on them. At least half of these were package tours and, as it became easier and cheaper with jets to reach resorts like the Costa Brava and Palma de Mallorca, the British inclusive tour holiday business increased in volume and moved steadily *down market*.[10]

Tourist Supply in Britain

Tourist demand in Britain preceded supply, and construction of an efficient international tourism infrastructure in Britain was unplanned and somewhat muddled.[11] Tourism supply – apart from the intrinsic attractions of the tourist destination itself – consists of accommodation and transport, plus ancillary services such as restaurants and souvenir retailing. This chapter deals with transport and, in particular, the revolution caused by aircraft, jet engines, and the growth of independent British airlines.

British Independent Airlines

After World War II, three British state-owned flag carriers emerged from legislation passed by the Labour government in 1946.[12] The government expected that in the post-war world Britain's civil aviation effort would be the exclusive responsibility of these nationalized airlines and it awarded them monopolies to carry out scheduled services in their designated areas. It was not anticipated, or considered desirable, that privately owned independent airlines would play a significant role in either domestic or international air transport, although they would be allowed to offer their services for private charter, much as a taxi is allowed to operate in a city with public transport. "It is not proposed to exclude private operators from charter and taxi work," a junior minister informed the House of Commons in 1946, "but I want to give a clear warning that any attempt to run regular services under the guise of charter work will not be tolerated."[13]

This is not the place to examine Britain's post-war policy on commercial air transport; it is sufficient to note that that policy followed a somewhat chaotic path between 1945 and 1965.[14] What is important to mention, however, is that civil air transport evolved in those twenty years in a manner that the politicians of the late 1940s did not envisage. They got it wrong; and for the very understandable reason that they did not foresee the *democratization* and huge expansion in international air tourism.

Initially, independent British airlines were precarious, "seat-of-the-pants" affairs, never far from bankruptcy. Typically they were the creation of an ex-serviceman who had managed to scrape together sufficient capital to buy one or two war-surplus Douglas C-47 ("Dakotas"; DC-3s in civilian use), of which there were thousands in Europe after the war.[15] Besides private charters and helping out in the 1948 Berlin Air Lift, their operations consisted of running services on behalf of the nationalized flag carriers, British Overseas Airways Corporation (BOAC) and BEA, whose initial embarrassing shortage of capacity led them to make use of British independent airlines as "associates," and offering the occasional vacation air tour. Scottish Aviation, for example, offered an "air cruise" in the winter of 1946, flying tourists from Prestwick (Glasgow) to the Costa del Sol, and on to Estoril: "Estoril, with its hotels, sports and entertainments, preserves a balance between the romantic character of the Peninsula and the requirements of contemporary civilisation … it is for this reason that *Scottish Air Express* has chosen to make it the centre for this air cruise … The fare of £120 per person payable in advance is completely inclusive and covers €€€, hotel accommodation, transport between airports and hotels, meals in flight and the service of the *Scottish Air Express* guides and representatives in Estoril."[16] The price of £120 to fly in a converted Liberator bomber to Portugal was very high for post-war austerity Britain, and it confirms that Scottish Aviation's customers were prosperous middle-class Britons – tourists in the pre-war mould – they were not the new British tourist of the 1960s.[17]

The salvation of British independent airlines was not tourists but soldiers. At the time of the Korean War someone in government had the bright idea that troops could be moved more quickly by air than by sea to international trouble spots and Britain's remaining colonial garrisons. These *air trooping* contracts with the Ministry of Defence kept British independent airlines airborne in the 1950s; as one authority has put it, it was their "bread and butter."[18] Trooping was easy, contracts were large, costs were low, and load factors guaranteed to be 100 percent. Furthermore, trooping was the one market from which the nationalized air corporations (BOAC and BEA), were specifically excluded, "making it in effect a means by which the government could provide private airlines with an indirect subsidy."[19] The first contract for a year went in 1950

Table 1.2 Total passenger numbers, British Air Transport, 1953–1961

Year	BOAC (Long-haul)	Index (1953=100)	BEA (Short-haul)	Index (1953=100)	Independent Airlines	Index (1953=100)
1953–4	286,582	100	1,656,779	100	252,550	100
1954–5	270,635	94*	1,874,316	113	360,686	143
1955–6	363,507	126	2,224,747	134	552,326	219
1956–7	383,862	134	2,461,065	148	725,988	287
1957–8	447,835	156	2,765,591	166	903,427	358
1958–9	470,959	164	2,828,715	171	949,892	376
1959–60	597,561	208	3,289,606	199	1,118,235	443
1960–1	790,718	275	3,990,957	241	1,517,421	601

*Year of the Comet Disasters

Source: Air Transport Advisory Council, *Annual Report*, 1960–61. Scheduled and non-scheduled, including trooping, colonial coach, and IT charters.

to the major independent airline Airwork for carrying 11,000 troops to the Mediterranean and West Africa (see table 1.2).[20]

Unfortunately trooping contracts diminished in the 1950s with Britain's withdrawal from its colonial commitments and strategic obligations "east of Suez"; by 1960 a replacement for the "squaddies" had to be found. It came in the form of tourists on cheap inclusive tours – indeed it may be said that the demise of trooping contracts was a major incentive for Britain's independent airlines to start inclusive tour operations.

The records of the regulatory body at the time, the Air Transport Advisory Council (ATAC), give us an idea of the rapid growth of these early air package tours, despite the entrenched opposition of the nationalized flag carrier, BEA. In August 1957, for example, the ATAC heard a large number of proposals by independent British airlines to fly to Basle and other points in Switzerland for summer inclusive tours. Airwork, Eagle Aviation, Hunting Clan Air, Millbank Tours, Wayfarers Travel, and Britavia all sought permission for up to ten return flights to Basle in 1958, where their passengers would then set off on coach and walking tours around Switzerland and the Italian Lakes. They had in common very high load factors and the use of obsolescent aircraft such as Vickers Vikings and DC-3s. Silver City Airways, in conjunction with the tour operator Gaytours, for example, planned three return flights a week in May and September 1958, and four return flights a week in June, July, and August. The vacation consisted of three days at Lucerne, followed by four at Interlaken. Gaytours was a Manchester travel agent, who had "previously carried their tours by surface transport but now wished to carry some of their passengers by air." When asked by the ATAC chairman why tourists for Switzerland should not fly on the scheduled BEA flights, which appealed against almost every application to the ATAC by independent airlines on grounds of "diversion" of traffic from its services, the Airwork representative pointed out the vital truth that "passengers travelled on (its) Inclusive Tour Services principally to obtain the benefit of the much lower air fare element that was obtainable on those services." According to another private carrier, Independent Air Travel, "there was an immense demand for IT [Inclusive Tour Services] services and this was likely to increase whatever the trend of other types of traffic. The research carried out by this company indicates that a very high proportion of passengers travelling on IT services *were travelling for the first time....* it was extremely rare for a passenger to say that he had hitherto been a regular BEA traveller."[21] Although these British tourists for Switzerland were not the yet the "new" tourist variety that appeared in the 1960s, the low prices of independent charter airlines were already a factor in the choice of an inclusive tour.

In 1960 the legislative framework governing independent airlines in Britain was changed. With the Civil Aviation (Licensing) Act the ATAC, which since 1952 had been a mere advisory body, was replaced with what seemed to be a more robust licensing authority – the Air Transport Licensing Board (ATLB). The new legislation placed private airlines on an equal basis with the nationalized air corporations, and gave the ATLB the power to grant licenses for both scheduled and charter operations. The ATLB immediately got busy; for example, in August and September 1961 it convened three days a week, mornings and afternoons, and dealt with nearly 1,000 Inclusive Tour applications for 1962.[22] Its policy was generous toward the award of IT licenses, although BEA and BOAC continued to appeal successfully against the license applications of the independents because they were "diverting" traffic from their scheduled services. They argued, not without some logic, that as state-owned enterprises, with a wider range of responsibilities and obligations than that of merely offering the cheapest possible flights to tourists (for example, fostering the products of the British aircraft industry and providing loss-making domestic services), they should be protected against privately owned and low-cost independents. In other words, their monopolies should be upheld.

There was another reason why the flag carriers were increasingly hostile to the independent airlines. The independents themselves were no longer small, "seat-of-the pants" affairs; thanks to a rapid process of merger and consolidation, and the flow of new capital into the industry from British shipping interests who were anxious to diversify from their declining passenger liner operations, the independents had become major airlines in their own right.[23] The two largest were British United Airways (BUA), formed by the merger of Airwork and Hunting Clan in 1960, and Cunard Eagle, which was the result of the Cunard Shipping Company acquiring a majority interest in Eagle Airways.

These new companies had the capital to buy new modern aircraft, including jets and this was a source of particular concern to BEA and BOAC. "The trouble with BUA," noted the *Economist* in 1961, "is that it is not a brave and struggling little airline grateful for the occasional pat on the head, but a sizeable organization backed by shipping money looking for investment."[24]

For a while the ATLB steered a middle course between the demands of the flag carriers and the petitioning of the independents. It was helped in this by adherence to the legal restriction on British price competition in inclusive tours known as "Provision 1," which stemmed from a long-standing IATA rule (Resolution 045), stipulating that package vacation prices should not be below the minimum *scheduled* return fare to the destination in question. In 1965 however, in a landmark decision, the Minister of Aviation Roy Jenkins rejected a BEA appeal against the ATLB's approval of forty-six new licenses to independent airlines, claiming that it was "in the interests of both the travelling public and British civil aviation that the market be as free as possible."[25] The mould was broken and the way was now open for a major expansion of IT supply. Fierce price competition followed in the late 1960s, with inclusive tours being advertised below the sacred "Provision 1" level. The result was a price war in the British tourist industry that not only drew the wrath of BEA and BOAC, who continued to claim that they deserved protection from the activities of independent airlines, but also undermined the viability of the independent charter airlines themselves, which were now struggling to pay the interest charges on their fleets of new *jet* aircraft (see table 1.3).[26]

The Importance of Jet Engines for International Tourism

The importance of the introduction of jet aircraft into the British IT vacation market, coinciding with the legislative "liberation" of independent airline operations in the 1960s and the influx of new capital from the shipping industry, can hardly be exaggerated. For the first time since 1945 British private airlines and the scheduled flag carriers flew the same aircraft.

Jet engines were critical to the growth and success of the inclusive tour. With the introduction of jets, the independent airlines gained both speed and range, so that, for example, up to three return flights per day could now fly to the Balearic Islands. Moreover, with high utilization these jet aircraft delivered major cost savings; between 1967 and 1971 costs on IT charter flights to Palma de Mallorca fell 27 percent in real terms.[27] There is another, more fundamental reason why jet engines are so important to the growth of modern tourism: *speed made luxury unnecessary.* When civil airliners were relatively slow in the early 1950s – averaging a cruising speed of around 250 miles per hour – they had to be luxurious and there was only first class accommodation. When jet

Table 1.3 Jet aircraft in the main European passenger charter airlines, 1975

Country	Airline	Operations	Charter Passengers	Jet Aircraft in Fleet
Belgium	Sobelair	European IT	539,383	2 x Boeing 707 3 x Caravelle
	Trans-European	European IT	462,474	3 x Boeing707 2 x Boeing720 2 x A300B
Finland	Kar-Air	European IT World charter Sched. Domestic	63,196	1 x Douglas DC.8
France	Air Charter International	European IT World Charter	320,000	2 x Boeing 727 7 x Caravelle
	Catair	European IT World Charter	128,000	9 x Caravelle
	Euralair	European IT	83,000	2 x Caravelle
Germany	Bavaria	European IT	568,336	6 x BAC 1-11
	Condor	European IT World Charter	1,853,253	1 x Boeing 707 16 x Boeing 727 2 x Boeing 747
	Germanair	European IT	630,081	1 x Airbus A300B 3 x BAC 1-11
	Hapag-Lloyd	European IT	445, 32	8 x Boeing 727
	LTU	European IT	599,209	4 x Caravelle 2 x Lockheed L-1011 Tristar
Netherlands	Martinair	European IT World Charter	626,700	2 x Douglas DC-8 3 x Douglas DC-9 2 x Douglas DC-10
	Transavia	European IT World Charter	788,742	1 x Boeing 707 5 x Boeing 737 2 x Caravelle
Scandinavia	Braathens	European IT Sched.domest.	415,000	6 x Boeing 737
	Conair	European IT	615,004	4 x Boeing 720
	Maersk	European IT Sched. Domest	500,000	5 x Boeing 720
	Scanair	European IT World Charter	737,200	2 x Douglas DC.8 3 x Boeing 727
	Sterling	European IT N.Atlantic IT	1,892,225	5 x Boeing 727 13 x Caravelle
Spain	Aviaco	European IT Sched. domest.	875,071	6 x Douglas DC.8 8 x Douglas DC.9 7 x Caravelle
	Spantax	European IT N.Atlantic IT Cargo charter	1,556,634	2 x Douglas DC.8 2 x Douglas DC.9 14 x Convair CV-990
	TAE	European IT	412,617	2 x Douglas DC.8 1 x Caravelle
	Trans Europa	European IT	387,763	5 x Caravelle

(*Continued*)

Table 1.3 Jet aircraft in the main European passenger charter airlines, 1975 (*cont.*)

Country	Airline	Operations	Charter Passengers	Jet Aircraft in Fleet
Switzerland	Balair	European IT Sched. domest. World charter	136,087	2 x Douglas DC.8 1 x Douglas DC.9
	Sata	European IT	325,000	1 x Douglas DC.8 4 x Caravelle
UK	Britannia	European IT European charter	2,285,000	13 x Boeing 737
	British Air Tours (BEA)	European IT	830,927	7 x Boeing 707
	British Caledonian	Scheduled domestic &. International, World charter	609,184	10 x Boeing 707 12 x BAC 1-11
	Monarch	European IT World Charter	778,690	3 Boeing 720 3 x BAC 1-11
	Dan-Air	European IT N.Atlantic IT Sched. Domestic European	2,306,373	2 x Boeing 707 5 x Boeing 727 12 x BAC 1-11 17 x DH. Comet
	Laker	European IT N.Atlantic Charter	960, 800	3 x Douglas DC.10 2 x Boeing 707 5 x BAC 1-11

Source: McDonnell Douglas Market Research Report, *The European Charter Airlines*, 2nd ed., Worldwide Horizons, Market Research Department, Douglas Aircraft Company, March 1977, MR-report, C1-800-4275, 1.

engines made them twice as fast, passengers could put up with more discomfort: the seat pitch could be reduced and half the cabin toilets removed to make way for more seats. With this *speed tourism,* tourists could arrive at their destinations without the need for the slightest degree of acclimatization to the changes involved, say, between a suburb of Manchester and a beach in Spain. Jets, then, not only changed the *cost* of international tourism and opened it up to a large new market of people who had never been able to travel abroad before; they also changed the *culture* of tourism and the relationship between the tourists and the people at their destination.

Jet aircraft were embraced so readily by the new, and still to some degree xenophobic, British tourist of the 1960s, partly because they were perceived to be so quintessentially British. The jet had been first proposed by the Englishman Frank Whittle in a 1930 patent (the fact that it was the German Hans von Ohain who built the first engine and flew the first jet plane in 1939, was largely ignored by the post-war generation of Britons). The British had led the world in jet engine design after the war and first applied it to civil aircraft propulsion in the de Havilland Comet 1 in 1952. [28] There was a widespread notion, born out of Britons' experience of aircraft in the war and a romantic attachment to the 1940 Battle of Britain, that the British "were good in the air," just as they had been masters of the sea a century before.[29] The jet engine was simply the latest confirmation of this belief.

The jet engine revolutionized both the airline and tourist industries. With the introduction of bypass engines in the 1960s, the airlines had the instrument to make air transport fully competitive with surface systems; it was the means to make air travel irresistible. Bypass engines were much quieter than the original military jets, cheaper to run, and more powerful – in short, they were an airline manager's dream. More power meant more passengers because bigger aircrafts could be built around bypass engines and existing ones "stretched." Thus, the jet airliners that appeared in the 1960s and which were so important for the European tourist industry by lowering the cost of flying, such as the Boeing 727 tri-jet and 737 twin-jet, and the Douglas DC-9, would not have been possible without the bypass jet engine.

The revolution was not, of course, limited to scheduled airlines and IATA members. Unlike the situation in the late 1940s when independent airlines had to make do with obsolete types like the DC-3 and Viking, while the flag carriers flew Lockheed Constellations and DC-6s, in the 1960s the independent airlines acquired jet aircraft at the same time as, and even before, the scheduled carriers like BEA and BOAC. In 1960 93 percent of European charter aircraft were piston-engines, by 1965 jet and turboprops already comprised 43 percent of the total charter airline fleet, and by 1975 the change to jets was almost complete at 82 percent from a total European charter fleet of 366.[30] In Britain the new charter carrier Britannia had no less than thirteen Boeing 737s (see table 1.3).

The Inclusive Tour Package Air Holiday (IT)

Europe was decisive in the creation of the international market for inclusive tours by air. Air holidays from north to south in Europe grew so fast they surpassed travel on scheduled services and many new resorts in the Mediterranean were virtually created by IT charter services (e.g., in Spain, Greece, Cyprus, and Turkey).[31] The key to their success was *exceptionally low fares*, exploiting the high price elasticity of demand for air travel as a means to widen the market. As two of the leading pioneers of the British independent airline business pointed out at an early stage, cost is the key parameter in package tours; the IT tourist does not care *where* he or she is going; the cost is everything and a £30 vacation on the Costa Brava did not compete with a £70 vacation on the Costa Brava, but with a £30 vacation at Clacton-on-Sea (in England).[32]

These low fares were achieved by designing a low cost system. Thus, aircraft seats were matched to hotel beds, and both were bought by tour operators in large blocks at advantageous rates for a whole season from charter airlines and hotels. The use of jet aircraft, which can fly half empty and still show a profit, was crucial to the success of the enterprise. The block booking of aircraft seats ensured high load factors to the charter airline, while the high utilization of the aircraft meant a high return on the capital tied up in the new jet aircraft. Early package tours in the 1950s from London to Palma de Mallorca with piston-engine aircraft like the DC-3 or Viking carried around forty passengers and took over seven hours, including a refueling stop at Lyon. With jet aircraft like the Boeing 737 or BAC 1-11, over 100 passengers could be flown in half that time, thus ensuring much higher productivity; in just four years from 1967 to 1971 the cost of IT flights to Palma fell by nearly 30 percent in real terms thanks to the use of jet aircraft.[33]

The result of the full implementation of the IT air system was that the price of a British package vacation hardly changed between 1967 and 1972 – an increasingly good deal for the British tourists. In fact, as table 1.4 shows, at a time of accelerating price inflation in the late 1960s and early 1970s, IT vacations were actually getting cheaper every year.

As always with major commercial innovations, in the development of the IT system one or two pioneers were ahead of the pack. These were entrepreneurs for whom low-cost air transport was an article of faith and for whom the scheduled flag carriers (BEA and BOAC) were reactionary monopolists and cartel members (of IATA). They were successful because they offered the

Table 1.4 Thomsons "Summer Sun" vacation, average prices at actual and price-adjusted values, 1966–1977

Year	Actual Price (£ sterling)	Index (1977=100)	Price Adjusted to 1977 values (£ sterling)	Index (1977=100)
1966	48.9	33	143.2	97
1967	50.7	34	145.0	98
1968	51.3	35	140.2	95
1969	53.6	36	138.8	94
1970	55.7	38	135.3	92
1971	51.6	35	115.0	78
1972	54.2	37	112.7	76
1973	62.1	42	118.0	79
1974	78.8	53	129.3	87
1975	90.6	61	118.7	80
1976	116.9	79	132.0	89
1977	147.6	100	147.6	100

Source: Thomson Holiday Research Department.

adventure of foreign travel at a price low enough to be within the reach of people for whom foreign travel had previously been impossible.[34] Two of these pioneers in Britain were Freddie Laker and J.E.D. Williams. Laker was head of BUA in the 1960s and in the 1970s the instigator and force behind *Skytrain*, the first low-cost, scheduled transatlantic airline. Williams, who is perhaps less well-known, was the intellectual force behind what was to become Britain's largest independent charter airline by 1972, namely Britannia Airways. It is useful to briefly review Britannia's history because it was typical of British independent charter airlines in the 1960s.

Britannia began operations in May 1962 with three aging Lockheed Constellations. It was the creation of Williams, an aviation consultant, and Ted Langton of the tour operator Universal Sky Tours. They started an airline called Euravia based at the little-used (and therefore cheap) Luton airport, offering a week's package vacation in Palma de Majorca for £53. In 1964 Euravia replaced the Constellations with ex-BOAC turbo-prop Bristol Britannias and changed its name to Britannia Airways in their honor. The 1965 breakthrough at the ATLB (outlined above) made the airline attractive to the press baron Lord Thomson who wanted to diversify from his newspaper empire and acquire something in the service sector that would give him a new source of cash flow. He appreciated the mass-market potential of jet-borne vacations for the workers and bought both Britannia and Universal Sky Tours. Thomson provided the airline with the means to buy the jets. While Constellations with 82 passengers had taken eight hours to Palma and back, jets with 117 passengers took four – thus ensuring much higher productivity. Traditionally charter companies bought second-hand planes from scheduled carriers (as Britannia had bought its Britannias from BOAC and many of the carriers had acquired Boeing 707s and Douglas DC-8s from their national flag carriers), but Williams broke radically with this tradition by buying the unproven Boeing 737-200, practically off the Boeing drawing board.[35]

This was accomplished not without difficulty because the chairman of the British Aircraft Corporation, Sir George Edwards, expected Britannia to buy the BAC 1-11 and exerted political pressure through President of the Board of Trade, Tony Crosland, to secure a British order. However, Williams stuck to commercial principles and remained determined to have the more powerful 737. In 1968 Britannia took delivery of its first 737 and by 1975 had thirteen, becoming the biggest non-scheduled airline in Britain (see table 1.5).[36]

In many ways, Britannia typifies and encapsulates the British charter airline business up until the mid-1970s: the concentration on low-cost Spain as a destination, the operation of a "one-type fleet" of efficient and low-maintenance Boeing 737 jets, the entrance of a wealthy backer (Thomson) at the right moment to buy those jets in 1965, and the use of a low-cost "provincial"

Table 1.5 Passengers on international IT charter flights – the leading carriers, 1963–1972 (in thousands)

	1963	1964	1965	1966	1967	1968	1969	1970	1971	1972
Britannia	64.3	105.5	168.2	283.3	302.2	432.6	665.8	688.9	1049.3	1447.9
Autair	21.3	39.9	27.9	–	–	–	–	–	–	–
Court	–	–	–	80.9	56.2	221.5	456.9	809.2	1151.5	1419.0
BUA/Bcal	–	151.8	209.8	357.5	378.4	379.9	1092.4	1079.3	1302.4	1244.8
Dan Air	–	48.9	54.3	66.4	57.9	166.5	437.1	605.5	981.3	1240.7
BEA/Airtour	–	–	–	–	–	–	–	416.5	543.5	712.4
Monarch	–	–	–	–	–	–	240.8	274.7	406.2	497.1
Brit.Midland	–	–	11.3	33.1	57.6	57.7	107.1	206.7	317.9	339.9
Laker	–	–	–	–	–	–	203.7	255.2	243.3	311.8
BEA	–	16.9	24.2	21.4	113.7	81.4	79.1	23.3	0.6	51.7
BOAC	–	–	–	–	–	–	–	–	7.9	40.9

Source: *Economist Intelligence Unit*, ITQ, 2, no. 7 (1973): 50; B.K. Humphreys, "The Regulation of Non-Scheduled Air Services in the United Kingdom 1960 to 1972: A Note," *Journal of Industrial Economics* 24, no. 3 (1976): 235.

airport at Luton. The use of provincial airports, beyond London, exemplified British charter operations, establishing direct connectivity between tourist generating catchment areas in the north of England and Spain. By 1979 almost half of non-scheduled traffic entering Spain from Britain originated in British provincial airports and their catchment areas.[37] Luton – virtually created by *Britannia* – became the main center for inclusive tours to the Mediterranean, thanks partly to its close proximity to the M1 motorway, which made it convenient for the northern English markets of the Midlands and Yorkshire.

Not all independent charter carriers did as well as Britannia. By 1974 the growth in European IT traffic to the Mediterranean, which had been averaging 28 percent per year since 1967, had been slowed by the oil crisis. In Britain the depression in the IT market was aggravated by industrial unrest (the "three-day week") and general economic recession. At the same time the process of business *concentration* that had begun among British independent airlines in the late 1960s had resulted in the domination of the IT market by just five main tour operators (Clarksons, Thomson, Horizon, Cooks/Lunn-Poly, and Cosmos). Competition among these companies, particularly the market leaders Clarksons and Thomson, led to aggressive marketing and a price war that did little to help the companies make *profits*. Although an IT vacation became an increasingly good deal for the British tourists, it placed a growing financial strain on the airlines and tour operators. Pressed by rising capacity and struggling to pay the charges on their new jet aircraft, many of them now found themselves facing bankruptcy, the most spectacular example of which was the

Court Line/Clarksons Group that collapsed in 1974, leaving stranded passengers all over the Mediterranean.[38]

The Response of the Scheduled Carriers

By way of conclusion it is worth to consider what the impact of the independent charter airlines' operations was on scheduled carriers like BEA and BOAC (in fact, all the European flag carriers), and what was their response. As we have seen, the scheduled airlines began services after the war in a cozy environment of state sponsorship and cartel (IATA) organization. Their customers were businessmen and their fares were high; it should be remembered that Tourist Class fares, which offered a modest reduction on the standard First Class fare, was only introduced in 1952. They concentrated their marketing on the provision of high quality (the only people who flew in cabins with a 34-inch seat pitch were soldiers on trooping charters!) and the maximum flexibility of booking. For most travelers price was immaterial and certainly not critical. When the scheduled airlines began to experience price competition from the independent charter companies, offering inclusive tours, their first response was one of affront and they turned to the government and the law to suppress these unwelcome upstarts. The scheduled airlines did not understand the charter airlines because they did not understand the radical change in demand that was taking place in the air travel market. The potential to enlarge that market was seen clearly and early by IT operators and visionaries like J.E.D. Williams, but not by the managers of state-owned airlines like BEA and BOAC, who still appeared to labor under the delusion that aviation was in some special way connected with national prestige and national interest. Yet they were flying against the wind; the two driving forces of modern tourism, namely the spread of car ownership and the fall in the real cost of flying, are essentially supply-led.[39] If they were to prosper, then the British scheduled airlines would have to seize the opportunity offered by the possibility of cheap air travel. Instead, it was the independent airlines that tapped the new market of tourists who had not previously flown and would not have been able to afford to do so if the fares had not been substantially cheaper than those offered by BEA.

It was also the independents who first appreciated the possibilities inherent in jet aircraft. It is fair to say that jets were more of a "problem" for the flag carriers than an opportunity, and initially they spent a lot of time debating the wisdom of imposing a "jet surcharge" on their passengers. Flag carriers like BEA, Air France, Lufthansa, and KLM, all to one degree or another seemed to be unable to fully exploit jet engines because they were locked into national civil aviation policies, which tended to decide their aircraft procurement strategy on political grounds. This was especially true of the British.

Table 1.6 Impact of inclusive tours on European scheduled air fares, 1969–1972

London to	Distance (miles)	Tourist Single Fare Summer, 1969–1970 (pence per mile)	Tourist Single Fare Winter, 1971–1972 (pence per mile)
Amsterdam	230	5.43	6.20
Basle	436	5.07	5.83
Belgrade	1,049	4.18	4.48
Bordeaux	449	5.29	5.67
Brussels	211	6.09	6.94
Budapest	917	4.40	4.62
Copenhagen	611	5.30	5.82
Dublin	290	4.10	4.55
Frankfurt	400	5.21	5.61
Hamburg	463	4.87	5.24
Helsinki	1,152	4.28	4.62
Milan	584	4.97	5.35
Moscow	1,557	4.96	4.96
Munich	580	4.67	5.03
Oslo	743	4.77	5.25
Prague	644	5.12	5.38
Stockholm	908	4.77	5.25
Vienna	784	4.45	4.98
Warsaw	910	5.19	5.46
Zurich	480	4.88	5.60
Average of routes with minimal IT competition	**670**	**4.90**	**5.34**
Alicante	902	3.87	4.11
Athens	1,392	4.39	4.57
Gibraltar	1,077	2.93	3.22
Las Palmos	1,796	3.30	3.30
Lisbon	966	3.90	4.00
Málaga	1,032	3.70	4.00
Malta	1,295	2.70	2.90
Naples	1,002	4.10	4.40
Nicosia	2,001	3.80	3.90
Palermo	1,118	4.10	4.40
Palma	826	3.70	3.90
Rome	892	4.30	4.60
Tangier	1,112	3.50	3.70
Tel Aviv	2,222	3.90	4.10
Venice	705	3.79	5.10
Average of routes with unlimited IT competition	**1,222**	**3.79**	**4.01**

Source: A.P. Ellison and E.M. Stafford, *The Dynamics of the Civil Aviation Industry* (Farnborough: Saxon House, 1974), 45–47.

Meanwhile, the privately owned independent airlines like Britannia went ahead and ordered jets as soon as they were able, and on strictly commercial grounds. They understood immediately what the flag carriers missed: that if you can carry passengers *fast* it does not matter if they are relatively uncomfortable, that the new British tourists of the 1960s cared nothing for the quality of the airline experience, but everything for the speed and efficiency with which they were delivered to the beach. It took IT operators like Britannia to seize the opportunity of the jet engine and particularly the bypass engine. They harnessed the jet engine to mass tourism – classic *Fordism* – and built around a single technological artifact, a new industry. Just as the jet engine turned the airline business into a regular business, so the IT business turned a military invention into a commercial success.

Gradually the scheduled airlines became alarmed at the advances of the charter operators and realized the value of cheap tours as a fast growing market, which charter airlines were stealing from under their noses. In 1960 they introduced an inclusive tour based fare, known as ITX, which could be used by travel agents to construct a package tour using scheduled services rather than charter aircraft. It was open to travel agents for 16.6 percent less than the relevant scheduled fare. In the same year BEA admitted that it was itself earning nearly 10 percent of its passenger revenue from inclusive tour sales.[40] A process of *convergence* set in as scheduled carriers sought to match charter carriers' prices, while the charter carriers sought to match the scheduled carriers' jet fleets. In short the distinction between scheduled and unscheduled airlines became blurred and ultimately disappeared. The charter operators had forced price of air travel down and forced scheduled operators like BEA to cut its fares. In 1971, for example, BEA announced cheaper fares on many of its European routes to combat the loss of traffic to charter competition; fares from London to Paris, Amsterdam, Brussels, Copenhagen, Frankfurt, Milan, Munich, Nice, Stockholm, and Zurich were all cut by half, while the peak-season fare to Rome was reduced from £92.30 to £41.15.[41]

In general, the effect of the British-led charter airline phenomenon of the 1960s was to lower the cost of air travel to the first post-war generation of tourists by exerting a downward pressure on the fare levels of routes where inclusive tours were available. As table 1.6 makes clear, where IT competition was minimal, on routes from London to other European capitals, the fare level, measured in pence per mile, remained higher than on routes to Mediterranean tourist destinations where there was a strong IT offering. Eventually this downward pressure would extend itself throughout the European air travel market and would ultimately lead to the appearance of ultra-cheap scheduled carriers in the 1990s like EasyJet and Ryanair.

Notes

1. The link between international tourism and the airline industry in the third quarter of the twentieth century is clear; note that world scheduled passenger air traffic increased ten times in volume from 31 million in 1950 to 314 million in 1970. *ICAO Bulletin*, February 1972, 46.
2. See, for example, J.-K. Walton, *The English Seaside Resort: A Social History, 1750–1914* (Leicester: University of Leicester Press, 1983), and J.-K. Walton, *The British Seaside: Holidays and Resorts in the Twentieth Century* (Manchester: Manchester University Press, 2000.) Also see S. Farrant, "London by the Sea: Resort Development on the South Coast of England, 1880–1939," *Journal of Contemporary History* 22 (1987): 137–62, and still valuable, J. Pimlott, *The Englishman's Holiday* (London, 1947).
3. See Peter J. Lyth and Marc L. Dierikx, "From Privilege to Popularity: The Growth of Leisure Air Travel," *Journal of Transport History* 15, no. 2 (1994): 97–116.
4. *Fordist* mass production in the first and second quarters of the twentieth century was followed by a *Fordist* lifestyle of mass consumption in the third, and this included international tourism. See David Harvey, *The Condition of Postmodernity* (Oxford: Blackwell, 1989).
5. Support for this view comes from a survey carried out in 1967 in which 71 percent of respondents claimed that the attraction of inclusive tours was not just the vacation's low price but the fact that they did not have to make individual arrangements or deal with foreign officials. *British National Travel Survey*, 1967, BTA January 1968.
6. Where the nineteenth-century tourist gazed at an Alpine peak and allowed himself to be uplifted by nature's grandeur, the modern tourist looks at a landscape and "thinks in terms of speed and immediacy: the strongest possible experience in the shortest possible time." David E. Nye, *Narratives and Space, Technology and the Construction of American Culture* (Exeter: University of Exeter Press, 1997), 22–23.
7. J. Urry, *The Tourist Gaze: Leisure and Travel in Contemporary Societies* (London: Sage, 1990), 9.
8. Manuel Valenzuela, "Spain: The Phenomenon of Mass Tourism," in *Tourism and Economic Development*, ed. Allan Williams and Gareth Shaw (London and New York, 1988), 39.
9. Valenzuela, *Spain*, 40
10. "Package Tours – Where They Have Been and Where They Are Going," *International Tourist Quarterly* 1, Special Report no. 42 (1981): 45. Also see British Tourist Authority, *British National Travel Survey, 1969* (London, 1970).
11. Douglas G. Pearce, *Tourist Development* (London and New York: Longman, 1989), 14.
12. These were British Overseas Airways Corporation (BOAC), British European Airways (BEA), and British South American Airways (BSAA). BSAA was taken over by BOAC in 1949.
13. Ivor Thomas, Parliamentary Secretary at the Ministry of Civil Aviation, Debate on Civil Aviation (Cmd 6712), *24.1.1946*, Hansard CO.NO.328.

14. See Peter J. Lyth, "The Changing Role of Government in British Civil Air Transport, 1919–1949," in *The Political Economy of Nationalisation in Britain, 1920–1950,* ed. Robert Millward and John Singleton (Cambridge: Cambridge University Press, 1995), 65–87.
15. Usual practice was to use one aircraft for service and the other for spares.
16. Scottish Aviation-Air Cruises to Portugal and Elsewhere, 1946–47. *Public Record Office*, Kew, PRO. BT.217/1079.
17. For more details see B.K. Humphreys, "Nationalisation and Independent Airlines in the United Kingdom, 1945–51," *Journal of Transport History*, second series, 3, no. 4 (1976): 265–81.
18. See B.K. Humphreys, "Trooping and the Development of the British Independent Airlines," *Journal of Transport History*, second series 5, no. 1 (1979): 46–59.
19. Peter J. Lyth, "Introduction," in *Air Transport* (Aldershot: Scolar Press, 1996), xvii.
20. M.D.N. Wyatt, "British Independent Aviation – Past and Present," *Journal of Institute of Transport* (May 1963): 109.
21. In 1956 the IT capacity approved for Basle was 27,356 seats out of the applied for 64,890. In 1957 it was 46,354 out of 98,969 applications. Air Transport Advisory Council, 13–14 August 1957, *Public Record Office, Kew BT.245/10.*
22. Memo by the company secretary, British European Airways, Board Paper 165, 2 September 1961.
23. Lyth, "Introduction," in *Air Transport*, xviii.
24. "The First Test," *The Economist*, 7 January 1961.
25. "A Smack in the Face for BEA," *The Economist*, 28 January 1965.
26. Civil Air Transport Inquiry-Submission by BEA, Edwards Committee, "BEA and the Holiday Maker," 1968, RAF Museum, Hendon Box 341.
27. F.F. Higgins, Tour Operating: Some Implications for Air Transport, Anglo-American Aeronautical Conference, London, 31 May–2 June 1977.
28. For the race to get the jet engine operational, see Edward W. Constant II, *The Origins of the Turbojet Revolution* (Baltimore: Johns Hopkins University Press, 1980): 178–207. For the history of the British aircraft industry, see Keith Hayward, *The British Aircraft Industry* (Manchester University Press 1989).
29. A useful explanation of these ideas can be found in David Edgerton, *England and the Aeroplane: An Essay on a Militant and Technological Nation* (Basingstoke: Macmillan, 1991).
30. McDonnell Douglas Market Research Report, *The European Charter Airlines,* 2nd ed., Worldwide Horizons, Market Research Department, Douglas Aircraft Company, March 1977, MR-report, C1-800-4275, 1.
31. Stephen Wheatcroft, *Aviation and Tourism Policies,* 12–13.
32. See Freddie Laker, "Private Enterprise in British Air Transport," *Journal of the Royal Aeronautical Society* (February 1966); see also J.E.D. Williams, "The Role of Private Enterprise in British Air Transportation," *Journal of the Royal Aeronautical Society* (June 1967).
33. *International Tourist Quarterly,* National Report No. 2: *Spain*; 1971, 3: 13–14. See also Rigas Doganis, *Flying off Course: The Economics of International Airlines*, 2nd ed. (London: Routledge 1991), 174.

34. Alan Snudden, "Success in a Package," *Journal of the Institute of Transport* (January/February 1990).
35. Geoffrey Cuthbert, *Flying to the Sun: Quarter Century of Britannia Airways, Europe's Leading Leisure Airline* (London: Hodder and Stoughton 1987), 11–45.
36. Cuthbert, *Flying to the Sun,* 50–60.
37. Douglas Pearce, *Tourism Today: A Geographical Analysis* (New York: Longman Scientific and Technical 1987), 86–93.
38. A major shipping concern, Court Line had got into air transport in 1965 when it bought the charter airline Autair International. It developed close ties with Clarksons Holidays, a tour operator specializing in the cheap end of the ITC market, and invested heavily in jet aircraft. Clarksons's losses in 1971 and 1972 led Court Line to take over the company as the only way to ensure passengers in its burgeoning capacity. By 1973 it was fatally over-extended in a depressed market and was forced to suspend business.
39. Allan M. Williams and Gareth Shaw, "Western European Tourism in Perspective," in *Tourism and Economic Development,* Williams and Shaw, ed., 13.
40. BEA *Annual Report and Accounts*, 1960–61.
41. *International Tourism Quarterly,* Issues in the News, 2. 1971, Economist Intelligence Unit, London, 4.

Chapter 2

The Transformation of the Economic Model of the Balearic Islands

The Pioneers of Mass Tourism

Carles Manera and Jaume Garau-Taberner

The Economic Base That Favored Tourism

The great transformation of the Balearic economy started in the mid-1940s and lasted until the first oil crisis in 1973. In fact, these decades redefined the model of economic growth in the islands. From 1960 on there was a real economic upsurge, fueled and stimulated by the spectacular development of the European economy. The islands' secure income was a determining factor, even though it is not the only explanation. Moreover, it was no longer to be the conventional products of the countryside or the urban workshops that would favor the change; it was the *foreigner industry,* to use the visionary expression coined by the Majorcan Bartomeu Amengual, secretary of the Chamber of Commerce, Industry and Navigation of Barcelona from 1902 to 1957, which became the source of this phenomenon. At that time Europe was recovering from the consequences of World War II. The improvement in standards of living together with appropriate legislation meant that an important section of the working class could enjoy vacations in countries other than their own. That is how tourist demand directed at the Mediterranean countries arose, countries where the relatively low cost of living offered comparative advantages to the leisure industry. The response of the Balearic Islands in the 1960s

Notes for this chapter are located on page 44.

was rapid and deserves the attention of economic historians. Nevertheless, our hypothesis, based on the available data, is that industrial and agricultural towns and shrewd entrepreneurs of modest origins and diverse provenance laid the foundations of an infrastructure which, built hastily and in a totally anarchic way, within a few years became the main Mediterranean tourist destination and an inexhaustible magnet for gastarbeiters. The development, as far as Europe is concerned, began toward the middle of the 1950s, as the flow of passengers from the continent by air was already substantial in comparison with those arriving by sea. But other measures also helped to complete this phase. The period from 1956 to 1959 is considered a turning point because it was then that the customs and visa processes were simplified and/or abolished, currency regulations were relaxed, exchange rates were modified and prices were stabilized, all factors that had a favorable impact on the initial stages of foreign tourism.

Between the beginning of the upsurge in tourism in 1960 and the 1973 crisis, the rise in demand was impressive, moving from roughly 600,000 visitors to 3,600,000. This remarkable growth was the cause of the speedy evolution of a complex and diversified offer, which had repercussions for the economic activity of the islands. The result is well-known: the archipelago became increasingly dependent on tourist revenues, which conditioned its economic structure. Moreover, the autonomous community of the Balearic Islands headed the list in Spain in terms of revenue per head of population and enjoyed a privileged situation in the context of the European Community (EC). The labor market reflected this decisive transformation at the very beginning of the tourism phenomenon.

The figures speak volumes (see table 2.1): in eight years, the tertiary sector increased by eight points in the composition of the active population, while the primary sector lost ten – which in fact moved to the service sector, and the secondary sector remained within margins that could be described as historic, although tangibly lower than those registered in the 1920s and 1930s (at this time industry in the Balearic Islands was regrouping almost 40 percent of its workforce). The construction sector became quite active, but it was traditional manufacturing, with its roots going back for centuries, that supported a quarter of the active population of the islands between 1955 and 1962. The gross value added indicators allow us to confirm this initial impression, because they reveal an important nominal increase during these vital years. Three facts attract our attention: first, the importance of services, which was already appreciable in 1955 (47 percent), a fact that reflects the dynamism of the sector in the five years that preceded the actual upswing. Second, the fall in the figures for industry: 10 percent between 1955 and 1962, if we exclude activity connected with construction, which shows an increase (from almost 5 percent

Table 2.1 The labor market and gross added value of the Balearic economy

Active Population Economic Sectors	1955 %	1957 %	1960 %	1962 %	Gross Added Value Sectors	1955 %	1957 %	1960 %	1962 %
Tertiary	29.59	30.13	29.61	37.29	Services	47.32	46.30	44.55	50.68
Secondary (not includ. construction)	23.58	23.86	24.98	24.38	Industry (not includ. construction)	32.82	32.53	29.11	23.24
Construction	6.67	7.08	7.60	7.41	Construction	4.79	5.87	4.58	7.41
Primary	40.16	38.93	37.81	30.92	Agriculture and fishery	15.07	15.30	21.77	18.67
	100	100	100	100		100	100	100	100

Source: C. Manera, "L'endarreriment econòmic de les illes Balears fins el turisme de masses: la construcció d'un mit" (forthcoming).

to a little more than 7 percent). Thus, industry maintains its proportion of the active population but its contribution to the regional gross added-value is in retreat, allowing us to assume that there are evident losses in terms of productivity. Third, the continuation and slight development of primary activities simultaneously fall slightly, in terms of its share of the active population. As a consequence, a proposed hypothesis, which must be evaluated by future work, is that at the moment of the emergence of mass tourism the economy of the Balearic Islands (see tables 2.2 and 2.3) was not in a critical situation at the internal level (new data support this from a comparative perspective).

By the mid-1950s, the Balearic Islands were above the Spanish average in terms of revenue per head of population (just over 20 percent), and in 1959 they were, in current pesetas, at a level of 76 percent of the GDP per head of population of the fifteen-member European Community. As far as this measure is concerned, quoted in constant 1998 values, the GDP per head of population in the Balearic Islands in 1959 was 881,000 pesetas per head, with the national average slightly over 678,000 and that in the Community 1,162,000 pesetas.[1] Comparing the economy of the islands with that of the most developed regions of Spain confirms that the islands were ahead of the Valencian region and lagged behind the Catalonia, Madrid, and Basque regions, even though the differences were not enormous. It is in 1961 that Spain reached a level of revenue per head equaling that of the Balearic Islands in 1955, which leads to the conclusion that the economic structure of the islands at the dawn of the rise of tourism did not have any insurmountable retarding factors that could have led to the frankly tertiary orientation which that surfaced in the 1960s. It is therefore unwise to suggest that it was pre-existing poverty that was the only factor that made tourism the main activity in the islands. The factors

Table 2.2 Revenue per head of population in constant pesetas of 1990

Year	Spain	Balearic Islands	Balearic Islands (Spain=100)
1955	355,124	428,105	120.55
1957	383,390	453,061	118.17
1960	382,023	447,038	117.02
1962	459,539	628,689	136.81
1964	507,507	745,666	146.93

Table 2.3 GDP per head of population in current pesetas

Year	Spain	Balearic Islands	Catalonia	Valencia	Madrid	Basque Country
1959	24,312	31,601	36,999	28,044	36,268	39,638
1961	29,633	38,530	45,652	33,280	43,912	47,540
1963	39,220	51,239	58,778	42,694	56,722	62,767
1965	49,364	64,859	71,800	51,983	73,145	78,059

Sources: E. Reig and A. Picazo, *Capitalización y crecimiento de la economía balear, 1955–1996* (Bilbao: Fundación BBV, 1998), 282; J. Alcaide, *Renta Nacional de España y su distribución provincial. Serie homogénea* (Bilbao: Fundación BBV, 1999).

that should be considered are different, and it is in this sense that we need to elaborate on an economic model where the polyvalence of the social agents becomes the principal motivating factor.

Growth, Tertiarization, and Crisis in the Model

Economic growth in the Balearic Islands is constant from 1955 until the end of the century, as the figures in table 2.4. Between 1955 and 1996, the gross value added rate rose by 5.09 percent, which is more than one point above the national mean of 3.97. It is the highest regional growth index of all the communities in forty years and is directly related to the international economic situation, whose vicissitudes would seriously disturb the islands' economic structure on two occasions; that is, at the time of the 1973 energy crisis and between 1991 and 1993. However, that only partially affected the flow of travelers to the islands, which maintained its upward tendency. In this respect the figures are spectacular: from 98,000 tourists visiting the islands in 1950, to one million in 1965, two million in 1969, three million in 1971, five million in 1982, and ten million in 1998. They therefore survived the critical periods quite easily. This influx of visitors produced an impact that radically changed the socio-economic structure of the islands. We are faced with a truly Copernican revolution in the economy of the islands, otherwise relatively unchanged since the sixteenth century, which was carried by an avant-garde spirit in the tourist enterprises. This phenomenon also generated the know-how that was exportable to other areas, which had similar characteristics but were less mature in tourist terms (particularly the Canaries, Cuba, the Dominican Republic, and China). The results were impressive: the tourist revenue in the islands moved from almost 439,000 million pesetas in 1990 to just over a billion in 1998, with a growth rate of 14.73 percent compared with 1997.[2]

Table 2.4 Growth rate of gross value added (in %)

Years	Balearic Islands	Spain
1955–1964	7.49	5.10
1964–1975	5.18	5.58
1975–1985	4.56	2.14
1985–1991	4.14	4.44
1991–1993	- 0.19	- 0.19
1993–1996	4.98	2.84

Source: E. Reig and A. Picazo, *Capitalización y crecimiento de la economía balear, 1955–1996* (Bilbao: Fundación BBV, 1998), 55.

These considerations highlight two fundamental factors. On the one hand, the break with the only historic method of passenger and goods transport, that is by sea, because of the development of air transport, a fundamental phenomenon in ensuring the movement of tourists. And also the survival of some hesitant but appreciable industrial activity, mainly in the shoe industry, in this context of tertiary development. On the other hand, the problem of the environmental impact resulting from this extensive growth, because of the pressure it exerted on land requirements and the consumption of energy. In this chapter we undertake an exploratory examination of these two factors.

The Transport Revolution

In the Balearic Islands tourism generated an important level of demand in the sphere of transport both of people and of goods. Air traffic increased because of the increase in international flights, mostly charter flights, leading to important investment for the construction of a new airport, which in a very short time became one of the most important in Europe in terms of number of passenger. Majorca became a fundamental node in the air network of the continent. Maritime traffic, of prime importance where goods transport is concerned, also increased because of the upsurge in consumption. In this case, newly constructed port installations and new transport systems facilitated this traffic.

Air transport of passengers gained importance in the early post-war years. Between 1940 and 1950, direct connections between Palma and the principal European towns were rare. For passenger traffic, connections were made via Barcelona, Madrid, and Valencia and were characterized by slight oscillations in demand, though with a clear tendency to increase. But in 1950 more than 90 percent of European travelers who visited the islands used air transport, whereas those traveling by ship rarely rose above 10 percent. The flights linked Majorca with some of the main European capitals by means of regular connections guaranteed by the most important airlines. This European network of the 1950s, whose main departure points were in North Atlantic Europe (Amsterdam, Brussels, London, Manchester, Paris), was – thanks to its air links with Majorca – successfully extended in the direction of the Mediterranean region.

Seen in the light of economic analysis, the figures for maritime traffic suggest different hypotheses and at the same time pose serious problems of interpretation. We want to emphasize that we are working with important variables, given the difficulty of reducing them to units of value at present. But from the point of view of the formation of transport networks, the data available are sufficiently trustworthy to allow us to determine their basic components. Between 1945 and 1959, Majorca's maritime trade with Europe developed with, as main partners, Great Britain (45 percent), Holland (16 percent), France (11 percent), Norway (7 percent), and Germany (7 percent). The requirements of the Majorcan economy, urgent in terms of energy resources and machines, explain this obvious orientation in terms of external trade, which in its turn determines the structure of this network which is clearly concentrated on the countries of Western Europe. Between 1960 and 1973, these fundamental axes were maintained, even if the course of the flow of imports shows some decisive variations: first, modifications arise at the level of goods brought from the previous centers of the maritime network compared with the network as a whole; second, new nodes are integrated into the network, which are important both for their contributions in terms of goods and in terms of expanding the network. Even if the main points of connection relating to exports from the port of Palma continued to be the same as in the preceding period (dominated by Great Britain, Holland, and Germany), where imports were concerned the divergence was clear in a certain number of cases. First, Britain was no longer a major connection because its imports dropped from 50 percent to 11 percent of the total of European imports to the port of Palma; a factor linked with its loss of importance in terms of energy provision. Another fact worthy of note is the entry of certain Eastern European countries with a flow of goods, which is by no means negligible, such as Romania (17 percent), the Soviet Union (15 percent), Poland (13 percent), and Bulgaria (8 percent), together comprising almost 53 percent of the total imports between the tourist boom and the 1973 crisis. This process is linked with the provision of products derived from oil.[3]

Thus, in the middle of this economic development, Iron Curtain countries replaced Great Britain as a supplier of energy to the Balearic Islands at exactly the same time as the British became the main tourists on the islands and consequently Great Britain became the main node in the air passenger transport network. This economic development is a typical example of using the situation of being an island to obtain, by means of flexible connections that make sea and air transport possible, the most favorable articulation of the two circuits. In this way the specialization of each network for an almost exclusive purpose (sea transport = goods, air transport = passengers) made it possible for Majorca to occupy an advantageous position at the heart of Europe.

A Tourist Economy against Increasingly Important Environmental Limits

The economic expansion of the islands gives rise to serious contradictions in terms of the environment, which become more and more important in view of the fact that we are dealing with insular economies whose backbone is European tourism, which increasingly appreciates the existence of an unspoiled environment and the abundance of natural sites. These economies managed to escape from critical cycles by means of new waves of expansion characterized by an increased consumption of land and, in consequence, negative effects on the countryside, their main source of income. This is how the conditions that existed at the beginning of the process of economic growth were reproduced following three very obvious vectors: the major increase in the number of visitors, the growth in tourist consumption and, above all, the expansion of the construction sector (see table 2.5).

Between 1955 and 1996, the growth rate of the service sector overtook that of agriculture and industry at the same time as the construction sector produced rates, which taken as a whole were higher than 5 percent. The impetus given by the tourism industry explains this effect. The large-scale development of the construction sector at this time was the main and most important economic manifestation: for the external economies that were created as a result of this urban development, the absence of planning represented a stimulant in the short term and a problem in the long term. The hotel infrastructure

Table 2.5 Growth rate of gross value added in the Balearic Islands by sectors (in %)

Years	Agriculture	Industry	Construction	Services
1955–1964	5.60	3.72	12.47	7.94
1964–1975	- 0.89	5.42	5.26	5.54
1975–1985	1.63	2.21	1.60	5.36
1985–1991	1.18	4.42	6.36	3.97
1991–1993	10.32	- 3.87	- 12.48	1.18
1993–1996	2.43	1.74	7.91	5.19

Source: E. Reig and A. Picazo, *Capitalización y crecimiento de la economía balear, 1955–1996* (Bilbao: Fundación BBV, 1998), 65.

proliferated in an anarchic development process, which lasted almost until the beginning of the 1970s; 83 percent of the hotels in Majorca listed in 1992 were built before 1974. The environmental impact connected with the destruction of the coast has repercussions for this economic development. But this economic model affected not only real estate, which was already limited in the islands, but also other areas that we examine below.

Table 2.6 shows that economic growth, directly connected with the increase in the number of tourists, demographic development, and the GDP rate, gave rise to measurable negative externalities. For example, in 1998, the islands led the Spanish regional table for the production of urban household waste at 1.80 kilogram per head per day, with the national average of 1.19 kilogram, while the ash produced by incineration continued to accumulate. In 1999, the pressure on water resources in the Palma-Calvia area, the most populated in the Balearic Islands, led to a daily consumption per head of population of about 200 liters, producing serious water shortage problems, which made it necessary to introduce measures such as purification and desalination. All these factors increase the consumption of energy to the extent that the solutions they required created vicious circles.

In fact mass tourism is the origin of important variations in the degree of energy consumption on the islands because of three determining factors. First, the growth in the economy and consequently in the levels of activity; second, technological development, which allowed a more active use of energy and favored the vertiginous rise in consumption; finally, variations in price relative to the different forms of energy, which brought a diminution in the final price. This quantitative leap originated from two basic sectors: the construction and the electricity. These two cases demonstrate a total dependence on external energy sources because the availability of fossil fuels on the islands is reduced and of a mediocre calorific quality compared with the needs of a

Table 2.6 The impact of the economic growth of the Balearic Islands

Indicators	Growth Rate
Coal imports (1997/1996)	17.19
Coke imports (1997/1996)	14.31
Water consumption (Palma and Calvià, 1999/1998)	5.43
Energy consumption	6.30
Solid urban waste production (Palma, 1997/1991)	7.94
Population (1996/1991)	7.28
Tourists (1998/1997)	9.17
GDP (1999/1998)	7.34

Source: C. Manera, *El coll d'ampolla ecològic del creixement econòmic balear, 1985–2000. Una perspectiva des de la historia econòmica*, paper presented at the Seminario de Historia Económica, Universitat de les Illes Baleares, 2000a.

production stimulated by increasing demand. In the area of construction, the activity of the cement industry increased in the 1980s on, which necessitated an increase in coal and coke imports, leading to this phenomenon being christened the "second tourist book." The figures are indisputable: from 22,000 tons in 1981 to 63,000 tons at the beginning of 1990. To their own production of cement, partly destined for export though mainly intended to satisfy the internal demands of the construction industry, one must add the important introduction of external cement supplies, which fulfill the requirements in this particular area. Moreover, the data concerning the consumption of electric energy per inhabitant indicate that tertiarization also represented an explosive increase in energy consumption: from 496 KWH in 1965 to almost 2,500 in 1988. That said the list of these variables together with economic indicators does not always show an improvement in terms of the energy efficiency of the economy as shown in table 2.7.

This data in table 2.7 show that, in an economic situation of strong growth in the regional GDP (which results ultimately in the islands surpassing all the Spanish regions in terms of income per head of population) this finally absorbs any possible small progress in terms of energy efficiency resulting from the adoption of more modern technology. It is only during periods of apparent recession that one can observe positive signs of energy use. In table 2.7, this is the case for 1991 and 1992 because of the impact of the Gulf War, which led to a short period of awareness of the scarcity – and consequently the expensiveness – of fossil fuels. But the later tendency allows little doubt: for every extra million pesetas of increased regional GDP it was necessary to inject almost two tons of oil or its equivalent destined for the different processes of production or consumption, with a tendency to increase. This figure contains a specific lesson

Table 2.7 Energy intensity of the Balearic economy (energy consumption per million pesetas of GDP in constant values)

Year	(A)	(B)	(C)	Intensity (C/A)
1985	794,420	719,879	1,261,908	1.59
1986	827,447	827,447	1,269,520	1.53
1987	894,149	954,146	1,460,693	1.63
1988	956,731	1,087,314	1,530,346	1.60
1989	983,043	1,208,192	1,593,790	1.62
1990	998,616	1,324,576	1,646,127	1.65
1991	1,029,889	1,489,233	1,161,831	1.13
1992	1,044,096	1,623,605	1,596,498	1.53
1993	1,003,028	1,680,451	1,635,094	1.63
1994	1,053,591	1,861,736	1,803,854	1.71
1995	1,101,585	2,034,046	1,876,799	1.70
1996	1,128,254	2,154,615	1,961,109	1.74
1997	1,177,622	2,309,125	2,114,300	1.80

(A) GDP at factor cost, in millions of constant pesetas of 1986.

(B) GDP at factor cost, in millions of current pesetas.

(C) Gross energy consumption in TEP.

Sources: Based on authors' personal calculation. The data concerning GDP were produced by the General Directorate of Programming and Economic Development, Council of Finances and Budget of the Government of the Balearic Islands. Our thanks to Maria Marqués for enabling me to access this data. The variables for energy are taken from the document "Statistiques énergétiques. Iles Baléares 1997" (Energy Statistics: Balearic Islands 1997), General Directorate of Industry, Council for Agriculture, Trade and Industry of the Government of the Balearic Islands, 1997.

that cannot be ignored because it affects an economy in which services and not industry are the leading sector: the case of the Balearic Islands demonstrates that tertiarized economic growth can meet with serious difficulties in terms of energy efficiency if it does not change its modes of consumption and encourage the development of technological development – which, in turn, is more efficient – with the aim of reducing environmental and energy costs and, as a result, the costs of production. Further statistical data on the tourism industry of the Balearics from 1960 to 2004 is presented in the appendix to this chapter.

Conclusions

From the economic point of view, and with the exception of some periods, the Balearic Islands have always benefited from an open economy. Their favorable situation in the Mediterranean made the archipelago an object of desire for various empires and an important link in their diplomatic, military, and commercial strategies. Their magnificent guaranteed income has supported a decisive commercial expansion with a great capacity for promoting changes in the products supplied by the islands from the Middle Ages until present day. The islands reached the end of the millennium in the incontestable leading position compared with the other Spanish regions, and occupy a favorable position compared with the most advanced European regions. Faced with these positive statements, two questions arise: What encouraged this situation? And why the Balearic Islands and not other economies possess similar advantages, or even better endowed, such as, notably, the other islands in the Mediterranean basin? The reply that is most frequently advanced as the most convincing is the arrival of mass tourism on the Balearic archipelago considered as a radical factor in breaking with the past. This is, no doubt, a correct diagnosis. But we also want to emphasize that such response is incomplete. We provide three final reflections as possible avenues of debate, and research.

1. *For the Balearic Islands the analysis of the internal factors of the economy – agrarian structure, impulses from their own market, manufacturing and industrial activities – has been supported and given depth by studying trade factors.* Poverty, as far as insular economies are concerned, leads ultimately to two scenarios: it either leads to autarchy with very few choices – and that is where isolation and social insecurity appear unrelentingly (e.g., Corsica, Sardinia, and Sicily), or it encourages the social agents – that is, the authorities, the merchants, the entrepreneurs, the small producers – to make the effort to discover the most favorable formulas for obtaining what their own country does not produce. And, what is more important, they try to keep the circuits intact to avoid new undesirable situations in the future. The Balearic Islands embarked on the strategy that aimed to seek and find alternatives to states of prostration. Maritime exports were also fundamental for financing the purchase of imports until the 1960s, including food, raw materials, machines, and energy supplies. The nature of these goods made it possible to deduce what changes were in progress in the productive structure of the islands, to the point where it is possible to question once more several positions that are invariably held with regard to the economic growth of the Balearic Islands. In the case of Majorca, we have shown that the bases of its production were much richer and more varied than research linked to the agricultural sector allowed us to presume; where Minorca is concerned, we have emphasized that its particular path of expansion is due less to the British and much more to the plans of local entrepreneurs. If one of the major problems of economic development is a lack of understanding of the markets and the uncertainty attached to them, there is no doubt that this hurdle has been

broadly surmounted by the Balearic economy in the course of its recent history. This constant contact with the world of transactions empowered both capacities and attitudes, both on the operational level where internal insular demand is the main stimulating factor, and on the level of negotiations with more distant markets, without mentioning those on a national level. In terms of this last point, the function of the invisible factors has probably been crucial to the growth of the Balearic economy. This subject is more widely understood thanks to recent chronological data on the rise of tourism, but it is no less true that before the appearance of these phenomenal returns on capital, the amassing of profits on business external to the islands' productive economy, the rewards from maritime insurance, the movement of capital resulting from the effects of change could have been the ingredients that finally set the framework for a positive balance of payments.

2. *The case of the Balearic Islands demonstrates a fundamental concept: the existence of unconventional elements, which also help us understand the economic growth of a country or a region.* This is perhaps the most original contribution of the Balearic model. The Balearic Islands, which are not blessed with an abundance of what have always been considered the fundamental conditions in modern theories of growth – accessible sources of energy, industrialization based on important sectors, and so on – have seen a sufficiency of economic propositions, emanating from a multitude of anonymous protagonists, which have accelerated growth. These projects, which were micro-economic in character, had macro-economic results, which is what we have been describing throughout this chapter. We have also been able to demonstrate that Majorca and Minorca have shown from the eighteenth century on, obvious evidence of entrepreneurial capacity, latent and available, which was not always manifest, but which organized and directed one of the major comparative advantages of the islands: the versatility of their labor force. It is precisely this capacity, manifested in the changes that affected the economic structures of the islands, that is responsible for the retroactive effects that accompany the new challenges. In other words, applying the orthodox methods used to analyze the composition of the labor market, the classical Clarkian sectorization, to the Balearic Islands has frequently led to conclusions presented as irrefutable – even though they were erroneous – on the nature of their economy. It is true that economic historians continue to use this parameter, as has been the case in this chapter, and it has a usefulness, which is convincing in several cases. However, a deeper understanding of the historical evolution of the Balearic economy permits us to observe situations

of mobility, multiactivity, and small-scale initiatives, which often have a tangential relationship to the conventional rules of strict sectorization. In Majorca and Minorca the dichotomy between agriculture and industry cannot be automatically assumed, to the extent that the characteristics of their respective evolutions from the end of the eighteenth century on, whose principal element is the strength of the workforce and of professional ability closely linked to trade, transform these two islands into two examples of an economic development which it is difficult to associate with more rigid conventional models.

3. *Tourism makes a precocious appearance in Majorca, unlike Corsica, Sardinia, Sicily, and Malta, or even the Spanish Levant. This is due to the existence of other important factors which, to a certain degree, are particular to the economic growth of this Balearic Islands.* The conclusion that we propose is that the Balearic economy was not a poor economy when the political and economic transformations of the 1950s took place in Spain, and that it was not poor because the islands' economic base, which had survived the poverty of the 1940s with extreme difficulty, nevertheless appeared sufficiently solid to recover by the 1960s become the most prosperous Spanish region in terms of income per head of population in comparison with the historically industrialized economies thanks to the use of the two formulas used in the past: production for sale and intervening between supply and demand. We believe that these are the historical foundations – admittedly not without problems, contradictions, and phases of recession – that provide the most adequate explanations of the process. The main points are the spirit and the skill, which meant that the islands knew how to negotiate with distant markets to be able to change currencies, to work out effective strategies aimed at reducing transaction costs and, most important, to be capable of transforming one economic sector into another by using the capital, which historically represented the growth of the economy. In this respect the Balearic Islands are closer to the economic evolution of the Levant region than to that of other regions possessing a classic industrial structure. In the case of the Balearic Islands it is a matter of the particular skill which it demonstrated in order to invest. The development of the Balearic economy from the expansion of the wine industry in Majorca in the eighteenth century to the progress of the manufacture of shoes, wool, and cotton fabrics in Majorca and Minorca, passing through the expansion of almond and fig cultivation as well as the irrigation culture of the "grande Baléare" in the nineteenth and twentieth centuries, until the appearance of mass tourism on both islands, should be considered as a continuous process, with an

independent logic in each island, but with the common traits described above. Thus, it is a history of a long sequence with a wide variety of repercussions, external economies, and motivating forces. There are decisive connections between the investments of the different periods we have analyzed: to talk of unidentifiable ruptures with the past – as is usually done when analyzing tourism, which one literally separates from the entire preceding economic process – only clouds our understanding of the economic development. Because this way of defining the problem ignores the most direct precedents that justify the tourist boom and consigns the important capital that has made this development possible.

Notes

1. J. Alcaide, ed., *Renta Nacional de España y su distribución provincial. Serie homogénea* (Bilbao: Fundación BBV, 1999).
2. M. Alenyà, ed., *Informe econòmic i social de les Illes Balears* (Palma de Mallorca: Sa Nostra Caixa de Balears, 1999).
3. J.M. Escartín, C. Manera, and J. M. Petrus, "Le role de l'île de Majorque dans la formation des réseaux de transports européens (1945–1973)," in *Les réseaux européens transnationaux XIXème–XXème siècles. Quels enjeux?* ed. M. Merger, A. Carreras, and A. Giuntini (Nantes: Ouest Editions, 1995).

Appendix

Table 2.8 Number of air traffic passengers and tourists, 1960–2004

Year	No. of air traffic passengers Mallorca	No. of air traffic passengers Menorca	No. of air traffic passengers Ibiza	No. of air traffic passengers Balearics	No. of tourists Balearics
1960	636,764			636,764	371,882
1961	819,469	2,972		822,441	485,919
1962	1,044,633	23,013		1,067,646	637,232
1963	1,226,811	24,985		1,251,796	738,516
1964	1,636,821	44,184	150,843	1,831,847	865,349
1965	2,046,196	52,620	186,814	2,685,360	1,155,550
1966	2,393,340	70,089	256,246	2,616,675	1,326,390
1967	2,734,534	89,557	338,766	3,162,857	1,531,580
1968	3,168,178	113,519	447,617	3,729,314	1,794,741
1969	4,078,968	170,788	690,281	4,490,055	2,381,096
1970	4,723,331	246,596	882,439	5,852,366	2,703,197
1971	6,166,447	296,018	1,196,173	7,658,638	3,603,085
1972	6,946,491	374,632	1,361,046	8,682,169	4,128,291
1973	7,096,715	478,634	1,544,023	9,119,372	4,310,595
1974	6,442,185	472,795	1,426,658	8,341,638	3,943,119
1975	6,812,370	541,413	1,520,217	8,874,000	4,144,713
1976	6,367,294	532,153	1,519,755	8,419,202	3,904,010
1977	7,055,815	517,091	1,653,687	9,226,593	4,252,708
1978	7,894,806	658,673	1,915,318	10,468,797	4,780,002
1979	7,952,979	787,070	2,100,168	10,840,217	4,944,068
1980	7,392,779	805,795	2,052,141	10,250,715	4,672,956
1981	7,930,977	830,591	2,175,663	10,937,231	4,984,084
1982	8,599,125	890,610	2,295,514	11,785,249	5,290,654
1983	8,737,827	903,614	2,334,453	11,975,894	5,457,325
1984	9,347,284	956,625	2,512,440	12,816,349	5,865,724
1985	8,804,152	921,048	2,257,244	11,982,444	5,387,158
1986	9,932,851	1,135,163	2,604,873	13,672,887	6,154,910
1987	11,342,842	1,480,301	2,945,574	15,768,717	6,998,710
1988	11,719,014	1,648,031	2,942,034	16,309,079	7,199,704
1989	11,536,174	1,641,159	2,813,175	15,990,508	6,710,229
1990	11,334,228	1,470,697	2,467,166	15,272,091	6,349,254
1991	11,773,158	1,490,478	2,533,061	15,796,697	6,518,522
1992	11,867,370	1,660,843	2,569,016	16,097,229	6,660,166
1993	12,436,599	1,728,015	2,745,132	16,909,746	7,130,966
1994	14,264,355	2,057,944	3,231,756	19,554,055	8,250,329
1995	14,733,467	2,073,783	3,359,220	20,166,480	8,468,138
1996	15,382,588	2,023,572	3,285,815	20,691,975	8,600,796
1997	16,562,090	2,235,600	3,539,817	22,337,507	9,280,500
1998	17,664,783	2,426,974	3,829,439	23,921,196	10,067,100
1999	19,233,162	2,617,180	4,185,633	26,035,975	10,820,000
2000	18,315,144	2,775,891	4,475,710	25,566,745	11,096,500
2001	19,132,436	2,825,151	4,426,505	26,384,092	10,928,500
2002	17,832,761	2,733,733	4,094,446	24,660,940	10,209,800
2003	19,197,770	2,704,038	4,156,493	26,058,301	10,495,926
2004	20,415,764	2,631,334	4,170,422	27,217,520	10,799,077

Source: C. Manera, *Història del creixement econòmic a Mallorca, 1700–1930* (Palma: Lleonard Muntaner, 2001).

Table 2.9 Cement and energy consumption, 1960–2004

Year	Consump. Cement Balearics (tons)	Gas-Oil Sales Balearics (tons)	Fuel-Oil Sales Balearics (tons)	Petrol Sales Balearics (tons)	Vol. Elec. Invoiced Balearics (MW/h)
1960					
1961					
1962					
1963					
1964	179,641				
1965	219,750				
1966	223,056				
1967	222,103				
1968	233,164				
1969	287,328				
1970	348,727				
1971	450,000				
1972	500,000				
1973	505,510				
1974	435,637				
1975	281,422				
1976	270,908				
1977	254,831				
1978	275,620				
1979	414,000				
1980	455,000				
1981	454,000	163,804		150,158	
1982	465,000	168,207		157,006	
1983	480,000	207,577		219,243	492,146
1984	479,000	208,947		230,800	522,171
1985	472,000	208,450		237,980	545,989
1986	524,280	220,066	172,780	254,883	598,657
1987	701,963	237,867	199,774	280,204	615,809
1988	736,547	247,815	218,297	302,735	648,306
1989	706,044	267,210	245,296	321,853	700,473
1990	715,993	288,357	269,231	330,566	729,874
1991	598,711	282,731	276,433	331,846	838,493
1992	524,960	264,871	271,732	332,444	853,476
1993	465,855	278,326	270,704	336,387	828,438
1994	556,331	303,272	314,298	353,363	855,872
1995	621,483	339,829	341,118	361,933	877119
1996	624,512	358,371	351,978	374,951	939168
1997	663,223	389,633	206,262	386,510	960178
1998	754,299	415,360	49,733	397,574	1116390
1999	927,671	486,302	75,062	405,007	1263378
2000	1,020,282	561,996	129,594	399,803	3,884,291
2001	1,085,016	627,245	150,110	399,389	4,173,449
2002	992,569	699,328	123,519	377,003	4,337,497
2003	993,653	872,449	77,419	383,801	4,749,844
2004	950,095	872,343	72,923	370,017	4,952,735

Source: C. Manera, *Història del creixement econòmic a Mallorca, 1700–1930* (Palma: Lleonard Muntaner, 2001).

Table 2.10 Offical population statistics of the Balearic Islands, 1960–2004

Year	Official population Mallorca	Official population Menorca	Official population Ibiza	Official population Formentera	Official population Balearics
1960	362,302	42,305	27,225	2,671	434,503
1961					
1962					
1963	377,613	43,439	35,616	2,710	459,378
1964					
1965	406,007	45,365	40,698	2,887	494,957
1966					
1967					
1968					
1969				3,066	529,430
1970	438,656	48,817	42,456	3,017	532,946
1971					
1972	466,843	44,871	43,840	3,091	558,645
1973	456,419	51,062	44,828	3,125	555,434
1974	464,048	51,704	45,820	3,169	564,741
1975	492,247	53,548	48,315	3,595	597,705
1976	512,342	54,643	51,303	3,637	621,925
1977	522,513	55,405	52,672	3,658	634,248
1978	529,019	55,984	53,974	3,725	642,702
1979	535,506	56,928	55,506	3,807	651,747
1980					
1981	534,511	57,243	59,933	4,222	655,909
1982	545,171	58,416	62,033	4,319	669,939
1983	562,193	60,006	65,228	4,513	691,940
1984	572,232	61,080	67,700	4,597	705,609
1985	581,546	61,967	70,813	4,725	719,051
1986	550,962	59,583	64,157	4,734	680,933
1987	567,191	61,284	67,109	4,731	700,307
1988	586,002	64,460	72,992	4,713	728,173
1989	601,621	66,868	77,397	5,031	750,967
1990	613,831	68,347	80,538	5,202	767,918
1991	568,065	64,431	72,309	4,338	709,138
1992	582,975	65,724	76,563	4,967	728,609
1993	610,574	67,541	81,782	5,229	765,126
1994	622,447	68,027	82,820	5,323	778,617
1995	629,445	68,731	84,373	5,435	787,984
1996	609,150	67,009	78,867	5,353	760,379
1997	n/a	n/a	n/a	n/a	n/a
1998	637,510	69,070	84,044	5,859	796,483
1999	658,043	70,825	86,953	5,999	821,820
2000	677,014	72,716	89,611	6,289	845,630
2001	702,122	75,296	94,334	6,875	878,627
2002	730,778	78,796	99,933	7,461	916,968
2003	753,584	81,067	105,103	7,607	947,361
2004	758,822	82,872	106,220	7,131	955,045

Source: C. Manera, *Història del creixement econòmic a Mallorca, 1700–1930* (Palma: Lleonard Muntaner, 2001).

Table 2.11 Statistical data on the tourism industry of the Balearics, 1960–2004

Year	No. of vehicles Balearics	Inflation rate Balearics	Unemploy-ment rate Balearics	Economic growth	Tourist expenditure (million €)	Tourist expenditure Growth
1960						
1961						
1962	14,780					
1963						
1964	21,685					
1965	26,755					
1966	35,182					
1967	44,371					
1968	53,862					
1969	65,544					
1970	78,777					
1971				11.79		
1972				10.58		
1973	120,938			4.91		
1974	136,988			- 1.47		
1975	147,177			2.65		
1976	158,083			- 0.85		
1977	170,173			3.03		
1978	185,104			5.34		
1979	201,557	15.97	5.37	2.90		
1980	217,161	14.16	7.94	0.40		
1981	231,976	14.75	9.81	4.49		
1982	247,052	14.23	11.72	5.67		
1983	261,389	11.83	13.92	3.76		
1984	269,161	11.29	14.14	5.46	1,597.9	
1985	286,766	8.35	13.89	- 1.46	1,504.2	- 5.9%
1986	295,589	9.24	14.33	8.66	1,868.2	24.2%
1987		4.98	14.17	8.62	2,057.9	10.2%
1988	337,617	4.74	11.12	5.32	2,241.7	8.9%
1989	352,829	5.92	10.66	2.10	2,230.4	- 0.5%
1990		5.80	10.49	0.56	2,072.7	- 7.1%
1991	372,323	5.10	9.91	0.36	2,224.0	7.3%
1992	405,285	5.13	11.33	0.34	2,326.9	4.6%
1993	433,358	4.09	17.62	1.98	2,666.5	14.6%
1994	476,164	5.24	17.72	7.46	3,512.8	31.7%
1995	558,092	4.96	14.27	3.99	3,858.9	9.9%
1996	578,935	3.80	13.45	3.24	4,053.7	5.0%
1997	606,733	2.35	11.75	5.65	4,465.1	10.1%
1998	642,648	2.00	11.11	6.42	5,112.6	14.5%
1999	680,362	2.34	7.92	7.70	5,652.4	10.6%
2000	704,559	3.63	6.32	3.77	6,050.4	7.0%
2001	738,368	4.1	5.95	2.60	7,593.4	25.5%
2002	752,997	3.9	7.61	0.88	6,808.1	- 10.3%
2003	752,224	3	9.71	1.10	7,385.8	8.5%
2004		2.8	9.16	1.50		

Source: C. Manera, *Història del creixement econòmic a Mallorca, 1700–1930* (Palma: Lleonard Muntaner, 2001).

Chapter 3

Tourism and Business during the Twentieth Century in Greece

Continuity and Change

Margarita Dritsas

General Observations

Because this chapter was originally prepared for a conference on business history (BH) and tourism, I shall start by pointing out that BH is a new area of interest for historians in Greece. Its development spans barely two decades, institutionalization is low, and the number of studies produced is limited. BH is seen as a sub-branch of economic and social history and has found a good base in the banking sector.[1] A limited spillover can be discerned in the study of Greek industry.[2] Most other areas or sectors have not interested historians or businessmen to the same extent, with even less interest toward tourism. The most recent development has been the foundation of a "Research Academy for Tourism" by businessmen in the hotel sector, former state officials in tourism and academics interested in, among other things, the history of the sector. In addition, one of the dynamic professional associations in the sector, the Greek Committee of the World Association "Women in Tourism" has introduced an electronic museum of Greek tourism (see www.tourismmuseum.gr).

Despite the elusive nature of the concept of "tourism," the study of the history of tourism has been prompted by the realization that it is today the largest economic sector in Greece. As a phenomenon, it arose in the wake

Notes for this chapter begin on page 67.

of industrialization and over the last few decades has become closely linked with the process of de-industrialization.[3] More specifically, in 2000 tourism absorbed 247,500 people (out of a total of 3,901,400) and the hotels and restaurants branch alone contributed almost 10 percent of the GDP generated by the service sector, which amounted to over 60 percent of total. Tourism's contribution to the balance of payments is also impressive (32 percent of the invisible transaction balance).[4] Moreover, the tourism industry has shown particular flexibility and ability to adjust, in order to deal with crises. Initiatives taken by enterprises, and the fact that business firms of various sizes exhibit a high degree of complementarity among themselves, seems to be one of the major factors of success. Tourism strategy, at least as far as the private sector is concerned, appears to be based on the belief that constant innovation and the use of imagination are necessary components. This is one of the key elements that emerged out of the research that has been underway for the last few years. Since the nineteenth century, when the first regular flow of visitors began to be standardized, the sector has been characterized by a burgeoning of new business firms. However, there has so far been no analysis or typology of these organizations, their ownership arrangements, styles of management and cultural traits. Unfortunately statistics do not help in this case. The only measure that exists is the number of hotels in operation registered by the National Statistical Service (and previously by the National Tourist Organization). Over the years there have doubtless been significant changes that need to be studied, such as the emergence of a state hotel sector in the 1960s, the appearance of large firms, and the invasion of international enterprises. Official statistics on other types of businesses – restaurants, souvenir shops, travel agencies etc. are hard to come by and therefore it is difficult to draw any generalizations.

The long absence of historical analysis left a vacuum, which over the years was filled almost exclusively by architects, town planners, economists, geographers, and others who usually make scant reference to the past. The last two decades have witnessed a lively interest in the study of tourism development and policy matters. Studies usually focus on current problems, mostly referring to general government policy or to regional development. Some studies deal with the impact of tourism on society and on culture. Another group of studies represent econometric attempts to measure tourist sojourn, income, and consumption by foreign visitors in Greece etc. Most analysts use statistics sparingly and simply reiterate hypotheses or findings formulated by foreign authors. Tourism studies were until recently largely restricted to vocational schools and institutions. Hence, there have been a multitude of books written for "educational purposes," which present either basic economic or sociological analyses, lacking in synthesis and in critical appraisal of the relevant literature, or deal with practical matters of how to run travel agencies and hotels.

Recent output, prompted no doubt by the reorientation of government policy, concerns specific types of tourist development; for example, ecotourism or the package tour, professional tourism, entertainment and sport for hotel guests. Very few of these studies give any, even partial, view of the history of the tourist phenomenon or the evolution of the major debates about tourism.[5] Most of this research shows almost complete insensitivity to history and historical research. Indeed, there is a total neglect of the relationship between tourism and history, and within that, of the connection between tourism and economic history.

Research in the history of tourism is in its initial stages but positive steps have been made. An analysis of the development of modern tourism in Greece has been attempted, outlining the decisive turning points and trends as a basis for future analysis. The trend marks the transition from individual to organized group travel and the emergence of important business firms such as, for instance, travel agencies, hotels, and even publishers who specialize in travel books. By doing so, they helped create a network of travelers, agencies, hotels, and so on. The process was epitomized by the organization of the revived Olympic Games in 1896.

Brief History

During the nineteenth century, most of the full-service hotels outside of Athens were to be found in larger towns both on the Ionian Islands, which were under British rule until the 1860s, and in Patras, a major town enjoying frequent contact with the West. Otherwise visitors had to rely on the services of innkeepers, and conditions were far from satisfactory. This early phase of tourist development was dominated by an unregulated pattern of private initiative, although it is also a fact that early Greek entrepreneurs responded hesitantly to the still uncertain flow of visitors. Once the Corinth Canal was opened, many tourists preferred to visit Greece by way of cruises. Travelers lived on board steam ships, thus avoiding problematic accommodation and bad roads, only using carriages from Piraeus to Athens to visit the Acropolis and other antiquities. For the early visitor, travel was a quest for the folklore of the country and for its art, represented mainly by ancient monuments. The beauty of scenic nature was not yet highly valued and the trend was aptly illustrated in early professional photographs taken, especially of Athens, where only ancient monuments and hardly any people or landscapes were portrayed as significant sites. The importance of natural beauty spots came to the fore in the twentieth century, as transport conditions improved. The opening of railways and, even more so, of new roads allowed the development of the Greek coastline.

The initial phase of relatively small inflow of travelers soon gave way to a more sustained trend, as the European middle class started to travel abroad. Tourism as a modern phenomenon was born as the outcome of industrialization. The revolution in travel and the new age in transport and communications (railways and steam ships) made travel possible for whole families and groups of tourists. The extension of education and the new consumer patterns created new needs and the purpose of travel was differentiated (recreation, business, education, health, etc.). Incomes had improved and social policy was making a significant advance in most European countries. This stage in Greece stretched from the end of the nineteenth century through World War I. The last decade of the nineteenth century witnessed the proliferation of good hotels, travel agencies, and other businesses servicing tourists. At the same time, and because tourism mostly maintained its old "Grand Tour" educational and cultural aspects, most of the national collections of antiquities and artifacts that were housed in sumptuous museums became available for tourist consumption. Tourism thus contributed to the growing institutionalization of "national heritage," opening the way for endless representations, uses and reproductions by imaginative businessmen of all those objects and ideas (i.e., replicas and pictures of monuments, but also artifacts, arts, customs, symbols). National heritage being central to tourist development, it is understandable why, although business firms have over the years converged internationally with regard to ownership, products, and services, the design of policy has remained the domain of national politics, stressing or inventing national specificities.[6]

During this time Greece started to host increasing numbers of foreign tourists whose ranks were also inflated by wealthy Greeks residing in Central and Eastern Europe and in the Near East. Before the beginning of World War II, many more hotels appeared both in central towns and also elsewhere in Greece. The clientele had diversified: In addition to foreign tourists who chose Athens and stayed in central expensive hotels, expatriate Greek visitors – especially emigrants from the United States – preferred to spend their holidays in comfortable little hotels built by Greek Americans near their home towns (e.g., Arcadia in the Peloponnese). Toward the end of the interwar period, tourism became a tool of nationalist propaganda, and tourism affairs passed under the jurisdiction of none other than the Ministry of Press and Propaganda, which answered to the prime minister's office. Under the authoritarian government of Ioannis Metaxas, tourists were encouraged to appreciate the "Hellenic Miracle" – numerous advertisements diffused messages of national respectability, modernization, and pride. They showed new roads, new boats, comfortable hotels, picturesque landscapes, and "unspoiled" nature. "Eternal national glory" was reflected in ancient sites and monuments, Byzantine churches, castles, national costumes, and so on.

Within the more general trend of eugenics espoused by fascist governments all over Europe, a particular form of tourism was actively promoted in Greece. Spa towns began to mushroom all over the country near important springs and became a popular form of recreation even for modest income customers. The value of springs and rivers as life givers ensuring a mystical bond between man and earth was stressed by referring to age-old traditions and myths.[7] Moreover, special legislation was passed to regulate questions of the ownership of waters, their use and exploitation, and bathing cures in warm spring waters were prescribed by the social security system. In another corner of Greece, the Dodecanese, another tradition started under the impact of Italian rule. On Rhodes, new facilities were built by the Italian state and the island became a holiday and rest destination for the Italian military and state bureaucrats.

Early tourist opportunities for investment were usually grabbed by two groups of entrepreneurs. On the one hand, by astute and well-traveled Greek and foreign businessmen – often architects and engineers – who included tourism in their scope, attracted by the promise it held for more construction contracts. On the other hand, by several Greek Americans who had spent several years as immigrants in the United States (they were some of the several hundred thousand who immigrated to the United States between 1880 and 1921). Many among them had acquired experience in the ownership and running of host businesses (restaurant and related activities) and were returning home bringing their savings with them, in order to invest them in hotel businesses in their hometowns. Perceptions of the viability of tourism had definitely changed, although real conditions continued to fall short of expectations. Hotels built during this time, often quite pretentious and clean at the beginning, were established in various localities away from the capital. But after a few years of good business, because of the highly seasonal character of this early and still restricted tourist flow, they found they depended more on local trade – commercial travelers, notaries public, judges, and so on, who were less particular and definitely less affluent. When during World War I and during the Great Depression of the 1920s money stopped coming in regularly, hotels soon ran down and/or changed hands, which instead of rejuvenating them brought about their decline.

At the end of World War I, positive forecasts of an influx of European tourists and the realization by businessmen that they needed government support for any worthwhile development resulted in the foundation of the first big firm, Hellenic Hotels-Lampsa S.A. Capital contributions came from the big banks (General Bank, National Bank of Greece, Popular Bank, Bank of Athens, Bank of Industry, and Bank of National Economy) and businessmen. The company modernized, renovated, extended the Grande Bretagne hotel, and employed expert foreign staff for its management.[8]

Tourism and the State

Alongside private initiatives, a series of government measures began to influence the operation of the tourism sector. Several publications had appeared praising tourism and the prospects of development it held. Suggestions made by the authors emphasized the need for forward planning and for designating tourist zones according to existing hotel and transport facilities.[9] Suggestions also included the creation of national parks and the development of mountaineering and ski resorts. Improvements in communications, the provision of infrastructure for the cities and manpower training were given priority. In 1929, special legislation was passed (Law 4377) with the purpose of encouraging the foundation of new and the improvement of old hotel facilities. Toward the end of the period, bank credit for the construction of new hotels started for the first time to be advanced by Greek banks to credit-worthy customers, subject to terms similar to those prevailing for industry and commerce (short-term loans at an average 8 to 15 percent interest rate with high collateral).

No sooner had this development taken off than the Great Depression set in and foreign tourism declined temporarily. The drop was counteracted, however, by the rise of domestic tourism. For the first time the prospects of the sector impressed state leaders and tourist development was included in general economic policy. The Interwar period also saw the creation of new institutions for tourism: The Hellenic Tourist Organization (HTO), a predecessor of the post–World War II National Tourist Board, was born in 1930 and a Committee for Foreigners and Exhibitions was created by the Ministry of National Economy. One of the first steps taken by the HTO was the publication of leaflets on beauty spots in Greece. Statistics began to be collected and special loans were given by banks for the construction of hotels and spa interests. An official list of Greek hotels was published in 1933, but a few years earlier the first Greek travel book had appeared, including a list of approximately 250 recommended hotels all over the country. In 1934 Army General I.D. Petrides was appointed vice president of HTO and of the permanent exhibition of Greek products. Tourism was an appendage of trade and royal visits were organized in order to promote import-export relations among trade partners. Furthermore, the Hellenic Association of Hotel Owners appeared in 1935. It was a sort of chamber of commerce of hotels, which was supposed to support them and provide training for hotel managers and employees. Four years later, its scope was extended to include the issuing of loans to hotel businesses as reflected by its new title, Organization of Hotel Credit.[10]

It was the Metaxas government that created the position of undersecretary of press and tourism in 1936 and began to publish a monthly bulletin. Most of it was dedicated to political propaganda of the authoritarian regime and only a few pages were taken up by news of international and Greek tourism. Authoritarian and corporatist regimes are known for attaching particular importance to education; accordingly, the Higher School of Tourism was founded in Athens, and scholarships were given to graduates for further studies abroad, usually in Switzerland, Germany, and so on.[11]

These were also years of high unemployment rates and uncertainty, years of budget deficits, foreign borrowing and consequently of urgent need to increase foreign exchange earnings and produce a healthy balance of payments. The stabilization of the drachma in 1932 made Greece a very cheap country to visit, while the contribution of tourism in the "invisible accounts" (i.e., emigrant, shipping remittances and tourism revenue) and export revenue kept rising (see table 3.1).[12] This dynamism was the basis on which tourism gradually began to be considered on a par with industrial activity, while at the same time it was looming as an instrument of regional development. Within the general framework of belated industrialization and slow development in Greece, which had followed a pattern common to the Mediterranean region,[13] both state interventionism and dynamism by the tertiary sector made sense. Toward the end of the period, the improvement of tourist facilities by law enforcement was attempted,[14] albeit with limited results.[15] Of the total of 331 hotels inspected in the country in 1930, only 15 were in Class A, and 10 of those were limited companies, whereas the rest were small family or individual firms and partnerships. Those that were joint stock companies (JSCs) had a share capital amounting to 71.6 million drachmas (representing 2.5 percent of total nominal assets of all JSCs registered), and a ratio of own/borrowed funds of 2:1. Out of the ten, four (including Grande Bretagne) reported profits but three (spa centers) experienced considerable losses. They were relatively big companies usually owned by public authorities with substantial assets keeping accounts and employing qualified staff. However, credit remained limited during this time and it was only after World War II that it began to flow more regularly to the tourism sector.

Table 3.1 Recent tourism indicators

GDP 2000			EMPLOYMENT 2000			INVISIBLES 2000	
1 Total	2 Service (%)	3 Tourism (% 2/3)	4 Total	5 Service (%)	6 Hotel and Restaurant (% 5/6)*	7 Total	8 Hotel and Restaurant (%)
100	72		100	61.2	10.4	100	32.5

*Of this, 53.9 percent is male manpower, and 46.1 percent is female manpower.

What has just been outlined is certainly not an indication of any systematic policy. Tourism was perceived as a substitute for the opportunities created in the past by the army. In the absence of a healthy primary or a developed secondary sector was considered a way to keep people out of the dole queue, in partial employment; it was of secondary importance in relation to agriculture or industry. Within the corporatist perspective, however, of the semi-fascist Metaxas regime, tourism was able to contribute to the employment of the female population – particularly in rural areas – and to the revival of the traditional crafts and home industry as complementary activities to agriculture. Tourism was by no means yet a "road to development." Little consideration was given to serious investment in hotels, shops, services, transport facilities, to retailing, wholesaling, and manufacturing. Promotion was not energetically pursued either. As a result little had changed with regard to the constitution of tourist groups. Most tourists were Greek expatriates (from the United States, Egypt, Cyprus, and Turkey) returning for short visits,[16] and outnumbering any Europeans (British, French, and German). This specificity of tourist flow had determined hotel density and geographical distribution. For example, because a significant number of emigrants came from the Peloponnese, it was no coincidence that in the 1930s this region had a remarkable 28 percent of hotel facilities. Of the twenty-seven hotels registered, four were in Andritsaena, a small mountain town of no more than 2,000 people, which had been an important source of emigration since the 1880s. Hotel distribution had less to do with the fact that the Peloponnese also contained some of the antiquities and archaeological sites most familiar to Europeans (Mycenae, Tyrins, Olympia, Corinth) or because its shores had been carefully mapped in previous centuries by European travelers, explorers, and scientific missions.

It appeared as though the core of tourist policy continued to be based on the older belief that travelers would visit Greek archaeological sites regardless of conditions, or that former Greek emigrants/tourists were more important, because they were in a position to spend more. Between 1930 and 1940, the total number of tourists remained modest, not exceeding 100,000 annually, of which almost one-third were group tourists staying for only one day to visit the antiquities in Athens. Short stays seem to have been a direct result of the low level of facilities, and the consequent preference for organized cruises, usually arranged abroad by foreign agents who had correspondents in Athens. In fact, over ten travel agencies, of which four were foreign, were situated in central Athens. Foreign exchange earnings amounted to US$4,500,000 and this was a definite if slow increase in tourism's contribution to the balance of payments. A contribution, which became increasingly important as inputs from other sources – emigrants' remittances, exports, and so on – diminished due to the effects of the economic crisis.

The Post-War Period

Following World War II, there was an unprecedented growth in traveling for recreational purposes and new consumer patterns emerged. A report compiled at the end of the war compared the situation with conditions prevailing before the war and underlined the definite improvement of hotels in the provinces. Recommendations for tourist development were now made by US agencies and included a large array of measures, many of which were adopted by government authorities. They included the financing of several hotels in the provinces and the appointment of the representative of the American Express Travel Agency in Greece as general secretary of the resuscitated National Tourist Board (EOT). The new policy placed emphasis on institutional modernization and regulation. New legislation included provisions for expropriating property for hotel use and regulated the operation of a Supreme Council of Tourism (tourism in many small islands was a result of this policy, e.g., Hydra and Santorini).[17] A Chamber of Hotels[18] was founded in 1948 to improve hotel organization, raise the standard of the tourist trade, and insure hoteliers, and so on. Capital requirement was urgent and in 1946 the Organization of Tourist Credit was founded with the function of approving applications for credit, and fixing the amount and other terms of tourist loans to be granted by the National Bank of Greece. Capital for the new institution was provided by the Central Bank and was guaranteed by the state.[19] Conditions for the taxation of hotel and tourist establishments were also regulated. In addition to the moderate amount of 35 million drachmas extended by the Organization it ceased existence in 1953, another $1.5 million came from American Aid sources in the form of five-year loans. After 1953, the newly founded Organization for Financing Economic Development (OXOA) started to provide credit, whereas a few state loans were also advanced through the National Bank of Greece to selected enterprises, along the lines that have been mentioned earlier. This policy eventually neutralized the "sufficiency/saturation" principle that had ruled for part of the interwar period and many new hotels were built and older ones renovated. The National Bank of Greece finally realized the potential of the new field and emerged as the dominant credit institution.[20] The inability of alternative institutions like the Organization for Hotel Credit to survive, however, meant that capital was still expensive and the prospects of expansion remained limited, especially for smaller units.

Financing was not the only difficulty for tourist development; problems such as the lack of a connection between travel and tourism as well as the lack of publicity were just as important. They too were placed under the jurisdiction of the state. Accordingly, the EOT became a planning agency and an advisory body. In 1953 a number of illustrated publications on tourist spots in Greece were circulated for the first time and early reports praised the use of motorcars in touring the country.[21] Innovations were introduced in terms of tourist products (e.g., sightseeing buses and boat cruises organized by the EOT). One of the basic features of modern Greek tourist development was born: the preference for the motorcar and road transport rather than for railways; it was bound to have long-term negative effect on environmental pollution and weak backward linkages with industry.[22] Nor did it lead to any economies of scale for suppliers of tourism. The guidelines lay, nevertheless, within the framework of the more general post-war economic policy of fast reconstruction and modernization pursued by the post-1949 government and the subsequent Karamanlis cabinets (1958–1963) inspired by the determination to do away with old mentalities and traumas and reintroduce Greece as into the European core.[23]

It was from this period that the shift toward the attraction of mass tourism began to be energetically pursued by the state. Major banks supported the effort. By 1961, the first state-financed/run hotels and motels for average incomes – the Xenias – appeared and 172 hotels of several categories around the country were included in the official tourist guide book.[24] The Hellenic Hotels-Lampsa S.A., was no longer the only big firm owning and managing hotels; "Astir Tourism and Hotel Co.," run by the National Bank of Greece, proceeded to construct and manage large modern and comfortable hotels in selected areas on islands and inland regions, such as Rhodes,[25] Corfu, Herakleion (Crete), Kamena Vourla (a spa center), Alexandroupolis (Thrace), and to develop modern beach facilities for both foreign and domestic tourism (e.g., Glyfada, Vouliagmeni, and other coast areas in the outskirts of Athens). The Bank also tried to create the foundation for research into tourism by financing the compilation and publication of several studies and reports.[26] After 1955 the new National Tourist Board was integrated into the Office of the Prime Minister, definitely losing its previous propaganda character to become a central agency for planning and implementing tourist policy. It had a modern structure of several directorates concerned with the organization of tourist activities, advertising, management of tourist facilities, supervision of hotels, administrative affairs, technical services, and so on.

One of the first steps taken was the launching of an ambitious promotion campaign at home and abroad: Illustrated publications were published for general distribution, a committee of art professors and other prominent personalities advised on the aesthetics of what was to be produced. The target group was now twofold, one of its components being American tourists and the other domestic travelers. Leaflets were printed in several languages informing tourists of the EOT products (available bus tours, cruises, and festivals). Collaboration also started between the EOT, local groups, and art institutions, such as the National Theatre, for the organization of a series of art festivals.[27]

Moreover, cooperation with foreign publishers was sought by the EOT, and advertisements for beautiful land and seascapes appeared in major American newspapers. Until 1954 the single most important category of tourists continued to be expatriate Greeks from the United States, Egypt, and Turkey visiting their home country[28] but it was realized that demand had to be diversified by means of a more systematic policy.

The Center for Tourist Studies was founded with the purpose of compiling a "Tourist Geography" and of organizing educational and research seminars on tourism. Mass tourism was to be encouraged in imitation of the Italian and the French, but especially of the Spanish, pattern. Greece was gradually acquiring the well-known characteristics of a Mediterranean destination (sunshine, sea, sandy beaches, and cheap food). Conditions of entry for foreign tourists (visa requirements, currency exchange regulations, revised customs rules) were improved; infrastructure and transport was diversified; the devaluation of the Greek currency in 1953 made it a very cheap vacation destination; a favorable credit policy convinced ship owners to diversify routes and modernize their fleets. One example is ELMES (Hellenic Mediterranean Lines), which as of 1962 modernized to cover tourist traffic between Brindisi and Patras in cooperation with Italian lines. The new ferryboat line contributed to an unprecedented increase in the flow of motorists from Europe.[29] Guides were trained to deal with sightseeing groups and the school of tourist guides opened in the mid-1960s. Finally, tourist promotion was systematized. In addition to printing posters and advertising in the newspapers, the EOT regularly took part in international exhibitions. Ultimately, tourist information offices were established in the main capitals of Europe and the United States. Investment in tourism rose and it was estimated that between 1959 and 1961, 1,120 million drachmas from public funds went into tourism development. Not only were hotels built, but bus terminals, leisure facilities, and town improvement projects were also undertaken. In addition to the National Bank, the Ionian Bank now also showed particular interest through a takeover. Its affiliate S.A. Ionian Hotel Enterprises built a new luxury hotel in Athens, which began operation under the management of the US-operated Hilton.

During the 1960–64 Five-Year Plan tourism was for the first time considered the third most important economic sector in the country and was incorporated in the framework of productive investment.[30] Since 1960, tourism had already been seen as a way to solve the economic problem of underdeveloped or undeveloped regions, such as remote mountain areas and smaller islands.[31] Proposals were based on geographic position (usually near areas developed for tourism such as Rhodes, Kos, Mykonos, and so on) and on the comparative advantage of natural attractions. This implied the preservation of local architectural styles and the exploitation of natural environment, climate, the possible existence of spas, and antiquities. In addition, it presupposed the building of infrastructure projects (hotels, harbors, roads, entertainment facilities, marketing, and coordination). The policy was also intended to solve long-term problems of income distribution, regional employment, and the revival of the economy in the depressed areas. Until 1964, not only were public funds devoted to tourist development but 56 percent of them were allocated to the construction of new or the improvement of existing accommodation facilities and their management. A series of incentives for private investment was also included in new legislation.[32] Tourism started to extend geographically in new areas away from the urban centers and toward the islands. The EOT contributed in many ways, one of which was subsidizing new shipping lines until they were in a position to make profits.[33] As a result, between 1960 and 1966 total bed capacity rose from 50,456 to 82,262 (62.7 percent). The number of hotel beds rose from 49,797 in 1960 to 78,019 in 1966 (56.7 percent).

Had this policy continued into the 1970s, the economy might have improved further and tourism might have developed more smoothly. But the political situation changed drastically and tragically in 1967 when a military regime took power following a coup d'état. Many of the conditions for sustained development created in the preceding years were overturned by the reorientation toward a consumerist approach, by short-term economic policies, and irrational decision making. Until 1973 emphasis was placed, on the one hand, on the construction industry by the increase of credit facilities and tax exemptions and, on the other hand, to indiscriminate tourist development. For the first time, banks were allowed to advance medium-term loans to construction firms for the building of apartment buildings, houses, and hotels. At the same time, commercial banks were permitted to finance long-term investment in hotel and tourist enterprises, whereas loans for tourist development came from other sources, such as the National Mortgage Bank and the Post Office Savings Bank. The Bank of Greece rediscounted unpaid bank loans to enterprises, most often tourist firms that ran into difficulties. In fact the average annual rate of growth of tourist loans rose from 11.3 percent in the period between 1960 and 1966 to 26.7 percent between 1967 and 1973.

Tax concessions were introduced for hotels and firms and foreign capital ventures proliferated. Indeed foreign investment rose from 4 percent from the period between 1962 and 1967 to 66.1 percent of all investment in tourism in 1968 and represented 37 percent of total foreign capital invested in all sectors. Of this, 51.8 percent for the years 1968–1970 was US capital, although West German, Swiss, and French contributions were also important.[34] Foreign investment was mostly concentrated in the hotel business, especially in undeveloped coastal locations, reinforcing the features of mass tourism. The policy showed no consideration for "national interests" and led to the creation of serious imbalances. Low quality tourist facilities and small inefficient firms proliferated only to fall into disuse soon afterward, damaging the reputation of Greek tourism. Speculation in real estate values and construction deals became rampant and regional imbalances were accentuated; fast tourist development was now seriously affecting rural areas. In big cities like Athens or Thessaloniki, and in areas such as Crete or Chalkidiki, the problems of infrastructure and ecological balance became unmanageable.

Post-1974 Business Practices

Greek tourism developed further after the collapse of the military regime in 1974, when the energy crisis subsided in Europe and when links between Greece and Europe became tighter. This also led to a change in the composition of tourist flow. By 1973, tourists from the United States, who were still the largest group (in 1970, the flow of visitors from the United States was thirteen times larger than in 1953),[35] were beginning to be replaced by European groups. Tourism remained a matter of national concern as was the case for all European Economic Community (EEC) member states (the first steps toward a common tourist policy were taken as late as 1982).[36] During this period Greece has confirmed its role in the world and European tourism and its comparative advantages were quantified and advertised.[37] The share of Greece in OECD European countries in terms of foreign visitors increased from 2.2 percent in 1970 to 3.5 percent in 1982, while the origin of tourists was reversed: EEC nationals having risen from 46.69 percent of total in 1971 to 69.50 percent in 1987, those from the rest of the world falling from 36.60 percent in 1971 to 10.07 percent in 1987. The model of mass tourism so common for the Mediterranean countries, based on the perception that climate and heritage were strong comparative advantages,[38] was further reinforced. The economic importance of tourism was also acknowledged, as a source of foreign exchange, a strategic contributor to the balance of payments, and in terms of creating employment. For public policy it became both an agent of change and a means of income redistribution, while attempts to attenuate some of the regional imbalances were included only in the 1976–80 plan. The role of local capital and the value of small non-hotel tourism were also emphasized as a means of local development. Large units and foreign capital investment were, consequently, discouraged whereas the involvement of new more modest entrepreneurs was promoted. Soon, however, the contradictions of this policy became obvious: decentralization failed; "popular base" companies (with the exception of shipping) lacked imagination and were hampered by organizational problems and by a profiteering spirit; small units, though flexible, did not enhance quality; political/party considerations interfered in the allocation of resources while insufficient attention was given to regional development. It all resulted in an unbalanced use of resources, more pollution, cultural clashes, and so on.

As of the late 1980s and more so in the 1990s, tourist development began to be influenced by more "selective" EEC investment (Integrated Mediterranean Programs) and a still hesitant co-existence of mass and "elite" tourism may be the prelude to a more general shift. The Development Plan of 1988–92 explicitly referred to the attraction of higher-income tourism and to the dominant role of private investment in the creation of large complexes.[39] Investment projects of over $300 million have been encouraged in hotels of rank "A" or above and new initiatives include agro-tourism, conference, educational and cultural tourism, marine tourism, ecological tourism, and so on. Signs of restructuring in the business sector are also appearing in the emergence of Greek hotel chains (e.g., Grecotel, a family firm operating since 1976) that pursue horizontal and vertical concentration strategies.[40] Despite any leakage effects, the growth of large tourist groups in Greece is already creating important linkages with other sectors of the economy, such as suppliers, the furniture industry, architecture, construction materials. In addition to private ownership, several banks continue to own important shares in hotels (e.g., Ionian Bank and three hotels including Hilton International and Hilton Corfu, the chain of Astir Hotels belonging to the National Bank of Greece).

Nonetheless, the tourist industry has been and still remains a highly heterogeneous sector marked by increasing polarization with regard to capital, ownership arrangements, and spatial location. Large numbers of small businesses, self-employed persons, and medium-size companies coexist with important national or transnational groups and foreign or Greek direct ownership is often combined with long- or short-term sub-contracting. Foreign interests in Greece appeared soon after the conclusion of peace after the Greek Civil War (1946–1949). One of the earliest long-term investment projects was started in the mid-1950s by the French Club Méditerranée, which organized village resorts at several locations in Corfu, Euboea, and the Peloponnese. It also soon integrated the "village" enterprises with a travel agency.[41] In the late 1950s the construction of the Hilton Hotel owned by American TWA was another large project that subsequently led to sub-contracting to the Ionian Bank. Later, Pan American Airlines established in Athens a link of the Intercontinental chain, while a controlling interest in the oldest Greek group Lampsas was acquired by Sheraton, a considerable 42 percent still belonging, however, to the National Bank of Greece.[42] Following the recent commitment by the government to privatizing the state-owned Xenia hotels, lively interest is being shown both by foreign and by Greek groups.[43] The penetration of non-Greek agents into the Greek market may evolve into a test of resilience for Greek tourist firms.

In contrast to big business – Greek and foreign – an overwhelming plethora of tourist enterprises are small family-owned or individual firms. They cover the needs of low- to average-income tourists, and deal with seasonality by combining employment in other sectors. The sub-sector consists of small outlets of sometimes less than ten rooms, run by families whose main income is generated within other sectors – industry, the civil service, public utilities, agriculture, or a combination of those. In some less developed regions, hotel services (rooms rented to tourists) are part of household work, run mainly by female labor and providing a comfortable second income. Since the early 1970s such facilities have mushroomed around the country and their status is often semi-official. Access to capital for them is limited and expansion is severely constrained.[44] The fragmentation of occupation among various positions and jobs leads to overall inefficiency, whereas profiteering at the expense of quality is a common defect.[45]

Intense antagonism in the private sector over the years and not always rational state interventionism have induced changes resulting in increased diversity, the coexistence of a variety of large and small concerns, family firms and corporate units, and the combination of several patterns of management and capital ownership. One important feature, however, that remained dominant until the 1980s has been the overall national character of the sector, as the penetration of foreign capital has been rather modest. Another is the overwhelming presence of family businesses and the prominence of female ownership and management.[46]

The Hospitality Business: Recent Trends

Tourism today is considered one of the strategic sectors of Greek development, and interestingly enough, even though Greece is within the European Union, common directives and legislation, let alone a common policy on tourism, are still undeveloped. Given the fact that tourism as a sector is not totally autonomous but depends to a great extent on the general economic situation, it is obvious that the role of the state as a planner and regulator is important. For the past few years, devolution of power to local and regional authorities has meant that they were also responsible for the introduction of policy and legislation. This has created a series of problems arising from the lack of coordination with central authorities, from the lack of experience of local officers, and from many conflicting local interests.

The Greek hospitality industry continues of course to be the backbone of the tourism industry. However, it should also be mentioned that there are around 3,500 travel agencies. A recent list containing the largest hotels in the country registered ninety companies. Criteria used were their turnover, profitability, and the duration of operation. They operate all year round, and the turnover in 2001 ranged between 33 and 2.7 million euros. Nevertheless, in addition to the 56 five-star hotels there are about 100 class A hotels. These large companies are considered the engine of tourism and of private investment.[47] They generally follow the pattern of other Greek businesses including those in the secondary sector. They are family owned and family managed and/or they belong to groups of companies. They usually also include more than one hotel unit, in Athens or in other major cities, and in other key locations, forming a total of over 500 units, 56 of which are luxury hotels.[48] They differ in size, the largest group being Daskalantonakis-Grecotel, numbering 12,000 luxury beds and having invested over €250 million in tourism during the last five years. The group includes thirty-one hotels, of which twenty-two are summer resort units in major tourist destinations inside Greece, that is, in Crete, Corfu, Rhodes, Kos, Mykonos, Chalkidiki, the Peloponnese, and Attica. Nine other units are located in Athens and in major towns like Thessaloniki, Alexandroupolis (Thrace), Larissa (Thessaly), and Kalamata (Peloponnese). Two more luxury hotels were expected to open in 2003 in Athens and Cape Sounion. Some companies are either more local in character but equally successful in terms of profitability, like TEAB S.A., controlling three hotels in Crete; or more specialized, like Sani S.A., with villas, hotel units and marinas in Chalkidiki, and Sporades Islands. Sani S.A.'s focus on marine tourism allows it to form a network of marine activities linking islands and parts of mainland Greece. Marine tourism began to gather momentum after the privatization of EOT assets and the sale of a number of previously state-owned marinas. Equally successful are smaller companies, or companies specializing in new forms of tourism, e.g., sea-therapy centers. At least three of the hotel chains are owned and run by successful businesswomen, some of whom represent the passage of the business to the second or third generation of the family (e.g., Capsis, Daskalantonakis, Mantonanakis, Mamidakis and Argyros).

Most of the big firms in tourism have a history of about two generations. In other words, they are young firms and embody the entrepreneurial spirit of the post-war period, and the impressive development of Mediterranean tourism. Then as now there was a close relation with the construction industry, many hotel entrepreneurs being engineers, town planners, or architects who diversified their building contracts. A good example is the Kokotos family, owners of the top quality Elounda hotels in Crete. Spyros Kokotos, an engineer, was the founder of the firm about twenty-five years ago. The hotels have been steadily expanding, without increasing the number of beds but adding continuously modern features and improving their infrastructure. Kokotos introduced many innovations to the structure of resort hotels. The commercial centers of the hotels were built like the central squares of Greek villages where guests could find coffee places and shops. His luxury hotels included individual swimming pools, open-air theatres for musical and theatrical performances, and small chapels for Sunday service. These hotels do not rely on tour operators for their operation, but address individual customers who look for peace and quiet. Today, the whole family, comprised of Spyros Kokotos, his wife and three children, is involved in the running of the business. (One son is an environmental engineer who ensures the coordination of new investment and projects, whereas the other is a specialist in sales and marketing.)

In the past decade, many of these units have expanded by embarking on new forms of tourism. Aside from marine activities and sea-therapy complexes, conference facilities seem to be the most popular.[49] Since 1999 and with the coming of the 2004 Olympic Games, the trend has been intensified, the value of land in mainland Greece but mainly on the islands having increased by many times. The fashion dictates large complexes of groups of small houses, or luxury apartments, in other words, new small villages for tourists. Some of the large construction firms are involved in ambitious projects. One example is the Porto Carras complex in Halkidiki (Macedonia). It owns 17,630 hectares of land and three already existing hotel units are being modernized, with a conference center being projected, as well as a sea-therapy center and the construction of bungalows around the golf course. At the same time, the old winery of the Carras family is planned to be modernized. Another large construction company, AEGEK is also involved in similarly ambitious projects on Corfu, Mykonos, and Crete and negotiations have been underway with foreign investors. In addition to construction firms, real estate companies have shown great dynamism with regard to tourist development projects.

The capital base of most of these companies is Greek in origin (including Cypriot capital in several cases) with very few exceptions – notably the Club Méditerranée S.A. – of mainly French interests.[50] Most of these firms have increased their profitability in the last two years. They seem to have established a firm base as they have not shown any interest in entering the stock exchange. In fact, only seven hospitality businesses are at the moment quoted companies, and they are limited either to very old firms with important foreign shareholding or to firms belonging to Greek banks. Among the latter are Astir S.A. (national Bank of Greece), Lampsas S.A. (National Bank and Sheraton), Hyatt S.A. (Greek and foreign capital base), and Ioniki Hotel S.A. (owner of the Hilton hotel and affiliated to Alpha Bank). Only three of the quoted firms are family-owned companies, which have a wider scope mainly as construction firms. At least four central units of the major chains were in the process of renovation prior to the 2004 Olympic Games, held in Athens.

When the Government dismantled the seventy-year-old National Tourist Organization a few years ago, this elite group of the hospitality business emerged as the central force for development. Over the last decade, government policy has become very problematic as several agencies have been involved in planning without clear jurisdiction of authority. EOT has been attached to several ministries over the last few years and there have been frequent changes of its executive officers. There was no continuity in the enforcement of policy, inadequate follow-up, and growing bureaucratization. The overall dominant mentality failed to realize the importance of tourism and the need for equal support with other sectors.

Greek tourism has been vulnerable to many external shocks. The explosive situation in the Balkans and the nervousness about air travel after 9/11 terrorist attacks have caused stagnation. Greek entrepreneurs and the state were obliged to reconsider their policies. As a result, all concerned tried to reduce costs and losses by introducing innovations, by rediscovering neglected Greek nature, and by stressing simplicity as one of the specificities of Greek culture (which is also more economical). In this sense many areas of the hospitality business have been reviewed. On the one hand, the policy targets higher income tourists, but, on the other hand, it specifies cheaper alternatives to activities. Some examples: Greek cuisine (cucina povera) now forms the core of tourist menus in all quality hotels; health tourism and the modernization of spas are efforts to replace the older variety of massive beach tourism; food and wine tourism, ecotourism, trekking, rafting, and so on. Serious efforts are also being made to lengthen the season and if possible to extend it to year round to allow a more integrated development of towns and regions and to reduce unemployment. Conference tourism is central to these efforts.

Government policy has been adjusting accordingly. Fifteen years ago, conference tourism was embraced as the new orientation of Greek tourism, which would allow the lengthening of the tourist season, the upgrading of Greece as a destination, and a viable quality alternative to mass tourism. As a result 25 percent of investment in Attica and Thessaloniki and 35 percent in the rest of the country came from public sources.[51] The government now takes into account the fact that tourism industry is highly internationalized. It focuses, therefore, on the technological modernization of peripheral small- and medium-size firms. One of the key instruments is the development of information technology and the improvement of communication systems, so that airlines, tour operators, travel agencies, hotels, shipping firms, car rental companies, and other businesses may be integrated. Strategic planning also takes into consideration the impact of tourism on public opinion. This is why a three-prong program including an e-tourism forum, an Integrated Information System, and an Observatory of Tourism is being designed. Electronic presentation of tourist Greece is also being promoted.

Despite this undisputed progress, however, certain facts remain unchanged. For instance, 70 percent of tourism is still concentrated in only seven of fifty-two regions. Some forms of tourism, which have been actively promoted by competitors (Italy, Turkey), like winter tourism and winter sun tourism are still very undeveloped, absorbing only 9 percent of foreign visitors. Their promotion has so far been based on a policy of incentives for hotel owners, which proved insufficient. It appears that instead a new perception of tourism is necessary so that smaller towns may acquire basic infrastructure and may offer services (shops, restaurants, museums, etc.) during the winter months as well and not only during the summer months.

If the hospitality business is central in importance, the same is not the case with entrepreneurs in the sector. The heterogeneity of tourism business, personal aspirations, and the effort to get access to state resources has resulted in the fragmentation of the sector. The chairman of the Association of Tourist Companies stated that a powerful association is the key to giving tourism the place it deserves in the Greek economy. It could be hypothesized that with the de-nationalization of the sector and diminishing tutelage by the state, a collective consciousness and collective action by business may be necessary in the future.

Notes

1. For a fuller account of BH development in Greece, see Margarita Dritsas, "BH in Greece: The State of the Art and Future Prospects," in *Business History Around the World*, ed. F. Amatori and G. Jones (Cambridge: Cambridge University Press, 2003).
2. Margarita Dritsas, *To Chroma tes Epitychias (The Colour of Success, The Paint and Varnish Industry 1830–1990* (Athens: Trochalia, 1995).
3. In 1937, the League of Nations specified that a tourist is "someone who travels for a period of at least 24 hours in a country other than that in which he usually resides." In 1963, the UN Conference on International Travel and Tourism preferred the word "visitor" to describe "any person visiting a country other than that in which he has his usual place of residence for any reason other than following an occupation remunerated from within the country visited." Both definitions, however, ignored the movement of domestic tourists.
4. The Association of Tourist Enterprises (SETE) estimated the sector participated in the GDP with over 18 percent, whereas it absorbed over 16 percent of total labor. *To Vema*, 16 June 2002, B13.
5. A.M. Williams and Gareth Shaw, eds., *Tourism and Economic Development, Western European Experiences* (London and New York: Belhaven Press, 1991); P.E. Murphy, *Tourism: A Community Approach* (New York: Methuen, 1985).

6. For example, those who went to Turkey have been presented with a narrative stressing the Roman character of the ruins of Pergamon, Ephessus (Kussadasi), Alikarnassos, and so on, rather than their Hellenistic tradition. Homer for the Turks is not a Greek poet, despite that *Odyssey*, *The Iliad* and *The Aeneid* are universally considered the foundations of classical Greek, Roman, and European literature and culture. If scientifically these claims are impossible to sustain, through tourism they are codified, diffused, legitimated, and consumed by millions of people, ultimately contributing to the alienation of tourists from true knowledge. Vulgarizing history also contributes to strengthening national and racial stereotypes. The only non-nationalist action refers to what is specified as world heritage promoted by organizations such as UNESCO.
7. Apart from the myths included in Homer's epics *Odyssey* and *The Iliad*, other myths should be mentioned such as the legend of Jason and the maritime enterprise of Thessaly; the nuptials of Peleus and Thetis (the hero of the land with the goddess of the sea), which symbolizes the reconciliation of natural elements.
8. A Swiss, Rudolph Schmidt, was the manager of Grande Bretagne for eighteen years and he contributed to training the first group of qualified hotel employees in the country before the creation of any special schools. Two more Austrians worked as maîtres d'hôtel. The hotel was since renovated many times and hosted major foreign political leaders on their official sojourn in Athens.
9. In these, authors were often comparing Greece with prosperous Switzerland only to conclude, however, that there was a time lag of a century in its tourist development because this was based only on natural endowment and on the traditional cultural heritage, while it completely ignored services and equipment. Boissonas, a regular traveler from 1903 to 1930 and a lover of Greece had distinguished three zones: Athens and the surrounding well-off suburbs offering luxury hotel facilities, comfort, good food, and entertainment (served by the Orient express and by steamboats from Piraeus); another in several main towns served by the Greek railways where some respectable hotel businesses had sprung up after 1910 (e.g., Thessaloniki, Patras, Delphi, Olympia); a third zone of unspoiled territory lay still undiscovered but made accessible further to the north, after the annexation of Macedonia and Epirus in 1913. See Boissonas, *Le Tourisme en Grece*, 10–16.
10. Emergency Law 1697.
11. Its operation was interrupted during the war and civil war years. It reopened in 1949 but its full operation did not resume until 1956.
12. Despite problems of measurement (only one part of revenue, that of foreign exchange imported, is computed whereas other forms, e.g., local consumption, are not), the rise of tourism revenue remains spectacular. Table 1 shows the growth of revenue from 1938 to 1995, as well as the percentage in terms of GDP, of the "invisibles," and export trade. With regard to the GDP ratio, it should be taken into account that, if we were to include also the gray area of unrecorded revenue from non-registered tourist facilities, the amount should safely be tripled.
13. G. Tortella, "A Latecomer: The Modernisation of the Spanish Economy, 1800–1990," in *The Industrial Revolution in National Context: Europe and the USA* (Cambridge: Cambridge University Press, 1996).

14. Law 5181 stipulated that no license would be issued to hotels that were found in need of improvements, including partial redecoration, removal of supplementary beds, improvement of sanitary facilities, and renovation.
15. Strict application of the law would have simply meant closure of most establishments. Listing of hotels by rank was also introduced but was vehemently resisted by hoteliers who until then advertised their establishments as luxurious without meeting even minimum requirements.
16. In terms of spending power they ranked quite high, at least those from the United States, and this determined state policy for a long time.
17. Emergency Law 588/45. See also *Eos*, 58–60 (1962), p. 194.
18. Law 688/7. 5.48.
19. Also see V. Liantouras, Hotel Credit in *A Dodekameron of Tourist Industry* (Athens, 1955), 121–29. The proceeds of a special tax were to be used as capital for loans and for loan servicing; they were estimated at approximately one billion drachmas during the first year. Interest was fixed at about 8 percent for five years while reliability of entrepreneurs/firms, earnings, and overall performance was also considered. As of 1951, however, half the amount of the tax levied was channeled to other activities, the mission of the organization having failed. Its closure in 1953 was a foregone conclusion.
20. HANBG XXXIV, E, 11, memorandum 2.5.1946.
21. Specialized publications proliferated after 1950; for example, "Tourist Week," published mainly for foreign visitors as well as a series of Tourist Guidebooks, for motorists in mainland Greece.
22. Given that Greece was not capable to promote car manufacturing, tourist development led to increased imports of motorcars, making the country more dependent on foreign imports.
23. One contemporary report mentioned that there was an effort to "make Athens into a small, second-rate Paris." See H. Hill, *The Economy of Greece*, vol. V, appendix IV.
24. Only twenty-three of these were to be found on major islands (seven in the Dodecanese, nine in Crete, five in the North and Eastern Aegean Islands, and only two in the Cyclades complex in Andros and Syros). See *Tourist Guide* (Athens, 1961).
25. Rhodes, in the Dodecanese was ceded to Greece by the Italians in 1948 and was then, among those regions with relatively developed tourist infrastructure and mentality. It was no coincidence that the School of Tourism trade was established there. The other relatively developed island was Corfu, a gate to Greece since the nineteenth century and still popular among the British tourists today.
26. In particular, a series of studies on tourism regions. See, for example, M.I. Logothetis, *Tourism in Rhodes* (Athens: NBG, 1961).
27. E.g., the Epeiros Festival inaugurated in 1960, including the Dodone performances of ancient drama in the ancient theatre. The purpose of the festival was the development of Epeiros, then still one of the poorest areas of the country. In the absence of organized hotel facilities, houses were offered by local population to host and cater for the needs of the visitors. The festivities program also included performances of local dances and exhibitions of local folk art. Pamphlets also advertised historical sights of the area (castle, museum, local village

community, cave, ancient theatre, art gallery, etc.). Most of this work was done by local volunteers.

28. In 1954 they amounted to 24,000, followed by French and British (15,500 each), and German (11,000).
29. See *Eos*, 58–60 (1962), 173.
30. Ministry of Coordination, Five-Year Plan, 56–58.
31. See M.I. Logothetes, *Tourism and the Economy of the Island of Nisyros* (Athens 1962), 42.
32. Law 3213/1953; 3430/1955; 4171/1961; 276/1969; 2687/1961.
33. For example, the ferry boat line from Patras to Zante or Patras to Rio. See M.I. Logothetes, *Tourist Studies* (Athens 1963), 17.
34. Nicos E. Alexandrakis, "Tourism as a Leading Sector in the Economic Development: A Case Study of Greece," PhD diss., University of Kentucky, 1973, 181.
35. Ibid., 154.
36. There were of course a series of directives referring indirectly to tourism (movement of travelers, customs regulations, foreign exchange, as well as investment for rural areas that could promote tourism) but no overall strategy was devised and tourism even in the 1980s was seen as complementary to other rural activities. See EEC Commission, Report to the Council No. EP (82)382 final, Brussels, 7 July 1982; also M. Logothetis "Greek Tourism in the EEC," *Touristikai Meletae* IB/1982.
37. Greece has 15,000 kilometers of coastline, 3,000 kilometers of sandy beaches, 337 inhabited islands, and a rich cultural heritage.
38. Sea and sunshine beach-orientated mass tourism along the coastline of Southern Europe and holiday packages were based on low-cost charter air fares or self-drive to the Mediterranean locations.
39. Leontidou, 105. The recent (from 1996 on) policy of privatization of the public sector, including EOT, confirms the determination of the government to bring about a quick modernization of the Greek economy.
40. An example is provided by the Grecotel group owning or managing around twenty new and older luxury hotels in the country. The same company has an important share in an airline, a tour operating company, a trade supply firm, and a bank. Grecotel is run by members of the Daskalantonakis family. Similar moves have been made by other family-owned hotel firms, such as the "Tourist Complex S.A.," run by Mrs. Dia Kapsis and combining French capital (Sofitel) with hotels in Crete, Rhodes, and Athens. This group has turned in recent years toward conference tourism. Equally important is the Mamidakis project of tourist villages in Rhodes, Crete, and elsewhere. These groups offer on-site conference facilities, leisure facilities, restaurants, and off-site facilities – transportation to and from airports, car rentals, and organized tours.
41. In 1987 one more camp was added in Olympia.
42. Holiday Inn was among other transnational associated hotel figures.
43. "The Battle of Hotels," *Kyriakatike Oikonomia,* 26 July 1998.
44. An important source of such capital is emigrants' or returned migrants' remittances and savings. Increasingly after the 1970s resources were also transferred

from agriculture or other sectors causing sometimes the abandonment of primary activities. Similar trends have been observed in Spain and Portugal.

45. Despite or because of aspirations of the owners to become affluent "entrepreneurs." See P. Tsartas, *Social and Economic impact of tourist development in the Cyclades region 1950–1980* (Athens: EKKE, 1989), 184–96.
46. With the exception of a handful of large hotels owned or run by multinationals (e.g., Hilton International, Marriot), most important businesses, including those in which transnational capital holds important shares, are managed by Greek families (e.g., Daskalantonakis and Grecotel, Manantonakis and Elounda Beach Group, Kapsis and Sofitel). Interestingly enough, most of these groups are headed by successful businesswomen, often, as in the case of Kapsis, with a tradition in female management of hotels. Both family and female control is dominant in smaller establishments essentially run on a household basis and frequent in other tourist businesses such as travel agencies and souvenir stores.
47. "Quality Tourism in Greece Gains Ground," *To Vema* 22 December 2002, B12–13.
48. For instance, the Divanis group, one of the biggest and most successful in terms of profits, includes hotels in Athens, Central Greece (Larissa and Meteora), and Corfu. In addition to hotels, a large conference center in Attica (Kavouri) and a spa are forthcoming. Other family owned businesses include the Mantonanakis group, which controls units operating as The Leading Hotels of the World and the best city resort hotel in Greece (Grand Resort Lagonisi) and a conference center.
49. Conference facilities have proliferated to such an extent that it is already estimated by the Institute of Tourist Research and Forecasts (ITEP) that only 10 percent of them will be used. In 1998, there were 27 conference centers in the country, or 335 conference rooms in 56 luxury hotels around the country. Of these thirteen were in Athens, six in Rhodes, sixteen in Crete, four in Corfu, one in Thessaloniki, two in Halkidiki, and one in Delphi. Most of them have a maximum capacity of 2,500 people (*Viomihaniki Epitheorisi*, April 1998, 74–79).
50. Even in the case of Club Med, there are plans to found a Greek company that would become the vehicle of development in Greece.
51. Subsequently the percentage was increased to 35 percent for facilities in hotels and to 40 percent for integral conference centers.

Chapter 4

The Development of the Portuguese Hotel Business, 1950–1995

Benedita Câmara

This chapter focuses on the development of the Portuguese hotel business between 1950 and 1995. Some writers decry the entrepreneurial fabric of the package vacation and mass tourism business in favor of city tourism. The first is described as fragmented, averse to multinationalization of the ownership of hotels, largely dependent on tour operators, and highly labor intensive. City-business tourism on the contrary is characterized by a high level of multinationalization of the ownership of hotels, which leads to high level of investments in capital goods and economy in the use of labor. The evolution of the Portuguese hotel business confirms a trend toward a particular pattern of tourism. Notwithstanding these characteristics I propose to examine if any changes have taken place between 1950 and 1995 in a number of areas mentioned by those writers. At the investment level this chapter determines how important foreign investment has been, and seeks to characterize the evolution of investment in capital goods in order to relate these to the growth in the number of occupations in the hotel sector that require staff with an average level of qualification. The chapter establishes whether there has been any improvement in a sector that is traditionally viewed as not absorbing a very large proportion of skilled labor. Finally, I examine whether any changes have taken place in average hotel size and in the quantity of labor used per bed or per room in order to determine if economies of scale and gains in productivity of labor have contributed to an increase in productivity in the Portuguese hotel business during this period.

Notes for this chapter begin on page 83.

The chapter is organized into five sections. The first section looks at the expansion of tourism in Portugal in the general context of southern European countries between 1950 and 1995 based on data about tourist arrivals and receipts. Section two describes the development of supply in the hotel business in Portugal. Section three discusses the pattern of investment in the hotel business, and section four analyzes the use of labor in terms of quality and quantity. Finally, section five presents the conclusion that the Portuguese hotel business, notwithstanding its vacation pattern, has changed and increased its competitiveness during this period.

Portugal and Countries in Southern Europe: Tourist Arrivals and Receipts

At European and global levels, tourist numbers grew consistently from the 1950s until the end of the twentieth century. Portugal has welcomed international tourists in significant numbers, mainly from Europe.[1] The numbers of tourist arrivals show that the starting point in the mid-1950s was very low. Compared with Greece, the most similar country in terms of numbers, Portugal had half the number of tourists.

In terms of tourist arrivals, between 1955 and 1956 and between 1959 and 1962 Portugal had the highest growth rate among southern European countries. If trends from the former period had been maintained in the latter, the average rate of growth in the three remaining periods would have been 320 percent, and not 242 percent (see table 4.1). At the beginning and the end of the 1980s, the two most significant tourist destinations in southern Europe recorded growth rates in the number of tourist arrivals lower than those of Portugal and Greece. At the end of the 1980s, Italy slowed down in comparison to Spain. The strongest period of expansion for Portugal took place in that decade, when it fell just short of Greece.

The period from 1950 to 1970 was characterized by stable exchange rates and low inflation; and the huge increases in tourism flow played an important role in many economies as an element in the export of services. An analysis of the average growth rates in annual revenues during these years shows that Portugal recorded significant growth in relative terms in the first period, mainly because it started out from a very low base (see table 4.2). Its growth rate in the second period is the lowest in relative terms. If Portugal had maintained the average rate of growth of the other three countries between 1977 and 1981 it would have grown at 504 percent and not at 300.7 percent. In the third period it recorded the highest rate of growth and in the fourth period the second lowest.

Table 4.1 International tourist arrivals

A: Average Annual Number					% Change Compared to Previous Average Annual Years		
	1955–1956	1959–1962	1969–1970	1972–1973	1955–56/ 1959–62	1959–62/ 1967–70	1967–70/ 1972–73
Portugal	217,226	358,392	1,225,050	2,247,950	+ 65.0	+ 242	+ 83
Greece	401,868	406,864	2,137,218	2,641,471	+ 1.2	+ 425	+ 24
Italy	6,600,000	9,412,500	13,222,125	14,890,750	+ 43.0	+ 299	+ 13
Spain	–	6,169,020	20,707,483	33,532,767	–	+ 236	+ 60

Source: Author's calculations based on *Trends in Economic Sectors: Tourism in Europe. A Study by the Tourism Committee* (Paris: OECD).

B: Average Annual Number (millions)				% Change Compared to Previous Average Annual Years	
	1977–1981	1982–1986	1987–1991	1982–1986	1987–1991
Portugal	2.1	4.3	7.3	+ 104.8	+ 69.8
Greece	4.7	6.0	7.9	+ 26.7	+ 31.8
Italy	45.6 *	50.2	53.5	+ 10.1	+ 6.6
Spain	39.7	43.4	52.8	+ 9.3	+ 21.6

*Between 1978 and 1981 only.

Source: OECD, Tourism Policy and International Tourism in OECD Member Countries, Annual Report, 1977–92, in Allan M. Williams, "Tourism as an Agent of Economic Transformation in Southern Europe," in *Economic Transformation, Democratization and Integration into the European Perspective*, ed. Heather D. Gibson (New York: Palgrave, 2001), 124.

Table 4.2 Average annual receipts, 1953–1993 (million current $)

A:	1953–1955	1967–1970	1977–1981*	1982–1986*	1992–1993
Greece	28.1	147.75	1,529	1,461	3,191.5
Italy	150.5	1,565.00[a]	8,915	14,943	21,746.4
Portugal	14.8	269.00[a]	1,078	2,886	3,873.8
Spain	–	1,401.00	8,372	17,062	20,798.4
B: % Change Compared to Previous Period					
		1967–1970	1977–1981*	1982–1986*	1992–1993
Greece		+ 425.8	+ 936.6	+ 57.4	+118.4
Italy		+ 939.8	+ 469.0	+ 67.6	+ 45.5
Portugal		+ 1,717.6	+ 300.7	+ 167.8	+ 34.2
Spain		–	+ 469.1	+ 103.8	+ 21.8

*Allan M. Williams, *op. cit*, table 4.3 adaptation, p. 129.

[a] Numbers for 1968 are non-existent.

Source: OECD, Tourism Policy and International Tourism in OECD Member Countries, Annual Report, 1977–92, in Allan M. Williams, "Tourism as an Agent of Economic Transformation in Southern Europe," in *Economic Transformation, Democratization and Integration into the European Perspective*, ed. Heather D. Gibson (New York: Palgrave, 2001), 124.

Gross revenues of Portuguese tourism at constant prices recorded dramatic positive growth from 1984 to 1985 and 1987. This rapid growth during the 1980s occurred at a time when economic circumstances had brought about a degree of instability in tourist flows, in exchange rates, and in prices. This means that the general context for the growth of tourism in Portugal was less favorable than that in which countries like Spain and Italy recorded strong growth (between 1950 and 1970).

Between 1965 and 1967 the average revenue per tourist in Portugal was much higher than the average for the rest of southern Europe. Portugal's US$123 average revenue per tourist contrasted with $32 in Yugoslavia, $67 in Spain, and $104 in Italy. At that time it was the government's intention to expand tourism but maintain its commitment to luxury tourism.[2] In fact from 1977 to 1981 Portugal maintained the leadership in terms of the average spending by a foreign visitor (392) in constant dollars, followed by Greece (325) and, at some distance, by Italy (157) and Spain (150). From 1982 to 1986 these numbers fell in Portugal and Greece (to 251 and 244, respectively) and rose in Spain and Italy (to 193 and 177, respectively). In Portugal this drop was due to exchange rate fluctuations and to the increase in the number of Spanish visitors who did not stay overnight in Portuguese hotels.[3] Finally, between 1987 and 1991, Portugal recovered its position at the top of the table of southern European countries in relation to average spending per foreign visitor (395 at current dollar prices), Spain taking second place (323), and Greece and Italy third and fourth place (with 291 and 279, respectively).[4]

Supply of Hotel Accommodation

Accommodation in Portugal represents the main element of tourists' expenditure and is also significant in overall employment in the tourism activity. In 1999, hotel accommodation's share of total tourist accommodation capacity, including tourist complexes and apartments, was 45 percent. My analysis of the total hotel accommodation is based on a narrow definition in that it excludes rural accommodation, camping sites, and the parallel market.[5] The supply of hotel accommodation between 1965 and 1995 grew at an annual average of 4.04 percent. From 1962 to 1969 and from 1995 to 1999, available total hotel accommodation capacity increased from 63,494 to 211,194 beds.

Initially the greatest quantity of accommodation was in hotels and one- and two-star pensions. Between 1965 and 1995 the percentage of five-star hotels doubled. The same improvement occurred with other kinds of accommodations but these changes in terms of star-rating cannot be described as qualitative. Quality management is a dynamic process full of subjective factors, which are difficult to gauge in any comparative and developmental approach.[6]

At the beginning of the 1950s, Portugal faced the possibility of expanding the tourist industry but it was only after 1965 that investment in this industry began to be addressed in an organized way. Among the main measures adopted to make the expansion of hotel business possible was an alteration in financial criteria. Loans were now granted by the government according to the number of rooms or beds instead of expenditure. In addition to the concern with the mechanisms of domestic funding there was also the interest in tapping international sources of finance for tourist development in Portugal. Sharing in the concerns expressed by the industrial sector, business leaders called for changes in the regulations for direct inward foreign investment.[7] It was in 1965 that the main legislation on foreign investment was published.[8]

In the intermediate development plan (1965–1967) the growth of tourism was seen as advantageous in balance of payment terms because it implied lower imports. In addition, the low qualifications of the workforce were not seen as an obstacle to the growth of tourism as it was going through a process of industrialization. The targets for the tourism sector at that time were to increase the rate of growth, the employment levels and exports (of services), and to improve living standards.[9] This plan adopted an approach that placed tourism in the context of national and regional development and two regions were targeted for major promotion – the Algarve and Madeira. Very high growth rates were recorded in the Algarve for between 1962 and 1969 and between 1980 an 1985, whereas Madeira had particularly high rates of growth in the 1970s. Between 1962 and 1965 and between 1995 and 1999 the supply of city hotels – deduced from the data for the regions of Lisbon and the Tagus Valley (IV) and of the North (II) that included the main cities – lost ground in relative terms to holiday tourism (table 4.3).

Table 4.3 Accommodation capacity (%)

	1962–1969	1995–1999
Continental Portugal	95.00	89.43
Madeira and Azores (archipelagos)	5.00	10.56
Regions		
Alentejo (I)	2.79	3.45
Algarve	7.84	39.90
Madeira	3.71	8.84
North (II)	15.66	12.84
Centre (III)	27.36	9.60
Lisbon and Tagus Valley (IV)	35.89	23.62

Note: I-Beja, Évora and Portalegre; II-Braga, Bragança, Porto, Viana do Castelo and Vila Real; III-Lisboa, Santarém and Setúbal; IV-Lisboa, Santarém and Setúbal.

Source: Estatísticas do Turismo (I.N.E).

Investments in the Hotel Business

The phenomenon of tourism has been studied from different angles. One of these approaches links the attraction of international tourism with the development of backward countries. Another relates tourism to delays in the process of development and with countless social and economic costs; while the third identifies costs and benefits and seeks to minimize the former and maximize the latter. Williams's article, "Tourism as an Agent of Economic Transformation in Southern Europe," falls into the third approach in that he differentiates between the operation of package holiday tourism and city tourism and plays down the adverse consequences of the former in terms of the degree of diversification present in national or regional economies. According to this view vacation tourism is presented as not being characterized by a high level of multinationalization of the ownership of hotels. This assertion is based on the theories of Dunning and McQueen on the low levels of foreign direct investment (FDI) in this business because in their view there are a number of reasons for the emergence of international hotel chains. Among those reasons the internalization of market transactions is understandable if "there are net ownership advantages for example, via branding, where there are location factor endowments." One of the main examples of this situation is illustrated by Hyatt users who expect to find Hyatts in all major cities. A number of authors infer from this that mass tourism – unlike city tourism and within this branch business tourism – as the product being sold (sun, sea, etc.) is largely indifferent to branding and location factor endowment.[10]

To a certain extent the figures about the evolution of foreign investment in the Portuguese hotel sector confirmed this assertion. In fact, between 1967 and 1988 the amounts of foreign investment as a proportion of total investment in the hotel business vary on average between 6 and 9 percent of all investment in the hotel business, except in the years 1971 and 1973.[11] Between 1978 and 1981 foreign capital was invested almost entirely in already existing hotels. In absolute terms and at current prices the periods of lower investment were the years 1976 to 1979, and the revolutionary period from 1974 to 1975 in particular. The highest levels of foreign investment occurred from 1985 to 1988. At constant prices, the levels of investment that took place in 1973 have not been reached again. For the period from 1974 to 1988, the highest rates were achieved in 1986. At this time, unlike in 1973, it was mainly Portuguese capital that led the expansion of the hotel business (table 4.4).

From the previous viewpoint, investment in hotels in southern European countries on the part of tour operators is stressed as being low because internalization is seen as unnecessary because the tour operators control and take advantage of the segmented nature of the hotel business. In this approach the

Table 4.4 Investment in the hotel business (annual averages) (1,000 escudos)

	Current Prices				Constant Prices
	I Portuguese capital	II Foreign capital	III Total	IV % of foreign capital and total	
1967–1970	8289,44	54,184	883,128	6.5	
1971–1973	329,308	1,921,216	2,250,524	85.3	2049
1974–1975	1,957,822	187,079	2,145,901	8.7	1437
1976–1979	1,379,246	93,468	1,472,714	6.3	538
1980–1984	8,148,981	362,252	8,511,233	4.2	1266
1985–1988	24,496,465	2,271,982	26,768,447	8.4	1530

Source: O *Turismo* (data from National Statistics Institute); Portugal Deflator for GDP at Market Prices, OECD Statistical Compendium.

"lack of internalization is facilitated by the development of particular circuits of capital during the tourism development cycle. The initiation of tourism leads to sharp increases in the price of land which generates capital which may be re-invested in tourism enterprises. This ensures that there is a ready supply of sub-contracts to the tour operators."[12] Land is characterized as non-produced capital, and is a significant element in measuring total inputs in the hotel business for the purposes of assessing the return on capital invested in this business. When we consider whether land accounts for a significant part of capital invested, the data available for Portugal enable us to state that the percentage of investment in land in the hotel business was very high only in 1971 and 1972. It decreased in absolute terms afterward and became significant again between 1985 and 1987.

A more important conclusion from this data (table 4.5) concerns the evolution in capital goods from the same point of view that sees vacation tourism as synonymous with labor intensive. Having in mind that in geographical terms Portuguese tourism tended to be what we can call sun-vacation tourism, it would also be plausible that the evolution of the ratio of capital goods to labor should tend to show stability or a reduction in hotel business. On the contrary, during the 1980s in the Portuguese hotel business – notwithstanding its sun and sea pattern – there were high levels of investment in fixed assets when compared with 1992 (table 4.5). The amount of investment in capital goods per member of staff in the Portuguese hotel business doubled between 1982 and 1984 and between 1985 and 1988 from 46.4k to 96k Portuguese Escudos

(PTE). To explain this data it is very likely that the increased availability of technology in the spheres of catering and information technology may have generated an increase in capital formation and a less intensive use of labor in the hotel business.[13] But before drawing such a conclusion we need to analyze in more detail the evolution of labor in the Portuguese hotel business.

Table 4.5 Investment in the hotel business by type of capital invested (annual average values) (1,000 escudos)

	1971–1972	1973–1976	1977–1980	1982–1984	1985–1988	1992
I–Purchase of fixed assets or capital goods	776,457	439,575	740,929	5,249,944	15,739,858	7,616,635
Land-A	419,130	114,604	74,260	144,014	637,239	11,611
Equipment-B	n/a	n/a	n/a	1,401,333	3,268,393	311,915
II–Immovable assets (property and business leases, expenses, other types of immovable assets)	n/a	n/a	n/a	393,692	704,944	2,509
III-Total	1,911,231	2,074,849	2,099,402	5,643,636	16,440,302	18,73,138
A/I%	53.9	26	10	2.7	4.04	1.62
A/III%	21.9	5.5	3.5	2.5	3.87	0.61
B/I %	n/a	n/a	n/a	26.7	20.7	4.09

Notes: Prior to 1981, II consisted of buildings and works. Equipment is separate from furniture and utensils, clothes and vehicles. Data for 1992 are for companies having more than five employees.

Sources: E. Reig and A. Picazo, *Capitalización y crecimiento de la economía balear, 1955–1996* (Bilbao: Fundación BBV, 1998), 282; J. Alcaide, *Renta Nacional de España y su distribución provincial. Serie homogénea* (Bilbao: Fundación BBV, 1999).

Labor in the Hotel Business: Quantity and Quality

In overall terms tourism is seen as an economic activity that creates jobs. It was mentioned earlier what the intermediate development plan (1965–67) stated in stressing this factor. The number of jobs created in the hotel business increased consistently, and it recorded an absolute growth of 76 percent between 1966 and 1969 and between 1993 and 1995. The percentage of people employed in the hotel business as a proportion of the working population and of the workforce as a whole grew between 1966 and 1989–92 from 6.05 percent to 8.06 percent.[14]

The supply of accommodation in less labor-intensive hotels (tourist complexes, apartments, and aparthotels) grew from 10 percent to 35 percent of the total from 1980 to 1995.[15] As far as the number of staff to beds ratio by class of hotel is concerned, there was a fall of almost half in hotels overall (see table 4.6). In aparthotels and pensions the fall was very similar, and insignificant in tourist complexes and apartments (appendix table 4.9). If we relate the number of employees to the number of rooms between 1969 and 1971 and between 1997 and 1999, we can see that there was a fall from 60 to 43 employees for every 100 rooms in the hotel business. In the case of hotels – both in total numbers as well as in the better classes of hotel – the fall in the staff to rooms ratio was very steep, 0.39 and 0.58 percent respectively.

Table 4.6 Ratio of number of staff to number of rooms

	In the hotel business as a whole	All hotels	Luxury or five-star hotels
1969–1971	0.60	0.90	1.46
1983–1985	0.60	0.79	1.28
1989–1991	0.53	0.67	1.05
1997–1999	0.43	0.51	0.88

Source: Tourism Statistics, I.N.E (various years).

This issue is very important because staff costs represent a major proportion of total costs in the hotel business, which faces strong international competition. For this reason, comparative costs – particularly labor costs – play a key role in the system of exchange. The first conclusion to be drawn is that between the 1970s and the 1990s, staff costs as a percentage of total costs grew in current price terms (appendix table 4.9).[16] Average costs per employee also grew continuously in constant price terms, except at the beginning of the 1990s (appendix table 4.10).

By examining increases in unit labor costs and trends in those costs to determine what percentage they represent of total costs, together with the efforts made to save on such costs, we have tried to emphasize the relationship between productivity gains and competitiveness in the hotel sector.[17] Several studies emphasize the decrease in the average price of an overnight stay by reference to general economic circumstances in any given year. By contrast we stress the importance of the improvement in the performance of the Portuguese hotel business in terms of labor productivity. Occupancy rates and labor costs as a percentage of total hotel revenue remained stable over a long period. Total hotel revenue at constant prices per employee also increased over the long term – the change in the growth rate was 87.2 percent between 1994 and 1996 (appendix tables 4.11 and 4.12). This picture is confirmed by the reduction in the number of staff to room ratio, in the number of beds to staff ratio (appendix table 4.13).

In most sectors of the tourism industry skilled labor is of little importance.[18] Jobs in hotels and restaurants are the visible aspect of employment in tourism. My analysis of the development of job classifications in the hotel trade shows that the number of managerial (group A) jobs fell, a factor that may be tied to a possible increase in the size of hotel firms. Not only did the number of employees in group B grow in absolute and percentage terms, but the jobs in this group became more diversified and more complex. The rate of growth in group C was much higher (209 percent) than the overall rate (93 percent), and they practically doubled in percentage terms. This would seem to be indicative of better management and organizational techniques. In group D there are no noteworthy differences in percentage terms, but there are pronounced differences in group G. There is also a noticeable reduction in the number of occupations covered (see table 4.7).

Table 4.7 Hotel staff

	1969				1991			
	Total number	%	Hotels number	%	Total number	%	Hotels number	%
A : Directors	2,071	11	809	7.4	1,125	3.2	528	2.6
Owners and managers					1,363	3.9	227	1.1
B : Administrative services					2,383		1,642	8.0
Receptionists	819	4.6	551	5	3,382	9.8	1,676	8.2
Total					**5,765**	**16.7**	**3,318**	**16.2**
C : Housekeepers and similar	433	2.4	362	3.2	1,717	4.9	1,122	5.4
D: Cooks and waiters	5,478	31	3,188	29	99,02	28.7	7,016	34.3
E : Personal services staff	1,373	7.7	1,098	9.9	6,437	18.7	3,037	14.8
F : Porters and cleaning	4,674	26.2	2,884	26.2	3,162	9.1	1,901	9.3
G : Laundry	1,568	9	963	9	1,662	4.8	1,240	6.0
H : Ancillary activities	1,449	8.14	95	n/a	1,292	3.7	176	0.86
I : Security	n/a		n/a		2,891	8.4	1,292	6.32
Total	**17,784**		**10,994**		**34,410**		**20,422**	

Notes: Numbers do not include hairdressers and beauticians. For 1969, personal services staff meant bar and cafeteria staff.

Source: Estatísticas de Turismo (Statistics of Tourism).

This change in job classification during this particular period was not yet related to outsourcing mechanisms. More than any other business the hotel trade suffers from major variations in demand according to the season or the day of the week, weekends, and even at different times of the day and entrepreneurs respond to this situation by flexible staffing and greater cross-sector mobility.[19] Among other possible options for increasing labor productivity are the contribution made by investment in capital goods already described in the case of the Portuguese hotel sector (table 4.5) and the contribution of economies of scale (table 4.8).[20]

In fact if we want to understand the positive evolution detected in the labor productivity of the Portuguese hotel sector, we must note that between 1962 and 1990 the ratio of beds to the number of hotels rose from 30 to 106 per hotel and the ratio of number of rooms to number of hotels rose from 22 to 47. The increase in the number of beds was higher in the better quality hotels notwithstanding the fact that they already had the majority of beds/rooms.

Table 4.8 Evolution of the ratio of beds to the number of hotels

Between the years	No. of beds/Total accommodation units	No. of beds/No. of high-quality hotels*
1962–1965*	54	145
1966–1968*	52	122
1969–1972*	67	214
1973**	90	556
1976–1979	73	419
1981–1985	87	432
1986–1990	97	460
1991–1995	112	469
1996–2000	122	476

* Includes luxury hotels plus first-class hotels.

** Only includes five-star hotels.

Source: Estatísticas do Turismo (I.N.E).

In order to explain this performance in terms of the productivity of labor among all the other possible aspects – investment in capital goods, staff training, the introduction of better management methods – gains due to economies of scale prevail. This contradicts the theory that claims that in general the corporate structure of the hotel business in holiday destinations is somewhat fragmented whereas city-business tourism is more concentrated. Although there is low concentration among Portuguese firms, the rate of growth here has been positive.[21]

Conclusion

As far as Portugal's hotel business is concerned, over the forty-five years covered in this chapter, the percentage of foreign investment remained low (under 10 percent). In terms of its pattern of vacation tourism the market share of hotel chains remained extremely low and independent hotels prevailed. The average size of hotels also increased and the effect of scale was the main factor that allowed gains in labor productivity. Another hallmark of vacation holiday tourism was that it was labor intensive and did not encourage investment in capital goods, even though there was some investment in capital goods in Portugal that contributed to gains in labor productivity. In the hotel trade Portugal responded to the increase in labor costs by improving productivity levels. This was one of the main mechanisms adopted in order to maintain the competitiveness of the Portuguese hotel business in international terms. Rather than looking at package vacation tourism in contrast to city tourism, it is more important to observe how Portuguese hotel business underwent changes between 1950 and 1995. The degree of international competition in this business tended to increase and the Portuguese hotel business responded to changes by increasing productivity of labor.

Notes

1. For the importance of Europe in regional share of international tourism by arrivals and by receipts see J. Lathan, "Statistical Trends in Tourism and Hotel Accommodation up to 1988," in *Progress in Tourism, Recreation and Hospitality Management,* vol. 2, ed. C.P. Cooper (London and New York: Belhaven Press, 1989), table 8.3.
2. *Plano Intercalar de Fomento para 1965–7 (Intermediate Development plan for 1965–7)*, vol. 2. Opinion of the Chamber of Corporations (Lisbon: I.N., 1965), 213–14. Revenues from tourism depend on the number of tourists and how much they spend. Given that accommodation is a significant element in a tourist's total spending, average length of stay is a key factor.
3. José Sancho Silva, "Receitas e Despesas atribuídas ao Turismo" (Revenue and Expenditure Attributed to Tourism), *Turismo* 22/23, Year II, Series I (1990): 13.
4. Allan M. Williams, "Tourism as an Agent of Economic Transformation in Southern Europe," in *Economic Transformation, Democratization and Integration into the European Union, Southern Europe in Comparative Perspective,* ed. Heather D. Gibson (London: Palgrave, 2001), 130. The existence of unregistered accommodation in the Greek islands (e.g., the Algarve) means we must exercise some caution in relation to these figures. According to data for 1990 and 1992, the aver-

age daily spending by a package tourist was 12.4 and 11.9 contos (1 conto = PTE 1,000) respectively, mainly on clothing and footwear, household and decorative items, while that for a tourist was 10.1 and 13 contos, mainly on accommodation. Spending by package travelers represented 17 percent of total spending by the two groups (Tourism Receipts. Development of the Method for calculating receipts attributed to Tourism based on Surveys of foreign-resident visitors, see *Direcção Geral de Turismo. Gabinete de Estudos e Planeamento* (Directorate General for Tourism. Research and Planning Office, 1994), 4, 10–14.

5. The hotel business in this chapter includes hotels in the traditional sense – hotels, aparthotels, *pousadas* (the state-owned travelers hotels), hostelries, motels, and pensions, as well as hotel businesses involving less intensive use of labor (tourist complexes and tourist apartments). In 1999, camping sites represented 54 percent of total accommodation capacity (Licínio Cunha, *Introdução ao Turismo* [Introduction to Tourism] [Lisbon: Verbo, 2001], 189–90, 220–21).
6. Rik de Keyse and Norbert Vanhove, "Tourism Quality Plan: An Effective Tourism Policy," *Revue du Tourisme – The Tourist Review* 3 (1997): 32–37; Eduardo Fayos-Solá, "Competitividad y Calidad en la nueva era del turismo," *Estudios Turísticos* 123 (1994): 5–10; W. Faché, "Methodologies for Innovation and Improvement of Services in Tourism," *Managing Service Quality* 10, no. 6 (2000): 356–66; Sérgio da Palma Brito, "Turismo, Ambiente e Ordenamento do Território (parts I, II, III e IV)" (Tourism, Environment and Territorial Planning), *Turismohotel Internacional* 25, no. 7 (November 2000): 12–15; 25, no. 1 (January 2001): 14–22; 25, no. 2 (March 2001): 10–13; 25, no. 3 (May 2001): 14–20; idem, "A Massificação do Turismo e o Turismo de Massas" (The Massification of Tourism and Mass Tourism), *Turismohotel Internacional* 25, no. 4 (July 2001): 10–15, 387–409.
7. *Plano Intercalar de Fomento para 1965–7 (Intermediate Development plan for 1965–7)*, vol. 2. Opinion of the Chamber of Corporations (Lisbon: I.N., 1965, 215.
8. Abel Mateus, *Economia portuguesa* (Portuguese Economy) (Lisbon: Verbo, 2001), 98. See also Luís Salgado de Matos, *Investimentos Estrangeiros em Portugal* (Foreign Investment in Portugal) (Lisbon: Seara Nova, 1973), 203.
9. *Plano Intercalar de Fomento para 1965–7,* 212 *(Intermediate Development plan for 1965–7)*, vol. 2. and vol. I, I.N., 1968, 418.
10. F. Archer, *Tourism: Transnational Corporations and Cultural Identities* (Paris: UNESCO, 1985); J.H. Dunning and M. McQueen, "The Eclectic Theory of the Multinational Enterprise and the International Hotel Industry," in *New Theories of Multinational Enterprise*, ed. A.M. Rugman (London: Croom Helm, 1982); Allan M. Williams, "Tourism as an Agent of Economic Transformation in Southern Europe," in *Economic Transformation, Democratization and Integration into the European Union, Southern Europe in Comparative Perspective,* ed. Heather D. Gibson (London: Palgrave, 2001), 120–21.
11. M.I. Roque de Oliveira, "Investimento Estrangeiro," in *Portugal Contemporâneo. Problemas e Perspectivas* (Modern Portugal: Problems and Prospects), ed. Manuela Silva (Lisbon: INA, 1986), 522.
12. Cals, *apud* Allan M. Williams, *op. cit*, p. 13 and pp. 130–33. In this view "tourism in the development of the southern economies is dependent on tour operators,

which are multinationals having their head offices in northern Europe." For an opposite approach to the relationship between risk and profitability, not in tourism as a monolithic activity, but in tourist developments and firms in the tourist sector see Frank m. Go and Ray Pine, *Expanding in a Barrier-Free Europe* (London and New York: Routledge, 1995), 159–61 and 164–67. For a technical approach see *Measuring the Role of Tourism in OECD Economies. The OECD Manual on Tourism Satellite Accounts and Employment* (Paris: OECD, 2000), 5–32.

13. For labor reduction in food service by the use of technologies, which increases flexibility in the use of labor schedules, space, quality, and efficiency, see M. Storey and C.G. Smith, "Developments within the Catering Equipment Industry in Great Britain," in *Progress in Tourism,* ed. Cooper, 187. M.R. Nowlis, "Technological Aspects of Commercial Food Services," in *Progress in Tourism,* ed. Cooper, p.229. And for the example of the hotel company Accor in using electronic machine to check in and check out guests, see ibid., 228.
14. Tourism Statistics; Máximo Pinheiro, editor Long series for the Portuguese Economy after the Second World War, vol. I – Statistical Series, Lisbon, Bank of Portugal, data of business in the high season. The reduction that took place in the subsequent three years also took place in Spain. The staff directly employed in the hotel business in Spain was 418,6 (in thousands) in 1964, 796,0 (in thousands) in 1973.
15. In 1995 aparthotels were to be found in the two main vacation destination areas, with greater emphasis on the Algarve (62.5 percent) than in Madeira (14.9 percent) (João Martins Vieira, *A Economia do Turismo em Portugal* [Lisbon: Publicações Dom Quixote 1997, 102–3).
16. The data for salaries in the Portuguese hotel business between 1950 and 1970 are not available. In the same period, the rate of annual growth of nominal value of salaries in Portugal shows a small increase after the mid-1950s and a drop in 1959, an increase between 1961 and 1964, and small decrease and stabilization until 1970, followed by another marked increase. Between 1950 and 1974 the increase was 40 percent and in general the nominal value of salaries was maintained above the inflation level (Abel Mateus, *A Economia Portuguesa: Crescimento no Contexto Internacional* (Portuguese Economy: Growth in the International Context: 1910–1998), 2nd ed. (Lisbon: Verbo, 2001), figure 2 of file CNHSL of the Statistical Database.
17. This point is important when we consider how productivity growth has been observed in services compared with commodity production. Angus Maddison points out that the general view is that productivity growth tends to be slower in services due to the intrinsic character of many personal services and partly because of measurement conventions, which sometimes exclude the possibility of productivity growth. Maddison goes on to explain how structural changes have been affected by different kinds of forces and influences: in particular, one of the forces mentioned is "the various sectors' differing pace of technological advance." See Angus Maddison, "Explaining the Economic Performance of Nations, 1820–1989," in *Convergence of Productivity. Cross-National Studies and Historical Evidence,* ed. William Baumol, Richard R. Nelson, and Edward N. Wolff (Oxford: Oxford University Press, 1994), 49.

18. François Vella, *Economie Poilitique du Tourisme International* (Paris: Economica, 1985), 40–41. A wide-ranging overview of tourism makes it possible to compare the number of unskilled jobs in the hotel and restaurant trades with the skilled jobs they generate. Swiss employment statistics for the 1990s mention that 74.2 percent of jobs in hotels and restaurants are unskilled, compared with 60.6 percent of jobs in the economy as a whole (Tourism Policy and International Tourism in OECD Countries 1992–1993, Special Feature "Tourism and Employment" [Paris: OECD, 1995], 30–38). In Portugal it is quite possible that the difference is smaller than in Swiss employment.
19. Entrepreneurs in the hotel business argued in favor of this point of view in the early 1990s (Portuguese Hotels Association, Ninth National Hotel and Tourism Conference, Estoril, 1993).
20. Deeper investigation of productivity gains in this sector involves a comparison with studies carried out on the domestic service sector. For the relationship between the time spent in work and the quantity of goods and services produced due to technical changes to perform certain functions with machines more automatic or more efficient (vacuum cleaners, automatic washers and dryers) than previously or better cleaning agents could have made the difference, see W. Keith Bryant, "A Comparison of the Household Work of Married Females: The Mid-1920s and Late 1960s," *Family and Consumer Sciences Research Journal* 24, no. 4 (June 1996): 370–71, 375–77; idem, *The Economic Organization of the Household* (Cambridge: Cambridge University Press, 1990,) 9–10, 120–21; Joel Mokyr, "Why Was There More Work for Mother? Knowledge and Household Behaviour, 1870–1945," *Journal of Economic History* 60, no. 1 (March 2000): 1–40.
21. "*Estatísticas das Empresas, Hóteis, Restaurantes e Agências de Viagens,*" INE (National Statistics Institute), Vol. 1992. In addition, it would also be worth looking at what types of firms have emerged in the hotel business. If one assumes that public (publicly held) companies are associated with large businesses, and privately held limited companies are associated with small businesses, this would also give us some further significant pointers. The data used to support this chapter covered only a small fraction of the period (from 1973 to 1980) so it is insufficient to make any conclusion because the modernization of the economy and of the entrepreneurial fabric, which should also be taken into account in this context, took place in subsequent years. In 1992, 86 percent of hotel and similar corporations employed over twenty workers. In 1980, a company (Torralta) was among the five largest corporations in the country, and employed 2,886 people (Portugal. Principais Sociedades, 1980, I.N.E., Central Services, pp. 26–27).

Appendix

Table 4.9 Labor costs as a percentage of total hotel sector costs (annual averages)

	A -Total staff costs (PTE, thousands)	B–Total costs (PTE, thousands)	%
1976	2,406,694	5,697,272	42.2
1977	2,907,562	7,120,154	40.8
1978	3,425,343	8,539,004	40.1
1979	4,609,060	12,266,964	37.5
1980	5,703,502	13,315,512	42.8
1981	69,69,936	19,803,407	35.1
1982	8,554,577	24,044,604	35.5
1983	10,964,697	32,147,919	34.1
1984	13,024,673	39,236,923	33.1
1985	17,180,886	51,838,100	33.1
1986	20,407,154	58,459,758	34.9
1987	24,338,053	68,781,099	35.3
1988	29,418,844	84,660,106	34.7
1990	36,008,487		
1992	80,411,599	138,537,315	58.0
1993	52,454,000	125,497,217	41.7
1994	59,338,802	139,645,661	42.4
1995	61,906,000		

Sources: *Estatísticas do Turismo; Anuário Estatístico; Estatísticas das Empresas, Hotéis, restaurantes, agências de viagens e Turismo.*

Table 4.10 Total hotel staff costs (PTE, thousands)

	I-Deflator	II–Costs at current annual prices	III–Costs at cosntant annual prices	IV–Staff (numbers)	III/IV
1977	100	2,907,562	2,907,562	29,295	99.2
1978	121.352	3,425,343	2,822,650	29,424	95.9
1979	151.9282	4,609,060	3,033,710	n/a	n/a
1980	184.7577	5,703,502	3,087,017	27,660	111.6
1981	222.0024	6,969,936	3,139,577	30,276	103.6
1982	267.0239	8,554,577	3,203,675	30,454	
1983	335.9806	10,964,697	3,263,491	29,943	108.9
1984	431.6479	13,024,673	3,017,430	30,138	100.1
1985	515.5446	17,180,886	3,332,570	30,111	110.6
1986	586.7821	20,407,154	3,477,808	33,856	102.7
1987	644.9849	24,338,053	3,773,430	35,006	107.7
1988	720.3719	29,418,844	4,083,841	37,026	110.2
1989	815.0499	n/a	n/a	37,825	–
1990	916.0026	36,008,487	3,931,047	39,372	99.8
1991	1028.204	n/a	n/a	40,317	n/a
1992	1128.112	45,915,420	4,070,112	40,847	99.64
1993	1202.198	52,454,000	43,63,175	38,176	114.2
1994	1268.966	59,339,000	4,676,170	37,707	124.0
1995	1326.024	61,906,000	4,668,544	37,743	123.6

Notes: Traditional hotels (O turismo). High season personnel data. Personnel data includes unpaid staff.
Source: *Estatísticas de Turismo*; O Turismo, D.G.E., Statistical Compendium OECD, Deflator, Private Consumption.

Table 4.11 Staff costs, average price per overnight stay, and rate of bed occupancy

	A	B	C	D		B1	C1
1984	33	9,673,900	1,293	35.9			
1985	31.4	12,081,100	1,573	38.6	1985/84	24.9	21.7
1986	31.2	14,726,400	1917	37.9	1986/85	21.9	21.9
1987	30	17,675,800	2,302	37.4	1987/86	20	20.1
1988	29.9	20,807,900	2,606	36.5	1988/87	17.7	13.2
1989	30.2	24,384,800	2,913	36.2	1989/88	17.2	11.8
1990	31	29,924,800	3,217	36.8	1990/89	22.7	10.4
1991	31.2	35,459,900	3,419	37.7	1991/90	18.5	6.3
1992	34.4	41,261,300	3,915	34.7	1992/91	16.4	14.5
1996			4,422				
1997			4,507		1997/96		1.9

Notes: A-percentage of total hotel sector revenues absorbed by staff costs; B–staff costs (escudos); C-average price for overnight stay at current prices (escudos); D–bed occupancy rate excludes tourist complexes and apartments; B1 and C1 change.

Sources: O Turismo, DGE; Análise de Conjuntura. Bulletin nos. 25 and 26, January/April 1998, 23.

Table 4.12 Total hotel sector revenues and number of hotel staff

	A -Revenue at constant prices (escudos)	B -No. of hotel staff	A/B	Change
1966	795,403,000			
1967	802,601,752			
1968	1,079,250,582			
1969	1,208,659,436	17,784	67963,30612	+ 15.72
1970	1,496,422,632	19,026	78651,45758	+ 17.16
1971	1,831,137,310	19,870	92155,87871	+ 14.65
1972	2,312,306,547			
1973	2,565,638,976	23,859	107533,3826	
1974	1,837,220,199	24,238	75799,16656	- 29.5
1975	1,618,831,966	23,888	67767,58063	- 10.5
1976	1,918,102,612	24,318	78875,83732	+ 16.3
1977	1,873,797,589	25,835	72529,4209	- 8.0
1978	2,264,730,562	25,644	88314,24747	+21.0
1979	2,775,198,650	32,769	84689,75709	- 4.1
1980	2,914,609,824	33,012	88289,40458	+ 4.2
1992	4,111,530,052	40,847	100656,8427	+14.0
1993	3,539,860,488	38,201	92664,07916	- 7.9
1994	4,190,785,729	32,928	127271,1895	+ 37.3

Source: Estatísticas Das Sociedades; Estatísticas de Turismo; Statistical Compendium, OECD – Deflator, Private Consumption.

Table 4.13 Ratio of number of staff to number of beds

	1999	1996	1995	1993	1991	1989	1987	1984	1983	1976	1975	1974	1970	1967
All hotels	0.24	0.25	0.32	0.27	0.32	0.34	0.35	0.38	0.38	0.40	0.39	0.43	0.45	0.43
Five-star hotels	0.42	0.40	0.53	0.41	0.53	0.52	0.51	0.64	0.59					
Four-star hotels	0.24	0.26	0.34	0.30	0.34	0.37	0.38	0.39	0.40					
Three-star hotels	0.18	0.19	0.22	0.21	0.22	0.26	0.27	0.30	0.32					
Total aparthotels	0.15	0.13	0.21	0.15	0.21	0.21	0.22	0.23	0.24	0.18	0.16	0.26		
Pousadas		0.56		0.61	0.68	0.70	0.70	0.76	0.76	0.81	0.74	0.87	0.68	0.69
Total hostelries		0.31		0.34	0.38	0.34	0.36	0.35	0.35	0.35	0.37	0.45	0.46	0.47
Total *pensions*	0.14	0.14	0.14	0.15	0.15	0.14	0.14	0.15	0.15	0.18	0.18	0.19	0.21	0.25
Tourist complexes	0.14	0.12	0.11	0.12	0.11	0.10	0.10							
Tourist apartments	0.09	0.09	0.10	0.08	0.10	0.10	0.10							
Overall total	0.19	0.18	0.21	0.19	0.21	0.22	0.23	0.28	0.29	0.30	0.29	0.32	0.33	0.35

Source: Tourism, Direcção Geral de Turismo (various years).

Chapter 5

Sending the Italians on Vacation

The Alpitour Group

Luciano Segreto

In 1997 there were about 39,000 travel agencies in the European Union. Predominantly located in Central and Northern Europe, most of them were small independent travel agencies offering global services (see table 5.1). Only a few of them could be considered tour operators, who offered specialized services both directly and through the travel agencies. In Italy in that year a survey listed close to 350 tour operators. In 1998 they produced a global revenue of €1.5 billion, rising in 1996 to 2.25 billion. In 1996 roughly two-thirds of that revenue was produced by the top ten firms in the list, and 19.1 percent by the leader firm, Alpitour.

This trend is widespread, and applies not only to Italy. In the United Kingdom and in Germany, two of the biggest European countries that send their citizen-customers abroad, the concentration process is even more marked. In 1998 the two biggest tour operators in Italy (Alpitour and Franco Rosso) controlled about 24 percent of the market, while the two largest firms in Great Britain controlled 50 percent, and the two top operators in Germany 44 percent. This suggests that there is a direct relationship between the number, the importance, and the concentration process in terms of the tour operators on the one hand, and the propensity of a country to import or to export tourists on the other hand.

The same source includes the first Italian tour operator, Alpitour in the eighteenth place, with a revenue of €0.5 billion, and 760,000 customers in

---

Notes for this chapter begin on page 101.

Table 5.1 Revenues of the top ten European tour operators, 1997 (in billion euros)

Tourist Union International (Germany)	4.02
Airtour (United Kingdom)	2.85
NUR (Germany)	2.55
Thomson (United Kingdom)	2.34
LTU Touristik (Germany)	1.56
First Choice (United Kingdom)	1.46
Kuoni (Switzerland)	1.41
Air Tour (United Kingdom)	1.36
Nouvelles Frontières (France)	1.32
Club Med (France)	1.23

Source: Touring Club Italiano, *L'Annuario del turismo*, a cura del centro studi del Tci, 1999.

1997, which is a quarter of those counted for Nouvelles Frontières, and one-ninth of those who chose the German TUI (no data are available for Club Med for that year). This situation reflects the different history of tourism in traditionally more advanced countries, which discovered mass vacationing in the early decades of the twentieth century. It is also rooted in the different national history of the firms, their evolution, the role of the stockholders and the shareholders. Ultimately, it is a kaleidoscope of the different trajectories of the European firms. The analysis of the Italian case, mainly (but not exclusively) through the presentation of the Alpitour case, offers more than one factor that supports this hypothesis.

The Origins

Alpitour was set up in Cuneo, a provincial town of Piedmont, in 1947 as a travel agency under the name Alpi. Initially, its main goal was to sell coach and train tickets, with a secondary task of organizing trips by hiring coaches to take customers to the most significant social events of that period, such as the Nice Carnival or the Jubilee Year in Rome in 1950. The first journeys included the trip and two nights in a hotel of average category. From its very beginning, the story of this firm is not very different from that of any other small-size family-operated firms in Italy. Nevertheless, it is not an easily told story because, as in many family-operated firms do not keep archives and/or do not permit the historian easy access. The researcher is forced to use alternative sources, with research often thwarted by a hostile environment. Newspapers, not to mention Internet sources, are places where the news is filtered, if not written, by the very actors the historian would like to study. The Alpitour story is no exception. The family has been approached several times but researchers have only managed to obtain answers to a limited number of written questions. This helped to avoid practical mistakes, but the situation was unsatisfactory, leaving a lot of questions without any plausible answers, if any answer at all. The alternative was to forgo the opportunity of telling an interesting story that offered the chance to compare elements of the Italian case with that of other European tour operators, hoping to confirm the similarities among family-operated firms in Italy (and in many respects in the rest of Europe), regardless of the sector in which they have become a key actor, if not the main actor, of the system in which they are rooted.[1]

The founder of the Alpi travel agency was Lorenzo Isoardi. The son of a small entrepreneur involved in the building sector, Isoardi was born in 1915 and, after training in the family business, he acquired experience as a real estate agent, but had no background at all in the tourism sector. This was also true of his wife, Rosetta Damilano, the daughter of a local wholesale dealer, who helped Isoardi to get the new company off the ground. While a large proportion of the business came from tickets sold to workers commuting to Turin and other industrial areas by coach, Isoardi had an ambitious mission for his travel agency: he wanted to offer an increasing number of customers good tourism service at a relatively cheap price, at the time when, following World War II, more Italians had the opportunity to spend part of their free time on vacation, thanks to the economic development and the increase in their incomes.[2]

At the beginning of the 1950s the total population in Piedmont was about 4 million people, and Cuneo had roughly 52,000 inhabitants. The geographical position of the region was strategically significant to the plan to increase trips to France (the connections by train and by road were quite good for a large part of the year and there were important discussions about the possibility of building a new tunnel under the Mont Blanc),[3] while the Alps were gaining in interest among many Italians as a vacation spot. The demographic development of that area during the 1950s and the 1960s due to the immigration phenomenon resulting from the expansion of the Turin industrial area (and especially that of Fiat plants),[4] contributed directly to the increase in the economic activities of the Alpi travel agency. The firm had to take the drawbacks of Piedmont and the Cuneo Province into consideration: the relative distance from the Mediterranean area, and the poor condition of the road network in that period. Its strategy had to be reconsidered in subsequent years in order to change the offer to the customer. Thus, the geographical reorientation of the Alpi proposals included new international destinations that could be reached by coach and, later, by the combination of coach and airplane. Spain was the first country to which the Alpi travel agency offered a package that included a six-day trip to Barcelona and Madrid, the cost of the coach and six nights in a hotel, selected from the average categories (two- or three-stars). The strategy of the firm was to increase special offers during low season in order to de-specialize its target and to increase the number of customers. In the meantime, this strategy meant that the smallest local tourist agents considered the travel agency's name sufficiently reliable to be worth doing business with.

From Travel Agency to Tour Operator

The development of a more complex strategy, based on the travel combination of coach and plane was the direct consequence of the attempt by the national airline company, Alitalia, to set up a national network of travel agencies selling airplane tickets. Alitalia, like many other national flag carriers, realized that air travel was slowly shifting from elitist to more general use. Alitalia contacted Alpi and they easily came to an agreement at the beginning of the 1960s, which permitted the travel agency to sell "all-inclusive trips." This offer was completely new to the Italian market. Because the proposals would have affected and/or interested a wider portion of the potential customers, it was possible to limit costs in the bargaining process with the transportation operators. In fact, in 1960 Alpi was able to print a catalog with about thirty destinations in Europe and the Mediterranean, which included flight destinations such as Spain, Greece, France, and the Mediterranean islands – which at that time considered exclusive and only for very rich people, began to be more than just a dream for a larger portion of the local population. Part of Alpi travel agency's fame owed to these kinds of all-inclusive trips, advertised in the local newspapers as "deluxe trips at half price." The firm was still local, and not yet known nationally. Nevertheless, it is quite clear that its objectives were very ambitious and the growth strategy implemented in those years was producing encouraging results.

Following a somewhat Schumpeterian approach for the development of the firm, the Isoardi family realized that the commercial activity of selling trips, despite its success, was small and had no promising prospects: Alpi had to introduce new products to increase its turnover and diversify its profile. Furthermore, specializing in the preparation of the excursions constituted a real opportunity to develop in a different sector, which needed new expertise to set up new "products."[5] This strategy also necessitated a partial restructuring of the firm. Alpi remained, of course, a family firm, but its structure became more complex, with specialized staff organizing the all-inclusive trips formula. This required new contacts and new links with partners and the segmentation of the market, in order to establish different offers for different customers. The most delicate task was to find the right partners, because the decisive element for a successful strategy was the level of services offered in the resorts, such as the quality of the hotels, their location, and many other factors characterizing the tourist offer. This new approach was no longer that of a travel agency, but that of a real tour operator, because it implied personal and direct contact with local tourism organizations and firms.[6] In the late 1960s the firm decided to introduce technology into its activities, a pioneer decision for the Italian tour operating sector at that time. The decision to change the name from Alpi to Alpitour in 1968 was symbolic and represented the actualization of the decision to push in the new direction.[7]

The formula offered by Alpitour was a success. Their strategy created a virtuous circle: new, more flexible and more successful offers to increase the number of customers, which led to even more offers and so on. The real boom began in the second half of the 1970s, after the reorganization of airline companies following the first oil crisis and state intervention throughout Europe, which favored mass development of this means of transport.[8] Alpitour was an exception in the Italian situation, because at that time its offer included, as it had for many years, trips to Greece and Spain, whereas other Italian tour operators continued to limit their offer to Italian seaside resorts. Moreover, Alpitour was able to offer even more exotic destinations, which were not a mass success, but they did contribute to the enhancement of the company's image among their potential customers. In this very sensitive economic sector, having a constant supply of new products – regardless of their importance from a quantitative point of view – was strategically important in being successful.

The Takeoff

Data about the economic performance of Alpitour are almost non-existent in the firm's archives. Apparently they are available – or have been kept – only since 1982. They clearly show an excellent trend, but one that does not hide the fact that those figures were still nowhere near those of the most important European tour operators. In 1982 there were about 100,000 Alpitour customers and the firm's revenue was 54 billion lira in current value (140.9 billion lira in 2000 value or €72 million). The increase one year later was astonishing: 135,000 customers and the turnover was, in current value, 83 billion lira (188 billion lira in 2000 value or €97.3 million). In 1984 the figures were even higher: 180,000 customers and 120 billion lira revenue in current value (246 billion lira in 2000 value or €127 million). In three years customer figures increased by 80 percent and turnover increased by almost three times, certainly much more than inflation, which in that period was around 8–10 percent, with a slow tendency to decrease. Those figures are much more impressive if one considers that during the same period the Italian Association of Hotels Owners calculated that between 1982 and 1983 there were 9 percent fewer Italian tourists in Italy and 5 percent fewer chose to vacation abroad.[9]

Those results were the first effects of the firm's new strategy of organizing its own flights, assistance to tourists throughout their vacation, setting up of a network of foreign branches in the most important tourism areas.[10] These efforts allowed Alpitour to enter a new dimension that implied the extensive use of TV advertising. The development of commercial TV offered new opportunities.[11] Its advertising campaigns became quite famous during the second half of the 1980s and the beginning of the 1990s: they were based on a jingle that succeeded in reaching a new target, both elite and mass tourism.[12]

Internationalization or Merger and Acquisition?

During the 1980s the merger and acquisition movement gained ground in the tourism sector. In 1987 the German International Travel Service set up a commercial alliance with the Dutch firm Holland International, while another German group, Tourist Union International, took over the French group Air Tour. Alpitour was the first Italian tour operator to react positively to this new situation. In 1988 it bought 25 percent of the Palma de Mallorca firm Jumbo Tours, one of the top five Spanish firms in this sector. A year later Alpitour became one of the members of a big Spanish project. The Italian firm invested 50 billion lira (€4.1 million) in the so-called Pool Shana – a European pool jointly set up by Scandinavian Startour, British Horizon, German Neckermann, and Dutch Arkereizen – to gain a shareholding in the Spanish group Royal Tour España (a firm managing several hotels on the Mediterranean coast) and in another Spanish group, Royal Tour, owner of a hotel chain and many residential resorts on the Balearic Islands.[13]

Alpitour's participation in this investment project was a European seal of approval for the Italian firm: to be accepted among some of the most important European tour operators was the reward of forty years' development, and the confirmation that Alpitour was the only significant, major Italian group in this sector. In the world of the European tour operators of that time, in Italy Alpitour remained a giant among the dwarfs, and, at an international level, a dwarf among the giants.

Like many other Italian family-operated firms, Alpitour suffered from insufficient financial resources at the beginning of the 1990s. The never-ending increase in customers during the 1990s (545,000 in 1992, and 775,000 in 1997) was not sufficient to guarantee the same increase in revenue, because the volume of investment necessary to maintain or increase that level was becoming oppressive. The initial response, the progressive shift of destinations from Italy and Europe to long distance ones (see table 5.2), had an effect on the strategy of the firm, and especially on its financial requirements.

Table 5.2 Customer distribution by destination, 1992 and 1997 (%)

	1992	1997
Italy	25.8	21.6
Europe	14.5	12.5
Medium-distance destinations	46.8	50.7
Long-distance destinations	12.9	15.2

Source: Gruppo Alpitour, *Relazioni e bilancio al 31 ottobre 1997*, Cuneo, 1997, 10.

The strategy of the group in the early 1990s was to increase the quality of the services and the range of the offer. To implement that vision the firm started a campaign of share acquisition, but Alpitour did not take control of any other firm. In 1990 Alpitour became an important shareholder in the Spanish company Donamar (one of the most important actors in the Canary Islands), of the Trieste tour operator Utat (a leading coach tour operator with a solid tradition in travel to Eastern Europe, a destination of much more interest after the end of the Cold War), and of Air Europe, an Italian private airline company controlled by the Fiat group, a couple of big Piedmont families linked to the Agnelli family, and the International Leisure group, a leading international tour operator.[14]

Fiat Involvement: The Start of a New Era or the Never-Ending Story?

The first contacts with the Agnelli group dramatically changed Alpitour. In fact, in 1992 the Isoardi family and the financial holding of the Agnelli family, Ifil, signed an agreement permitting the latter to buy 30 percent of the capital of Alpitour, paying 43.5 billion lira in cash (55 billion lira in 2000 value or €28.5 million) through the issue of new reserved shares and convertible bonds. Implicitly, as a result of this financial operation, the economic value of the firm was considered to be as high as 145 billion lira, that is one-third of the revenue produced in 1991, quite a ratio for this kind of agreement.[15]

Agnelli group's interest in the tourism sector was part of a wider diversification process begun in 1986 by the Ifil group headed by Umberto Agnelli, the brother of Gianni Agnelli. The portfolio diversification was based on the expectation of an increase in the profitability of the financial company by reducing risk through the geographic and sector equilibrium of the new investments. In the 1980s Ifil was one of the most dynamic firms in the Agnelli group; especially after the effective commencement of the alliance with the French financial group Worms. This agreement (operated through a shareholding in the Exor group, the international financial holding of the Ifil group) opened the door to a series of important opportunities in some very dynamic sectors, such as food (the Bsn-Danone group, the major French sugar producer Saint Louis), insurance, transportation, tourism, and hotel chain companies (the Accor group).[16]

From Ifil's point of view, the investment in Alpitour was very promising. In 1991 Alpitour had a revenue in 1991 of 450 billion lira (603 billion lira in 2000 value or €311 million), and a staff of 580 members, official branches in four big Italian towns, 3,000 travel agencies selling its products, and shareholdings in many foreign companies, especially in Spain. Alpitour was, without doubt, the number one travel agency in Italy, controlling 15 percent of the national market.

As far as the Alpitour group was concerned, the new shareholder put fresh capital at the firm's disposal. In fact, new resources were necessary for investment planning, especially in the resort sector, which the firm had not developed as desired during the 1980s. In fact, in the following year, the firm embarked on a grand scheme of constructing new hotels and holiday villages, especially around the Mediterranean, but also in other areas of the world. In the 1990s the Alpitour group set up a specific structure, with sub-holdings (Jumbo Tours and Horizon Holidays) and specialized firms, such as Hoy Viajamos, Jumbo Tours Italia, Renthotel and Promotourist, to organize the selection, organization, and management of their hotels and villages abroad, as well as an insurance company – Alpitour Reinsurance, established in Dublin. Another firm, Jumbo Renta, was the direct owner of all the hotels, villages, and holidays resorts of the group.[17] Most of Alpitour's eighty hotels around the world (in Spain, as well as in Northern Africa and the Caribbean Islands) are "Hotel Italian style," which means that Italian tourists can find Italian cuisine, as well as personal assistance, leisure and everything they need managed by Italian staff. And the same model can be found in the Alpitour villages (in Minorca, for example).[18]

During the 1990s, Alpitour's strategy in the Italian market also changed greatly. The merger and acquisition process on an international scale that characterized the 1980s was now redirected to the domestic market. The most important difference was that Ifil led the game. The Turin financial holding of the Fiat group considered the tourism sector to be of major future significance. Their involvement in Club Med, despite some trouble, confirmed that this investment was strategic. The project Ifil had in mind was to establish a new Italian firm that would be in a better position to compete on international level, by integrating its offer with that of Club Med. The central point of this plan was a concentration process, which would have included the top four Italian tour operators – Alpitour (already controlled), Francorosso, I Viaggio del Ventaglio and Valtur (jointly controlled by the Bank San Paolo-Imi, a shareholder of the Fiat group, and an important partner of the Agnelli family, and Club Med, which had about 23 percent of the Valtur shares in its portfolio).[19]

However, something went wrong during the discussions between Ifil and San Paolo-Imi. The latter refused Ifil's offer to join the scheme. The project went on anyway, but without their being able to develop it completely. In 1998 Alpitour agreed to merge with Francorosso, the second largest Italian tour operator, whose historical development was not very different from Alpitour's previous trajectory. In fact the firm had been set up in Turin in 1953 by another Piedmont family, headed by an entrepreneur Franco Rosso, as a travel agency organizing trips to France and Switzerland. The Francorosso travel agency understood the appeal of long distance destinations much earlier than any other Italian tour operator. As early as 1967 this firm was able to organize vacation-related travel to Japan, Polynesia, and South Africa. In 1972 Francorosso was one of the tour operators connected with charter flights to London and to Africa. During the 1970s the firm set up a separate company, Francorosso International, to manage its international activities.

In the 1980s Francorosso controlled an exclusive hotel resort in Kenya, organized along the all-inclusive model. In the same decade the company started a program of constructing tourist villages and it was among the first European tour operators interested in promoting vacations in the Maldives. The local government gave Francorosso the permission to build two villages (later named "Sea Club") on two undeveloped islands.

The firm also increased its activity in the Mediterranean region. During the 1980s Francorosso bought several hotels and villages in Greece, Spain, Turkey, and Northern Africa. All these old and new structures were called "Italian Holiday," because the management, the assistance, the organization of every kind of activity was supported by Italian staff. In 1994, Francorosso signed an agreement with the US tour operator Marlboro Country Travels in order to introduce to the Italian market the kind of vacation product the US company specialized in, which appealed to the so-called spirit of adventure, suggested by the stereotyped image of the American West.[20]

In 1996 the firm announced that a deal with an important European partner was under discussion, the first step before entering the stock exchange. It is not clear what really happened during these discussions with the mysterious European partner, but something went wrong. Thus, Francorosso's entire dream, including the stock exchange hopes, collapsed.[21]

It is clear that the trajectories followed by the two tour operators were quite similar from the start. The merger was a sort of natural conclusion of two parallel stories. Nevertheless, the strong position of Alpitour gave the Isoardi and Ifil firm pre-eminence: in 1997 the revenue was already around 900 billion lira, exactly double that of 1992, when the Ifil group bought its shareholdings; and there was a staff of nearly 670 people, with about 700,000 customers planning their vacation via Alpitour.[22] The merger also redefined the balance of shareholders. In fact, Ifil invested 49 billion lira, whereas Alpitour paid 33 billion lira for its shareholding. In order to clarify the structure of the group, the new partners decided to set up a new holding company, Blufin, which was intended to have authority over the owner structure. A new picture of the group taken after that merger gave Ifil 43.5 percent of Blufin's capital, the same proportion as the Isoardi family, and the Rosso family kept 13 percent.[23]

The new leading position of the Alpitour group encouraged the development of the same strategy with other Italian competitors. In 1999 the group took a minority shareholding in two other firms: 49 percent of Viaggidea and 35 percent of Viaggi dell'Elefante. The former was established in the early 1980s and specialized in the organization of the Caribbean vacations, and later to the Indian and the Pacific oceans.[24] The latter was set up in 1984–85, and specialized as a tour operator for the Far East destinations, and particularly for travel of a strongly cultural character.[25]

This merger and acquisition strategy cannot conceal the fact that this process of development was very limited compared with that of the biggest European tour operators. For a very long time the only international partners of the Alpitour group were the Spanish firms Jumbo Tours and Donamar. The reason for this is linked in part with the peculiarity of the Italian tourism market. Its characteristics make any synergy with other European competitors based on a common structure and know-how difficult. In Italy, as mass tourism was developing, the economic actors developed a strategy based on two variables: product and promotion. This approach had something to do with the novelty of the "vacation product" for the Italian population, and its new and increasing interest in buying holidays and trips abroad. On the contrary, in Germany or in Great Britain, where the biggest European tour operators are located, the competitive element shifted quickly toward price. The internationalization and/or multinational process were the first answer to that kind of competition.[26]

This situation has begun to change at the turn of the twenty-first century. In 2000 the Rosso family sold its 13 percent shareholding in Blufin to the Ifil group for 42.6 billion lira (€22 million) after the Isoardi family declined to buy 6.5 percent, that is, half of that shareholding, even though it was entitled to do so by the existing agreement among the three partners. The transaction implied a valuation of the Blufin holding at 327 billion lira. After its founder's death in 1999, the family was represented by his son Guglielmo (born in 1945) and daughter Maria Luisa (born in 1942). One of the first decisions taken by the second generation was to sell its shareholding to Ifil as well: Ifil paid about 200 billion lira (more than €100 million) for 43.5 percent of Blufin, thus giving this holding an asset value of 459 billion lira, almost 40 percent more than a year earlier. As a result of the decision to maintain strong roots in the original territory, the Isoardi family remained on the board of Blufin and Guglielmo Isoardi was confirmed as chairman of the Alpitour group and member of the board of the Ifil group. The Isoardi family nevertheless did not leave the tourism sector. Through the financial holding Italiana Halley Partecipazioni (Italian Halley Shareholdings), they still own the Spanish firm Promotourist, the owner of hotels in the Canary Islands and Minorca, while other tourism activities are controlled through Teknema, a holding company based in Luxembourg.[27]

Only three months later the Italian tour operating sector was shocked by the news that the German group Preussag – a former conglomerate in coal, steel, and power production sector, and for years an active tour operator through the number one in Europe, TUI, with a revenue of €22 billion Euro – had bought from Ifil 10 percent of Holding Nht (New Holding Tourism), based in the Netherlands, the Ifil holding controlling Blufin. Preussag joined the shareholders in addition to the Ifil group in order to make the Italian tour operating sector more dynamic. Preussag's intervention seems to have opened the door to new investments, as the German partner declared their intention of setting up an airline charter company, Neos, in Italy to sustain Alpitour development.[28] In 2001, in the French press, there were rumors that TUI, who had just gained control of Nouvelles Frontières, wanted to merge the Italian subsidiary of this famous French group with Alpitour. Some discussions probably took place between the Preussag group and Ifil. No consensus was reached. Thus, three years later, in January 2004, this promising alliance was over. After a transaction valued at €50 million, Ifil was again owner of all the Alpitour shares and made the decision to liquidate Nht, after transferring to Alpitour the controlled shareholdings in two international firms, Welcome Travels group and airline company Neos.[29] In the same year the Agnelli family holding sold their Club Med shares to the Accor group, refocusing their portfolio and its investment strategy. In this situation Alpitour was transformed into an operative holding for the tourism sector, both as tour operator and controlling all the sub-sectors, such as incoming customers, hotels, resorts, distribution, and airplane transportation.[30] In 2006 newspapers reported that Ifil no longer considered this investment to be strategic.[31]

Conclusion

The tour operator sector in Italy is represented by the Association of Italian Tour Operators (ATOI), which has about fifty members, but there are at least 200 firms claiming that they are tour operators. In 1990 the top sixteen firms generated 50 percent of the revenue, whereas in 2000 the same amount was produced by the top eight or nine firms. Nevertheless, one should not forget that in 1996 the total revenue produced by all these firms combined was 6,000 billion lira or €3.1 million, while the German giant of the sector, and number one in Europe produced a revenue of about 8,000 billion lira or € 4.13 million.

The story of this sector is no exception in the familiar history of Italian companies: mainly family-operated small-scale firms, facing little price competition, with a high level of concentration.[32] All these ingredients may have led to the difficulties the Italian industrial system has been facing in recent years: a relative decline, sometimes being subjected to some variety of foreign economic colonization. Generally speaking, this is not unusual situation for the tourism sector. Unfortunately, it is also becoming customary for the entire Italian economic system. The story of Alpitour represents the evolution of the tourism sector in this country: a family-operated firm in its initial stages, a long-term development with increasing success among Italian customers, some financial difficulties because of lack of capital, the intervention of a big group, the reduction and then the elimination of the family ownership, some concentration process and new strategy to increase the profitability of the sector where income, at least in Italy, is still far too concentrated in a short period, while the costs for the structure cover the whole year.[33] This is apparently, a situation without a solution, if one considers some non-economic factors such as the Italian habit of concentrating vacations in the summer or the new trend, noticed by journalists and sociologists, of dividing vacations between different periods of the year, reducing the number of days of each short vacation, which is often transformed simply into a long weekend.

Notes

1. A. Colli, *The History of Family Business, 1850–2000* (Cambridge: Cambridge University Press, 2003).
2. M. Gregoretti, "Vacanze con l'Avvocato," *Panorama*, 23 February 1992, 183; for the history of the firm see www.alpitour.it; P. Battilani, *Vacanze di pochi, vacanze di tutti. L'evoluzione del turismo europeo* (Bologna: il Mulino, 2001), 230–41.

3. P. Lafond, "La France et le miracle économique italien, 1945–1963," PhD diss., Université de Paris XII, 2004.
4. V. Castronovo, S. Lanaro, P. Bevilacqua, G. Mori, M. Aymard, S, Anselmi et al. *Storia d'Italia dall'Unità a oggi, Le regioni, Il Piemonte* (Torino: Einaudi, 1998).
5. M. Boyer, *Il turismo: dai gran tour ai viaggi organizzati* (Trieste: Editoriale Libraria, 1997), 77–89.
6. A. Biella, *L'industria del viaggio organizzato* (Milan: Franco Angeli, 1996), 27–30.
7. R. Bosio, "Positivi i risultati Alpitour verso quota 180 mila clienti," *la Repubblica*, 9 August 1984.
8. On this specific point, see respective chart by Peter Lyth in this book.
9. "In rosso i conti dell'azienda vacanze," "*Il Sole-24 Ore*," 9 August 1984.
10. R. Bosio, "Positivi i risultati Alpitour. Verso quota 180 mila clienti," *Il Sole-24 Ore*, 9 August 1984.
11. V. Codeluppi, *Iperpubblicità. Come cambia la pubblicità italiana* (Milan: Franco Angeli, 2000); D. Pitteri, *La pubblicità in Italia. Dal dopoguerra a oggi* (Rome and Bari: La Terza, 2002).
12. The jingle said: "Self help tourist? No Alpitour? Ahi … ahi … ahi …," and it was targeted to convince tourists leaving for exotic destinations that the quality of their vacation would have been increased very much by relying on the high standard services of the tour operator, without losing any social or cultural contact with the visited country.
13. G. Palmieri, "I grandi del turismo vanno alla conquista dell'Europa," *Il Sole-24 Ore*, 3 November 1984.
14. R. Bosio, "Alpitour, la vacanza è business," *Il Sole-24 Ore*, 23 November 1990.
15. Agnelli nel business vacanze. Ifil compra il 30 percento di Alpitour," *la Repubblica*, 8 February 1992.
16. S. Pensabene, "L'altra Fiat esce dal guscio," *Mondo economico*, 1 May 1993, 82–84; V. Castronovo, *Fiat 1899–1999.*
17. Gruppo Alpitour, *Destinazione terzo millennio*, cit., p. 4; E. Ippolito, *Jumbo Tours Italia, la mossa concreta di Alpitour*, in "TTG Italia,," 17.1.2000, p. 5.
18. Gruppo Alpitour, *Bravo Club: I villaggi di Alpitour* (Cuneo, 2000), 18–19.
19. M. la Ferla, "Tutti in ferie con gli Agnelli," *L'Espresso*, 15 January 1998, 129–30.
20. G. Ferraino, "Turismo, maxipolo di Francorosso e Alpitour," *Corriere della Sera*, 18 December 1997.
21. N. Sunseri, "Club Med e Valtur, destini incrociati all'ombra della Mole," *il Lunedì della Repubblica*, 16 December 1996.
22. "Alpitour punta a mille miliardi," *Corriere della Sera*, 16 March 1997.
23. Gruppo Alpitour, *Destinazione nuovo millennio*, 13.
24. L. Allegrucci, "Alpitour si allarga con Viaggidea s.r.l.," *Italia Oggi*, 11 November 1999.
25. F. Briglia, "Vacanze culturali, arriva Alpitour," *Italia Oggi*, 1 July 1999.
26. A. Biella, *L'industria del viaggio organizzato*, 92–94.
27. G. Ferraina, "Turismo, Ifil conquista il 100 percento di Alpitour," *Corriere della Sera*, 1 February 2001; Isoardi investe sugli hotel tramite la halley Partecipazioni," *Plus24*, 2 December 2006.

28. M. De Feo, "Ifil, allanza nel turismo con la Preussag," *Corriere della Sera*, 19 May 2001.
29. See www.tui-group.com/de/pressemedien/pressemeldungen/2004/pm20040109_italien_verkauf.html.
30. Borsa Italiana-Ifil, *Relazione trimestrale al 30 settembre 2004.*
31. *Panorama*, 12 May 2006.
32. F. Amatori-A. Colli, *Impresa e industria in Italia dall'Unità a oggi* (Venice: Marsilio, 1999).
33. Ifil, *Relazione semestrale 2006*, Turin, June 2006.

Chapter 6

Rimini

An Original Mix of Italian Style and Foreign Models?

Patrizia Battilani

Rimini is a medium-size town on the Adriatic coast, which in the second half of the twentieth century became the main Italian seaside tourist destination. Rimini's tourism history is very interesting for many reasons. First, because of its long history as a tourist resort that dates back to the first half of the nineteenth century, second, for its extraordinary skill in changing its image, product, and variety of holidays, third, because of its organizational model that has always been based on small businesses instead of large corporations and finally, because of the attention paid to the experience of other resorts: during the nineteenth century to the Belgian and French resorts and during the last four decades to the United States.

This chapter analyzes Rimini's tourism development from the first half of the nineteenth century to the present day. The chapter presents the different stages of growth and the development of a new image and type of vacation, as well as three case studies that shed light on the organizational model, and on the copying of foreign technology and examples.

Despite its early beginning as a tourist destination, Rimini did not become well-known until the interwar years and real growth did not come until the 1950s. Rimini's post-war history could be summarized in four stages, following Butler's Resort Cycle model. Rimini's development, which corresponds to the third stage in Butler's model, started in 1945 and lasted until 1967. This was a period of considerable growth in tourist numbers, especially of foreign tourists, who made up 40 percent of the total during the 1960s.

Notes for this chapter begin on page 123.

The year 1968 signified the beginning of a decade of stagnation, during which Rimini began to feel the competition of recently developed resorts (especially in Spain and Yugoslavia), and foreign demand fell off considerably. Nevertheless, the tourist sector did not go through a crisis, as the drop in foreign tourist numbers was more than compensated for by the considerable increase in the number of Italians choosing Rimini for their vacations.

The stagnation was overcome by the reorientation of Rimini's tourism model. Between 1978 and 1988 Rimini became an entertainment capital, with the opening of numerous discotheques, arcades, and theme parks. Although foreign tourist numbers remained static, Italian tourist numbers rose. The year 1988 became Rimini's record year, with 8.5 million overnight guests. This growth was abruptly interrupted by an extraneous factor: in 1989 there were 2.5 million fewer overnight guests due to the problem of marine algae (mucilage). Rimini seemed to be starting to decline. However, during the 1990s, a second reorientation toward conference tourism permitted a slow but gradual recovery from the 1989 shock, although numbers never returned to their 1988 level. Since 1990 local administration and private entrepreneurs have been investing in conference tourism alongside the more traditional seaside variety.

Thus, what has emerged in Rimini's tourism history is the ability to offer new products and new kinds of holidays. Until the beginning of World War I, business leaders pursued the dream of Rimini's becoming an exclusive resort, in the interwar years hotels and entertainment structures directed their attention toward the middle classes, and in the 1950s and 1960s Rimini became the most famous Italian mass tourism resort. During the 1970s, as competition from foreign resorts had grown, Rimini's business leaders invented the leisure industry. Discotheques and arcades were the new reference point for tour agencies. Finally, after 1989 the marine algae crisis, local administration and hoteliers invested increasingly in conference and trade fair tourism.

It could be of some interest to investigate the organizational model that allowed Rimini's success and renovation. For this purpose I have analyzed the development of three important Rimini companies: the Calesini Hotel Company set up in 1964, the Paradiso Club discotheque that dates back to 1957, and Aquafan, a water theme park, opened in 1984.

Tourism in Rimini before World War II: The Important Legacy of the Past

Rimini's fame as a seaside resort goes back to at least 1843, the year in which two young landowners, the Counts Baldini, built the town's first bathing establishment. Bathing in the sea had already become something of a custom, and was popular with local people from all social classes. However, until World War I, business activities connected to seaside bathing proved far from profitable, and often the local council had to step in and both create the more important tourist infrastructures and save those set up by private concerns. The Baldini family's bathing establishment ultimately had to be bought by the council to prevent it from bankruptcy.

Tourism during this period was characterized by three main features: (1) the attempts made to create a tourist resort for the upper classes, with luxury structures, which often operated at a loss, and the plan to turn Rimini into a famous tourist resort for the aristocracy, proved a failure; (2) the strong commitment of the local administration to the tourism sector, consisting in investment and involvement in rescue operations designed to furnish the town with those structures required for the development of tourism; (3) the interest of the entire town in the tourism business: for example, the largest local bank granted loans, many local people opened bars and restaurants for less well-off tourists, and various non-profit associations were founded to organize entertainment and recreational activities in the town.[1]

In any case, the first real tourism growth in Rimini did not come until the interwar years when the number of bathers increased from 18,750 in 1922 to 74,953 in 1933. Hotels and, above all, guest houses quickly grew from 23 in 1923 to 109 in 1933, thanks to the success of all-inclusive pricing. The number of villas, homes, and apartments also grew. Their owners were generally shopkeepers or professionals who used rental fees to supplement their main income. In those days the tourists who came to Rimini were 90 to 95 percent Italian. This was also the era when summer camps spread; in 1937 they housed almost 40,000 children from working-class parents.

The interwar years represented a turnaround in Rimini's tourism history, when it became clear that only investment in entertainment and hotel structures would stimulate tourism development. In fact, great attention was paid to entertainment activities, such as parties and concerts, most of which took place in the luxury hotels. The local administration also organized different types of events: festivals, light opera, music, sporting events, and other recreational activities. Above all, dancing was very popular. "It is a miracle that the chairs do not dance" the local fascist journal, *The People of Romagna*, reported in 1928. A few dance halls were set up. But the most expensive investment was the opening of the Nirigua Park in 1922, one of the first Italian theme parks.[2] Unfortunately the numbers of tourists were not sufficient to guarantee the profitability of this investment and the park closed five years later. Furthermore, during the 1920s Rimini's institutional and private investors became aware of the importance of entertainment for the development of tourism. The local newspaper *Il Corriere dei Bagni* reported in 1923: "the main problems in Rimini are to provide all those things which could attract demanding customers and at the same time guarantee profits for the investors. The season is short because our beaches do not provide sufficient man-made attractions."[3] Another aspect of this new entrepreneurial mentality was the creation of professional courses. In 1937 a three-year vocational school was organized for young people who wanted to work in hotels and in the tourism sector. Many language courses were also set up.[4]

One of the most important developments in the interwar years was the introduction of the airport. In 1930 the first aircraft from Milan landed at a home-made landing area created in a farmer's field. The airport opened in 1938.[5] By the end of the 1930s Rimini became part of the European network of air destinations: Milan, Rome, London, Venice, and Vienna.[6] In 1939 the first night flight from Milan landed, carrying businessmen who wanted to spend their weekends in Rimini. Clearly, only a few privileged tourists could fly to Rimini in those days because the aircraft were still small (two or three passengers) and the flights were very expensive. However, the link between air transport and tourism has been established. Another important change was the increase in the number of small, cheap, and not prestigious guest houses, which converted Rimini into a destination for the middle classes.

It can be concluded that the fascist era left an important imprint on Rimini's tourism development through its interest in entertainment and modern transport infrastructures. During the interwar years Rimini began its conversion into a mass tourism resort.

The Great Tourist Boom after World War II

World War II interrupted the steady growth of tourism in Rimini, as elsewhere. Nevertheless, when the war was over, tourists immediately flocked back to the town, despite the fact that the beaches had yet to be cleared of unexploded shells and military vehicles. By 1947 the number of visitors had returned to its pre-war levels.

Nevertheless, it soon became evident that times had changed and a new kind of visitor would determine Rimini's success in the years to come. It was clear that the renewal of the luxury hotels and entertainment structures would be very complicated. No private investor showed any interest in buying and renovating the grand hotels or other luxury hotels because it would have been prohibitively expensive, with uncertain profitability. Apart from this, a few important hotels were bought by northern Italian companies and converted into seaside camps for their workers' sons. The Kursaal and the bathing establishment were demolished by the local administration that owned them, because during the interwar years they had become a meeting point for numerous supporters of the fascist government and they were perceived as symbols of the past regime. The *Ausa*, a local newspaper, reported in 1947: "Before the war there were a few hotels which could cater for the most demanding customers … None of them have been brought into use again."[7]

The tourism industry recovered very quickly, despite the fact that wealthy people did not return to Rimini. The hotel renovation was also aided by financial help in the form of the Marshall Plan, whose funds were granted and employed to renovate the town's existing hotels. During the period from 1950 to 1967, the number of hotels in Rimini shot up from 212 to 1,491. This growth was largely uncontrolled in the absence of any town-planning scheme. The new hotels were generally small (rarely having more than 10–15 rooms) and in the inexpensive or budget class (one or two star). They were usually family-run, each member of the family having a specific role to play. The family in this case included parents, brothers and sisters, grandparents, and extended family. A typical arrangement might have been as follows: the grandmother did the cooking, the wife the buying, the husband looked after customers and booking, while other members of the family worked part-time on the advertising aspect. Often hotels were not run by their owners, but were rented out. The same families who ran the hotels also had contacts with individuals who privately rented out rooms, so that during the peak season some customers could be provided with rooms outside of the hotels, while coming there to eat their meals and to use its facilities. After a number of years, such families could then think about buying their own hotel using the accumulated profits of past seasons together with a bank loan or mortgage if necessary. After such an investment, however, some families continued to manage a number of different hotels, that is, their own plus the ones they had rented.

Hotels offered their customers accommodation and meals, but rarely bothered with leisure facilities; in fact, they often did not have any common rooms for guests to use apart from the dining room. The organization of leisure activities was entrusted to the town (its public administration, tourist board, and non-profit associations), in keeping with established tradition. Only the high-class hotels, like the Grand Hotel, organized entertainment for their guests and, on occasion, for the entire town as well. What kind of entertainment was provided at that time? If we look at the list of entertainment organized for the summer of 1954 (from 20 June to 8 September), we find the following events: three yachting regattas, six sporting competitions (tennis, motorbike racing, car racing), three tournaments of various kinds (bridge, aircraft modeling), five art exhibitions, aircraft and automobile shows, local selections for beauty competitions (Miss Italy, Miss Universe), a light opera festival, the Sea Festival, and a Grand Ball. Excursions were also organized to nearby towns (Ravenna and San Marino), as were trips of various kinds.[8]

This brief summary of the available activities would not be complete without a mention of the town's dance halls. The most important was the Embassy, a dance hall set up in 1951 in a marvelous nineteenth-century villa on the seafront by two brothers from Rimini, the Semprinis. During the 1950s and 1960s it became the luxury reference point for the most demanding clientele. Then, in 1957 an exclusive restaurant on Rimini's hill was converted into a night club, the Paradiso Club, by the same Semprinis.

Very few recreational activities or sports were organized on the beach, however. Apart from the bars, there were just bowls for the adults and the occasional swing or slide for the children. Marketing was organized using informal channels, such as mailing lists drawn up from names furnished by members of the family during their trips abroad to learn languages, for example. Often the foreign travel agents themselves contacted the hotels and then gave their names to customers. Foreign tourists went to Rimini without having to be enticed by advertising: in fact, this could be defined as the era of passive marketing. These years of rapid tourist development were thus characterized as follows: small hotels offering basic services (accommodation with a shared bathroom, together with meals) at an affordable price within a family setting; various forms of free entertainment organized by the local council or by non-profit associations, together with some rather prestigious ballrooms.

During the 1950s and 1960s, the success of Rimini (and of Italy in general) as a vacation destination was largely due to its ability to organize some basic tourist facilities before its Spanish and Greek counterparts could do so, and to offer itself as a resort with something for tourists from all the social classes, now discovering the delights of tourism. In fact, Rimini pioneered seaside holidays, quickly gaining leadership in this field, something which it held on to unchallenged until the 1960s. This leadership was based on Rimini's willingness to invest in tourism: its vitality was proven by the speed with which the town tried to set up an airport for tourist charter flights. Rimini had a military airport, and in 1958 managed to obtain government permission to use it for civil purposes. Thus, on 12 July 1958, the first charter flight, coming in from London, landed at Rimini airport. During the early years, the airport was run by a non-profit organization, Rimini Aeroclub, the only one with the necessary expertise to do so. Once again, non-profit, co-operative organization played an important role in the development of Rimini as a resort. In 1962 the tourist boards of Rimini, Cattolica, Bellaria, and Riccione, together with the Forlì Chamber of Commerce, founded the Aeradria Company, which took over from the Aeroclub, with the aim of running the airport and further developing air traffic. The airport quickly became a vital infrastructure for the growth of tourism in Rimini. This airport, although only open during the summer months, quickly became the number one Italian airport for charter flights, and during the 1960s the number of foreign travelers using the airport was only equaled by those traveling into the large Italian airports situated in Rome and Milan. In fact, the percentage of tourists who chose to fly to Rimini increased rapidly: during the early 1970s, some 40 to 60 percent of all visitors to Rimini flew in.

These charter flights were mainly organized by foreign tour operators, and although this showed the strong attraction the town exercised at the international level, it also proved to be a weakness. In fact, as observers at that time rightly pointed out, "If the foreign charter companies that currently bring thousands of tourists into Italy were to decide to re-direct them towards other countries, we would not have the necessary organisational and marketing capacities to take their place." Even here, Rimini's marketing approach was very much of the passive variety.

A Decade of Stagnation: 1968–1977

The boom years for tourism in Rimini came to an end in the late 1960s, with the beginning a slow decline in the number of foreign visitors to the town. Many of the conditions for Rimini's supremacy among the Mediterranean resorts no longer existed. New competitors had emerged: the Spanish and Yugoslavian resorts, and to a certain extent the Greek, had developed their own facilities; their hotels and airports for charter flights meant that they now represented a valid alternative to Rimini. Often these alternatives were cheaper. Even the type of hotel that in those years had contributed toward Rimini's fortune (with few bedrooms and no common areas for socializing) became increasingly incapable of satisfying changing customer requirements. Moreover, the layout of the town itself was not particularly attractive, with all those hotels bunched together in a totally random fashion, with no green spaces in between.

Furthermore, given the fierce competition from rival resorts at the time, the traditional passive marketing approach was no way to defend the town's specific identity. At least three types of strategy had to be adopted at this point: a reformulation of its marketing strategy, an improvement in the facilities offered by the town, and an improvement in the quality of Rimini's hotels.

The town council was the first to voice the need for renewal, when in 1965 it passed a town planning scheme incorporating a new concept of tourism. Campos Venuti, the architect who coordinated the new town plan, had the following to say about the turnaround in 1965 in an article he wrote in 1982:

> When the 1950s expansion reached its limits, the town architects of that period failed to hide their concern, and at times horror, at what had been done ... The professional sphere was split between two completely different approaches: the first was that of the

> hard-line town planners who faced up to the Romagna region's coastal resorts using structural categories such as the battle against land rents, the policy of public service provision, and local relations between coastal and inland areas. It goes without saying that in Rimini, town renewal operations were far from easy … The town-planning approach underlying the 1965 town plan tended to turn the previous strategy upside down.… In fact, it tried to slow down new building, there was a significant increase in the number of areas targeted for public services, and the last remaining empty spaces between the coastline and the town were transformed into public parks.

Furthermore, the relationship between the coast and the inland areas was re-examined, with trips to the ancient hilltop villages suggested as an alternative leisure activity for tourists in Rimini. Finally, businessmen were asked to commit themselves to renovating the town's hotels, with bathrooms in all rooms, the creation of common rooms, and the construction of swimming pools in most hotels. One of the objectives was to merge hotels to make bigger ones.

What were the results of this plan? One definite result was that it managed to contain the building of new hotels and guest houses. Second, the layout of the town improved. However, the renovation of existing hotels proceeded at a very slow pace, partly because, despite the loss of a percentage of foreign customers, the hotels continued to make profits thanks to the considerable increase in the number of Italian tourists. The business sector, unlike the public sector, thus failed to realize that the Rimini model needed to be radically rethought, and that in order to withstand the competition from Spanish and Yugoslavian resorts, either prices had to come down dramatically or the tourist market had to offer a wider range of services. The result was that the renovation and renewal of the town's hotels was put off to a later period.

Private enterprise tried to do something about marketing and advertising the town's attractions. In 1968 a co-operative Promozione Alberghiera (Hotel Promotion) was set up by ten or so young hoteliers from Rimini (including the manager of the Grand Hotel) together with the town's tourist board. The main aim of the co-operative was to promote the quality and public image of Rimini, and, given that the individual hoteliers were no longer capable of doing so, to deal with the various tour operators as a single body. The most important of the town's hotels joined Promozione Alberghiera, whose members numbered 217 in 1997. The co-operative, which still exists, has always been characterized by intensive marketing and the search for new products and markets. Thus, in the 1970s, when tour operators began to pull out of Rimini Airport, the co-operative began to get directly involved in the organization of charter flights; similarly, in the 1980s the co-operative saw conference tourism as an important new opportunity for Rimini.

The years between 1967 and 1978 went by without the town managing to create a new tourist product capable of supporting a new period of growth.

However, it cannot be said that no new ideas or projects were forthcoming: the 1965 town plan and the foundation of Promozione Alberghiera in 1968 clearly show that this was not the case.

The First Reorientation and the Creation of the Leisure Industry: 1979–1989

Toward the end of the 1970s tourist numbers started to recover once again, thus marking the beginning of a new positive phase for tourism in Rimini. Tourism in Rimini during the 1980s was characterized by three main aspects.

1. Foreign tourist numbers remained stationary and even Rimini Airport showed worrying signs of a crisis. A growing number of tour operators pulled out of organizing charter flights to Rimini, preferring Spanish resorts instead. The Aeradria Company that ran the airport tried to contribute to the relaunching of Rimini's image, funding promotional campaigns in the main European markets (Great Britain, Scandinavia, and Germany). However, the problem was not just one of marketing: Rimini simply could not withstand the competition from Spain and Greece. In fact, a survey commissioned by Aeradria and conducted by an Italian market research company, showed the Italian resort to be more expensive than its rivals. The survey compared the average 1984 price asked by the main European tour operators (Cosmos, Thompson, Horizon, Global, Martin Rooks, Blue Sky, Falcon, Flair) for a seven-day vacation in a number of Spanish, Greek, and Yugoslavian resorts, to those in Rimini. The latter Rimini was 22 percent more expensive than the Spanish resorts, and 16 percent more expensive than the Yugoslavian ones. It turned out to be slightly cheaper than the Greek resorts because of the lower cost of transport. Furthermore, the gap between Rimini and the other Mediterranean resorts had increased between 1981 and 1984, and this seemed to indicate that it would continue to widen in subsequent years. Rimini was more expensive, and yet it failed to provide an image that justified this difference to European tourists.
2. During the 1980s it was the rapid rise of Italian tourists that enabled the town to reach its all-time record of overnight guests in 1988: 8.5 million, of whom only 27 percent were foreigners. Thus, within the Italian market, Rimini maintained its capacity to attract tourists, despite the existence of cheaper alternatives. Within Italy, Rimini has managed to preserve its identity and fascination, and to justify the greater expense of a vacation spent there.

3. Renovation of the town's hotels proceeded very slowly during this period. In 1977 the number of one- and two-star hotels began to fall, but from 1985 on there was a first significant increase in the number of mid-range hotels. One reason for this was that the continual increase in the total number of overnight guests meant that local businesses failed to fully realize Rimini's loss of competitive edge. We can only conclude that it was certainly not the recategorization of the town's hotel stock that underlay Rimini's success during this period. In fact the town's new image was that of entertainment capital.

As we have seen, Rimini had always been characterized by the presence of leisure and recreational facilities: its tourist appeal had never been based solely on sea, sun, and sand and the town had always offered a certain amount of entertainment for visitors. I have already mentioned the opening of the Embassy and the Paradise Club during the 1950s. Between 1967 and 1973 three new important night clubs opened: the Mecca, the Baia degli Angeli, and the Altro Mondo, which had the capacity to hold 2,000 people. Despite this long tradition of amusement structures, the first half of the 1970s was a watershed in the history of Rimini's amusement sector because of the opening of the first US-style discotheques. More precisely, during the 1970s many entrepreneurs at first converted their night clubs into a mix of night club and discotheque and then simply into a discotheque. The Paradiso Club, the Mecca, and the Altro mondo were the first to begin this transformation. Toward the end of the 1970s it was the Embassy's and the Lady Godiva's turn. Finally during the 1980s a new wave of investment set up many new larger discotheques like the Slego, the Bandiera gialla, and the Cellophane, which could hold thousands of people on many dance floors.

Finally, Rimini's business leaders had been aware of the importance of entertainment structures from the beginning. However, during the 1980s the scale of things changed somewhat. In fact, the major investments now being made, related to the opening of discotheques and arcades. The number of new licenses granted for such purposes rose from an average of twenty-four to eighty to ninety a year. Rimini became the trendy disco capital of Italy, and young people from all over the country flocked to the town not only during the summer months, but during weekends all year round. Rimini, which up to this point had been a family holiday resort, became the best-loved resort among young people. This is yet another reason for the slow pace at which hotel renovation proceeded. The new waves of younger tourists spent a lot on entertainment, but preferred to stay in smaller, cheaper hotels rather than in large luxurious establishments. The expansion of its entertainment infrastructure together with its variety made Rimini a unique resort within the Mediterranean region.

To understand how this resort became the disco capital of Italy, anticipating new fashions and attracting well-known people, from actors to politicians, from fashion stylists to sport champions, we need to look at the history of the Paradiso Club, a sort of symbol of the new Rimini. The club's origin goes back to 1954 when Annunziata Mirti, a middle-aged widow with two children, decided to build her house on Rimini's hill and opened an exclusive restaurant on the first floor of her villa. In 1956 she decided to rent the business to the Semprinis and to Guido Mulazzani, who at the time were also managing the Embassy. The restaurant was converted into a night club, which welcomed its clientele at a late hour when the Embassy had closed for the night. For fifteen years the most famous bands and singers played in this very successful night club. The turnaround year in the history of the Paradiso Club was 1971, when Annunziata Mirti's thirty-year-old son, Gianni Fabbri, took over. He had a long and varied CV. As a teenager he worked for some years in Germany and Great Britain to learn the languages, then he came back to Italy and took the hotel school certificate, after which he accumulated important work experience in various luxury hotels and dance halls (among them the Riccione Grand hotel) before moving to Milan and being employed by an important food processing company. In 1971 he returned to Rimini and started the transformation of his mother's night club into a discotheque: although bands and singers continued to play at the Paradiso Club, disk jockeys, go-go girls, and strobe lights were also introduced.

By the end of the 1970s, the Paradiso Club, which in summertime employed about twenty-three people, had become a trendy discotheque. It was run by Gianni Fabbri and two assistant directors: by a hotel school teacher Giulietto Turchini in the summer, and in the winter by Giorgio Utili, who was busy running a bar in the summer months. Gianni Fabbri, Giorgio Utili, and the architect Gianni Gavioli who planned the frequent renovations, got inspiration from their visits to European and American night clubs and discos: in 1976 they went to Paris and in the following years it was London, Ibiza, Berlin, New York, and Miami. The Paradise Club remained a trendy disco for twenty years thanks to huge and frequent investment, which every four to five years completely redesigned its image and structure. Besides having become the favorite of celebrities from sports champions to politicians, actors and actresses, the Paradiso Club was often mentioned in newspapers and magazines. During the 1980s, following the success of his first club, Gianni Fabbri opened two other discos, the Pineta at Milano Marittima and the Pascià in Riccione, which were also very successful.

In 1993 the Paradiso's balance sheet registered a small loss, which signaled the beginning of a new phase in its history and in the amusement sector in general. The golden age of the vast discos had come to an end because young people started to ask for more segmented and differentiated spots. The Paradiso tried to anticipate the new trend by radically changing its layout and by creating many different atmospheres to cater to every type of clientele. This huge investment, which built the Paradiso Club of the 1990s, allowed it to maintain its top position among Rimini and Italian discos but could not avoid a drastic reduction in profits and heavy losses in 1996 and 2000. In 2001 as a consequence of negative results, Gianni Fabbri sold the Paradiso to a pool of entrepreneurs who decided to keep it open only during winter and to continue to promote their open air disco in Riccione in summer. The history of the Paradiso as a trendy night club and disco had come to an end and Rimini started a second reorientation.

At the end of the 1980s, the growth of tourism for young people began to be incompatible with family vacationing. The reputation Rimini had gained of a night-time, transgressive resort that attracted thousands of young people was one that families found increasingly less appealing. Moreover, the town had its share of social problems: drug trafficking and prostitution were on the increase, and so on. Thus, at the end of the 1980s, cracks began to appear in this model of tourism for young people, and there was an increasing need to clean up the town's public image, and present it as a less transgressive, more family-oriented holiday resort.

The Second Reorientation – Rimini as a Conference and Trade Fair Center: 1990–2000

Despite the huge success of the 1980s, Rimini's tourism model continued to have its weak points, including the following: (1) the failure to completely renovate and renew its hotel stock (partly due to the continued preference for low prices rather than improved services); (2) the difficulty in managing its image as a youthful, transgressive resort but also a quiet place suited for families; and (3) the loss of international competitiveness compared with Spanish and Yugoslavian resorts.

In 1989, people suddenly became aware of these limits when an external event threatened the very survival of seaside tourism in Rimini. This was the year of the so-called mucilage problem; the sea became covered in algae and it was impossible to bathe in it. In just one year, overnight guest numbers fell by 35 percent, causing widespread panic among the business community as nobody knew how and when the sea would return to normal. This was the context within which Rimini formulated a second reorientation of its model of tourism, aimed above all at strengthening new forms of tourism. Special importance was given to conference tourism and theme parks. Once again

Rimini had not discovered a completely new formula, much as it had with the discos. In fact, Rimini boasted a tradition of trade fair organization going back to the years immediately following World War II, and in 1968 it had opened a brand new trade fair center. The availability of a structure like this made it possible to organize not only an increasing number of trade fairs during the 1970s and 1980s, but also a series of exhibitions, conferences and sporting events, to the extent that Rimini became one of the most important trade fair and conference centers in the country, second only to Milan and Bologna. The mucilage crisis meant that conference tourism took on a new role, as by definition this was a form of tourism that did not need the sea, and so could survive and develop despite the crisis. It was in these circumstances that the need for a new, large-scale trade fair complex emerged, as the 1968 trade fair center was too small, despite the extensions that had been added over the years. The new trade fair center was opened in 2001.

The first theme parks had been set up toward the end of the 1960s: *Fiabilandia* (Fairytale Land) in 1969 and the following year *Italia in Miniatura* (Miniature Italy).[9] During the 1970s and 1980s they became an important sector in Rimini's leisure industry. However, after the mucilage crisis they began to play a different role, becoming strategic in the construction of the new Rimini image. The turnaround year in the history of theme parks in Rimini province was 1987, when Aquafan, the most popular water park in Italy, was set up in Riccione.[10]

On 14 June 1987, Aquafan opened, after a two-week delay due to bad weather. The initial theme was "Il fantastico Parco d'Acqua, Riccione" (The wonderful water park at Riccione). Being a completely new concept, the theme park had to describe what it was (a water park) and where it was located (Riccione). Starting up was not easy and, despite increasing revenues, the first few years were unprofitable. The main reasons for this included huge initial investment, high fixed costs, bad weather, and a lack of organizational experience that led to high staffing costs. However, by the beginning of the 1990s, Aquafan had become well-known and the park attracted thousands of visitors, thanks to successful advertising campaigns and after being used for some well-known television shows.

From the start there had been a discotheque, the Walky Cup, inside the park. In 1993 night entertainment was further developed with the construction of a second discotheque, the Aquarius, which soon became the set for television and radio shows. The success of the night sector depended crucially on the collaboration with Italia Deejay, the most popular radio station in Italy, which used its famous disk jockeys to host shows at Aquafan's discotheques.

Between 1990 and 1993, despite great success in terms of numbers of visitors and gross revenues, the profit remained low. Things improved in 1994, when

Claudio Villa, who had a lot of experience in the entertainment sector, was appointed a new general manager. He reduced costs by reorganizing the work of employees, strengthened the night sector, and invested in new daytime attractions. Since 1994 the profit has increased more rapidly than gross revenues.

In addition, in 2000 the Valdadige (the holding company for Aquafan) jointly with Narvalo (the company for Riccione Delphinarium) invested €70 million and set up a 110 square meter theme park dedicated to our planet and oceans, the Oltremare (Oversea) park. The two theme parks, Aquafan and Oltremare, located on the hill of Riccione (a few kilometers from Rimini) and jointly managed, represented one of the most important amusement centers in Europe and registered 1,800,000 visitors annually.

This development of trade fairs, conferences, and theme parks led to numerous other changes. First, it required a rapid transformation of the town's hotels, given that business tourism is much more concerned with the quality of service offered by hotels than traditional seaside tourism is. In fact, during the 1990s there was an acceleration in the process of reducing the number of cheap hotels and a proliferation of mid-range ones: furthermore, many hotels made the qualitative leap into a higher class (today there are some thirty-five four- and five-star hotels). This also meant an overall increase in the services offered to customers by the various categories of hotels. Moreover, the mucilage crisis led many hoteliers to have swimming pools built; in fact, all the town's mid-range hotels now have a covered pool (it is worth pointing out that a total of forty-seven pools were built in 1990, as an immediate answer to the crisis).

The other important change made possible by the development of business and theme park tourism was the lengthening of the tourist season. In fact, trade fairs and conferences generally take place in spring or fall, and so the months of May, June, September, and October have become characterized by a significant tourist presence. Similarly, the theme parks open from April to October.

During the 1990s the growth in conference and theme park tourism softened the blow dealt by the seaside's declining appeal. In fact, the fall in tourist numbers in 1989 was not immediately reversed, as the sea took several years before it returned to its normal state, and even the most faithful of customers began to look elsewhere. Many tourists, especially foreign ones, have never returned to Rimini. Many tour operators went as far as removing Rimini from their catalogs. The most important fact is that even the recovery in foreign tourist numbers during the second half of the 1990s involved to a large extent new nationalities. Until the end of the 1970s, Germans, together with the charter travel English and Scandinavians, had been the ones to vacation in Rimini in the greatest numbers. However, in the 1990s their place was taken by Russians and other East Europeans. Thus, the partial recovery of foreign tourists was due uniquely to the identification of new markets.

What form does tourism in Rimini take today? The current model is one based on the quality and variety of hotel and beach services, and on a wide range of choice in entertainment and leisure activities. Diversification and personalization are today's keywords.

A Case Study: The Growth of a Family Business

The unplanned growth of hundreds of small to middle-size hotel companies has been one of the most interesting features of the Rimini tourism industry. Economists have frequently quoted the relevant literature to explain the impressive blossoming of firms in Rimini during the 1950s and 1960s. This case study illustrates how these small to middle-size firms started up and acquired the necessary working knowledge.[11]

The Calesini family (Armando, his wife Vanda, and his brother Domenico) entered the hotel industry in 1964 when they rented the Hotel Albion, a thirty-room hotel located on the seafront. The twenty-five-year-old Domenico was the only family member to have had formal training in this field: after attending a trade school in hotel skills he accumulated experience as hotel manager all over Europe (Germany, Spain, Luxembourg, and Great Britain). None of the other Calesinis had any hotel management experience: the wife was a shopkeeper and her husband a civil servant. Each member of the family had a specific job: Domenico welcomed the customers, allotted the rooms, and oversaw catering operations, whereas Vanda was responsible for buying, her mother for cooking, the others helping in different ways.

They invested all their savings in the project, including profits from the sale of the shop to start their business and above all to pay the hotel rent in advance. The local banks would not grant any loans without a mortgage. At the beginning only one member of the family, Vanda, worked full time in the hotel, whereas the others kept their previous jobs until the profitability of the hotel was proven.

The following year the Calesinis rented a bigger hotel with seventy rooms, the Rosabianca, and took on six staff, all unskilled people from Rimini. Typically they were housekeepers willing to do all types of duty (cleaning, laundry, etc.). They worked more than ten hours a day and were employed on a fixed wage.

The Calesinis did very little advertising apart from nurturing existing customers with Christmas or Easter cards accompanied by the next season's brochure. However, they did keep in touch with a few foreign travel agencies (French, German, and English). Some of them were Domenico's contacts from when he worked abroad. Foreigners were a significant percentage of their customers.

The year 1966 was an important year in the family's history because with the profits accumulated over the previous two years and thanks to a bank loan, the

Calesinis bought a villa near the sea and converted it into a thirty-five-room hotel, the Junior. Domenico got married and rented a hotel with his wife. The villa was renovated to medium quality hotel standard; each room had its own bathroom, and television and telephone were introduced. The hotel's slogan became: "clean, comfortable with good cuisine!" This was quite a rare strategy at the time, adopted by only a few hoteliers. In fact, the above-discussed 1963–64 tourism crisis was short-lived and had not encouraged any private investment in hotel renovation. As can be seen in table 6.1, in 1966 the sharing of bathrooms was common in Rimini hotels. With the Hotel Junior open, the Calesinis were now managing two hotels. In addition they also accommodated some of their customers in small guest houses or apartments very close to their hotels. This kind of organization allowed them to satisfy all different types of demand and customer budgets.

Table 6.1 Ratio of rooms to bathrooms in Rimini hotels, 1956–1996

Year	High-quality hotels	Middle-quality hotels	Low-quality hotels
1956	1.06	2.07	4.56
1961	1.11	1.42	2.26
1966	1.12	1.04	1.89
1971	1.08	1.09	1.49
1976	1.00	1.07	1.38
1981	1.00	1.06	1.36
1986	0.97	0.96	1.05
1991	0.96	0.96	1.01
1996	0.93	0.95	0.98

Source: Forlì and Rimini Chamber of Commerce, Rimini Tourist Board.

The increased capacity and the centralization of the many functions (industrial relations, buying, marketing, tax administration, etc.) represented an attempt to exploit economies of scale whereas the ties with the small guest house managers and apartment-building owners allowed the maintenance of a certain degree of flexibility and reduced the impact of possible crises. The Calesini strategy was threefold: economies of scale, flexibility in production level, and diverse level of service.

In 1970 a new phase of expansion started. The Calesinis bought Villa Elena, an eleven-room guest house, close to Hotel Junior and rented a fifty-room hotel (Vanda's sister had been put in charge of managing it). Overall, the Calesinis managed one guest house, the hotel they owned, and the two hotels they rented. During this period the support of the main local bank was very important because the profits accumulated over the previous years were not enough to finance growth. The local bank granted a loan amounting to 120 million lira.

In 1976 the Calesinis rationalized their activities. Villa Elena was annexed to Hotel Junior in order to create a higher quality hotel with fifty-four rooms, several meeting rooms inside (one dining room, one breakfast room, a large cocktail room), and an attractive garden outside. As already mentioned, the 1970s was a decade of radical change in Rimini's tourism history. Although increasing international competition reduced the numbers of foreigners, the level of overnight guests was maintained. In fact during the 1970s an increasing number of Italian people became accustomed to going on vacation and Rimini welcomed this new demand. The result was the substitution of foreigners with domestic demand. In fact, although Rimini was hard hit by the competition of the Spanish seaside resorts, the simultaneous growth of Italian demand averted a serious hotel industry crisis. Some astute hoteliers became aware of this competition and upgraded and renovated their hotels; however, the majority did not realize that times had changed and continued to offer a low standard of service.

The Calesinis chose to renovate. This choice allowed them to attract a new kind of customer, for instance, congress and trade fair participants. The hotel services were upgraded to cater for these new and more demanding customers: each room had its own television and telephone, parking facilities were introduced, catering was greatly improved, introducing an à la carte menu and varied cuisine (it was necessary to take on a chef) and different tariffs were implemented (full board, half board, bed and breakfast, etc.). In 1981, they were among the first to computerize their hotel accounting.

The rented hotels that could not be renovated were reserved for less demanding and lower budget customers, as the Calesinis tried to attract these customers too. They concentrated their efforts on out-of-season school trips by offering low priced services to students and high standard services to teachers. Many of these teachers became regular seasonal customers. Soon out-of-season school trips became a great success and enabled the Calesinis to cover the year's rent before the season began.

During the 1970s it became increasingly difficult to employ Rimini residents and the Calesinis went to southern Italy looking for staff, as did many others. Rimini was no longer a poor, agricultural area whose inhabitants accepted any kind of job. Now it had become a rich town and its residents looked for stable employment and would not accept temporary jobs in the hotel industry.

In 1988 the town reached its all-time record of 8.5 million overnight guests, after a decade of growth. In 1987 the Calesinis expanded their activities by renting a thirty-room hotel and buying a twenty-room guest house. It was sold the following year in order to buy joint ownership of the four-star Savoia Excelsior Hotel, one of the most prestigious hotels in Rimini, albeit in need of renovation. This luxury hotel dated back to 1905 and throughout the twentieth century had accommodated many of the most famous guests passing through Rimini. Unfortunately, the planned renovation required a huge investment to which the joint partner did not agree. Because the Calesinis could not finance the whole investment by themselves, they decided to sell their share and buy a smaller hotel. Consequently, at the beginning of 1990s they bought the seventy-nine-room Admiral Hotel, located on the main street, and converted it into a four-star hotel.

Nowadays, the Calesinis own and manage two hotels, the fifty-four-room Junior Hotel (three star) and the seventy-nine-room Admiral Palace Hotel (four star). Because they wanted the Admiral Palace to become part of an international chain, in 1999 they signed a franchising contract with the internationally known Choice Hotel Group. The Calesini group now has forty-two employees (some of them only in the summer) in addition to the family members, although it has maintained the family touch. After accumulating experience in hotel management all over Europe, the oldest son has become responsible for marketing, communication, and the booking of the two hotels, whereas the youngest son (after receiving a degree in economics) has become responsible for the accounts and staff management. Vanda is still responsible for buying and Armando for hotel provisions (food and table and bed linen). All the family members participate in strategic decisions. The economic strategy of the two hotels is determined jointly, but their performance is valued separately on the basis of revenue index.

This case study has allowed us to shed some light on Rimini's economic structure. First, it emerges that company growth has been financed by accumulated profits and bank loans. The small initial investment of most entrepreneurs has not been sufficient for the construction of big hotels and big companies. Small hotels have been converted to middle-size ones only after significant accumulation of profits. Second, the Calesinis' history has demonstrated the risk-taking propensity of Rimini families, who more than once have invested all their savings in their companies. Third, it has highlighted the role played by the middle class (shopkeepers, employers, etc.) in providing new entrepreneurs for the tourism industry.

Concluding Remarks

Two aspects in the development of tourism in Rimini stand out. First, it is based on small businesses instead of large corporations. Thus, the key organizational model is, and has always been, that of the service industry. What have been the advantages and limitations of this organizational form?

The main advantage has been the great wealth of business talent that has emerged not only in the setting up of a considerable number of hotel businesses, but also in the presence of many other activities, such as trade fair business or amusement parks. It is this wealth of business initiative that represents the way forward for Rimini after a period of stagnation. In fact, in the case of both the entertainment industry and conference tourism, the reorientation of the tourism model was based on the development of the already-existing activities that had not been fully exploited until then.

The main limitation of this organizational form has been the slow pace at which hotels are renovated (it takes much longer for 1,500 small and medium-sized businesses to accept the fact that it is time to renew their structures than it does for a few large businesses). The second limitation relates to the difficulty of constructing a standardized image of the Rimini tourism offering and of its marketing, given so many small businesses operating locally. However, this limitation can be overcome by means of the creation of specialized companies that perform this function on behalf of the entire business network.

The second aspect in the development of Rimini's tourism is that its business community has always learned from the experience of other resorts. In 1843, the Counts Baldini built their bathing establishment after a two-week visit to Viareggio where in 1828 the first Italian bathing establishment was built and where, during the 1870s, the local administration invested hugely to improve the tourism infrastructure and to develop the image of a luxury seaside resort. In those days Nice, in the south of France, was the prototype to follow and its Promenade des Anglais structure was reproduced in Rimini.[12]

At the beginning of the nineteenth century a new publicity slogan proclaimed Rimini's aspirations: "Spend your holidays in Rimini, the Ostend of Italy." The Belgian seaside resort remained a reference point for other resorts until the 1930s. In 1920, one Rimini newspaper wrote: "It's nice and comfortable to twiddle one's thumbs in the sun in front of the aristocratic villas of the Ostend of Italy."[13] In 1921 the same newspaper pointed out: "It's necessary to take away Rimini's ugly things if we want to live up to the name of the Ostend of Italy."[14]

It was only during the 1930s that this attitude changed completely and the people of Rimini became aware that they were living in one of the pleasantest and best-known seaside resorts in Italy and perhaps in Europe. It was not necessary to follow any foreign models for many decades and the advertising simply described Rimini as the most beautiful and attractive beach in the world.

In 1957 the Italian writer Guido Piovene in his *Travels around Italy* reported, "Since the war Rimini has been converted into an American style resort, which is unusual for Italy." This consideration is certainly exaggerated because until the 1960s the Rimini business community did not try to copy any American model. Things changed in the following decades, above all in the amusement sector. For example, in 1963, after the opening of the first aquarium in Riccione, the company's managers employed an American team with a lot of experience in aquatic breeding and in doing dolphin shows. The aquarium was later completely renovated, on the basis of American model. Other American models were imported during the 1970s, when dance halls and night clubs were converted into discotheques.

Finally, construction of the water park was based on US model. Aquafan offered many attractions, most of them managed by North American companies. It also copied many features from the Americans, like customer care, uniforms for the staff, and the availability of fast food restaurants. However, it never looked like an American theme park, first, because it had never been as theme-based as the American ones were, and second, because it was open both night and day. This decision contrasted strongly with the American evidence of incompatibility between day and night entertainments, as Scott Ziegfield, one of the most prominent theme park consultants, noticed in 1993. Ziegfield has written many books[15] and collaborated on the realization and renovation of Disney World, Epcot, and Universal Studios in the United States, Blackpool Pleasure Beach in the UK, and Phantasialand in Germany. In 1994, during a journey to Riccione and Aquafan, he wrote: "The theme park sector has some basic rules. Since the 1930s one of them is that a theme park cannot remain open during the night, because all the attempts have been revealed as unsuccessful.... However Aquafan, which is also open during the night, is the most popular park in Italy.... It is an exception."[16]

To sum up, Rimini's entrepreneurs have very often copied foreign models and imported new kinds of amusements and services. However, they have never forgotten to customize foreign models to Italian tastes. The result has been an original mix of Italian style and foreign models.

Notes

1. P. Battilani, "Rimini and Costa Smeralda: How Social Values Shape Recreational Sites," in *Water Leisure and Culture*, ed. Susan C. Anderson and B. Tabb (Oxford: Berg, 2002).
2. The Nirigua park was located in the part of Rimini that became an independent town called Riccione in 1922.
3. Riepilogando, Corriere dei bagni, 30 August 1923.
4. "Una scuola alberghiera," *Il popolo di Romagna*, 20 November 1937; "L'apertura del corso di specializzazione alberghiera," *Il popolo di Romagna*, 4 December

1937; "Corsi di Addestramento per lavoratori di alberghi," *Il popolo di Romagna*, 4 March 1939.

5. "Per le più potenti ali d'Italia," *Il popolo di Romagna*, 16 April 1938.
6. "La linea aerea Roma-Londra," *Il popolo di Romagna*, 4 May 1931.
7. "Rimini, il suo mare e il Piano Erp," *L'Ausa*, 30 July 1949.
8. Rimini Tourist board, 15 days in Rimini: summer, Rimini, 1954.
9. Italia in Miniatura was opened by a small businessman, Ivo Rambaldi, who had invested the family's entire fortune in the project. After his death in 1993, his sons carried on where he had left off, and in 1996, Italia in Miniatura registered 600,000 visitors, with a total revenue of 13 billion lira.
10. Aquafan was set up in 1986 at Riccione (close to Rimini) by Luciano Tirincanti, a hotelier who also managed some discotheques in Riccione, and Aldo Emilio Moretti, who had a lot of international experience in the hotel industry and was familiar with the structure of the North American theme water parks. The former provided the land, the latter financed the investment together with Ceti, a thermo-hydraulic cooperative from Cavriago (near Reggio Emilia), which, having participated in the construction of a water park in Lignano (a famous beach in the north of Italy), was interested in entering the business. In 1987, when the construction began, Valdadige Costruzioni also became involved. This was a famous building company managed by Antonio Benzi, an engineer from Rimini, who lived in Verona. In 1989, the Valdadige company set up Valdadige Futura and entered the entertainment industry, because its general manager considered it anti-cyclical in relation to its core business. The new company bought Aquafan and quickly made it the most popular water park in Europe.
11. I thank Carmela Pasquini for the archive work in question and for having given me the opportunity to use this important case study.
12. A. Del Piano, "I bagni di Rimini," *L'Ausa*, 5 August 1911.
13. *L'Ausa*, 31 July 1920.
14. *L'Ausa*, 30 April 1921.
15. Scott Ziegfield was born in Montana in 1921. He wrote many books, among them *Story of Leisure Gardens*, *Games Manufactures in 20th Century*, and *Leisure Management*.
16. Scott Ziegfield, "Noi americani non ci avevamo pensato," in *La Classe non è acqua, Aquafan* (1994).

Chapter 7

The Expansion Strategies of the Majorcan Hotel Chains

Antoni Serra

Forty Years of Mass Tourism in the Balearic Islands: The Birth of Big Majorcan Chains

Tourism in the Balearics has experienced tremendous growth since the 1960s. At the beginning of that decade, in a Europe where air transport was highly regulated, with extremely high fares that made it nearly impossible for medium income classes to travel, tour operators found a way to make holiday travel affordable for wide sectors of the European population.

The Chicago Convention of 1944 established the framework for international civil transport aviation in the following decades. At the Chicago Convention, it was thought that non-scheduled flights would have no significant economic importance in the future.[1] Therefore, they were only slightly regulated. The single condition imposed was that the flight seat could not be sold directly to the customer: it had to be a component part of a package that would include at least accommodation at the destination, plus any other services that could be incorporated. Taking advantage of this weak regulation, European tour operators started the impressive development of regular charter flights to the Mediterranean. In doing so, they had the complete cooperation of the Spanish government which, at this time, was facing serious balance of payments problems and was desperately seeking foreign exchange to allow investment in the industrial sector and modernization of the economy. The Spanish authorities gave tour operators blanket permission for incoming flights, sacrificing, in some way, its flag carrier's – Iberia – commercial interests. And flights started to come to Majorca. Majorca therefore deserves a prominent place in

Notes for this chapter begin on page 142.

the origins of the history of mass tourism in Europe as it was the first destination seriously developed by tour operators. Since these early days, the history of tourism in the Balearics has been one of continuous growth in tourist arrivals; with intermittent slow downs (mid-1970s, early 1990s, and 2002).[2]

A series of positive internal and external factors helped mass tourism to grow continuously for nearly half of a century in the Balearics because the core island product was attractive; sustainability (in whatever sense it can be taken) was not seen as an issue; the prices were competitive; tour operators found the product easy to sell and profitable; the service delivery was competitive and profitable for suppliers even on a highly seasonal basis; developers could profit from their investment in facilities; and staff shortages were not a problem. The overall image of the Islands was extremely positive.

Therefore, the model for tourist development in the Balearic Islands has been based on volume, price competition, and standardization of the holiday experience, with an offer mainly focused on sun, sand, and sea and relying exclusively on tour operators for capacity distribution.[3] It was the tour operators who were making the effort of promoting and distributing hotel capacity. It was the tour operators who were close to the market and to the consumers, thus having a huge influence on the image conveyed to the markets. This has been a constant feature of the Balearics' tourism model until recently. Consequently, marketing hotels was almost the same as selling capacity to the big tour operators and negotiating prices with them. It was in this context of rapid, strong tourism expansion, that the current major Majorcan hotel chains (or the companies they belong to) were created.

Majorcan Hotel Chains – the Four Big Players: A Brief Historical Review

The four biggest players in order of importance in terms of the number of hotel rooms are: Sol Meliá, Riu, Barceló, and Iberostar – these rank in the top fifty hotel chains in the world. Table 7.1 illustrates their overall importance at the end of 2004, according to the Hotels Corporate 300 Ranking. As it can be seen from the table, Sol Meliá is the most important, ranking thirteenth in the world; Riu is the second in the group of four and ranks twenty-sixth in the world; Barceló and Iberostar are companies of similar size, and they have experienced the strongest growth in recent years.

Sol Meliá

Sol Meliá was founded in 1956 by Gabriel Escarrer, the actual president of the company, when he started to run a small hotel in Palma de Majorca. The amazing

Table 7.1 Hotel companies and numbers of hotels and rooms

Rank 2004	Company	Rooms (thousands)	Number of hotels (thousands)
1	InterContinental Hotels Group (United S)	534,202	3,540
—	—	—	—
13	Sol Meliá	80,834	328
26	Riu Hotels and Resorts	34,000	110
32	Barceló Hotels & Resorts	28,145	112
33	Iberostar Hotels & Resorts	28,104	91

Source: Reed Business Information, *Hotels Corporate 300 Ranking* (New York: Reed Elsevier, 2004).

expansion of tourism in the Balearics during the 1960s allowed the expansion and consolidation of the company, which a few years later was already a small hotel chain, Hoteles Mallorquines Asociados, operating exclusively in the Balearic Islands.[4]

In 1976, the company began its expansion into mainland Spain (Costa del Sol) and to the Canary Islands, at the same time changing its name to Hoteles Sol. In 1984, the company acquired the Spanish hotel chain Hotasa, part of the Rumasa Group, which had been expropriated by the Spanish government in 1982 in one of the most controversial economic measures in the recent economic history of Spain. Rumasa comprised thirty-four urban hotels and this acquisition represented an important step forward in the expansion of Hoteles Sol and an important strategic shift in its former strategy of specialization in the tourism sector. With this acquisition, the group became the leading hotel chain in Spain being active in both the tourism and the urban sector. In this year, the international division of the company was created and the Bali Sol hotel in Indonesia was the group's first hotel outside Spain.

In 1987, the group acquired the international hotel chain Hoteles Meliá and started marketing two different brands: Sol Hoteles (aimed at the tourism sector) and Meliá Hoteles (aimed at the business traveler). The 1990s witnessed the major expansion of the group based on management and franchise contracts. During this decade, a multiple brand policy was implemented and part of the company went into the stock market. In 2000, Sol Meliá acquired the Spanish hotel chain Tryp, consolidating its leadership in the urban hotel sector in Spain.

Nowadays, Sol Meliá is the top hotel company in Spain, South America, and the Caribbean region. It holds the third position in the European ranking of hotel chains and is ranked thirteenth in the world. It has 328 hotels in thirty countries throughout Europe, America, the Mediterranean Basin, the Middle East, and the Asia-Pacific region.

Barceló Hotels & Resorts

Barceló Hotels & Resorts is the hotel division company of the Barceló Group, a vertically integrated company that covers nearly all the value chain in tourism. The Group's origins go back to 1931 when Autocares Barceló, a small transportation company, was founded by Simón Barceló in Felanitx (Majorca). Nearly twenty-five years later, in 1954, the company started activity in the travel agent industry. In 1960, the brand name Viajes Barceló was introduced. And in 1961, the first hotel of the chain was opened in Majorca.

During the 1960s the hotel chain consolidated and expanded to the rest of the Balearics (Ibiza and Minorca). The 1970s witnessed the beginning of activities in mainland Spain (Benidorm). In 1981 the acquisition of the tour operator Turavia took place, the first step to the internationalization of the group.

In 1985, the hotel chain started its international hotel operations with the opening of the first Caribbean hotel (Barceló Bávaro Beach) in Punta Cana, Dominican Republic, making Barceló the pioneer Spanish hotel company in the Caribbean. During the 1990s the company underwent impressive international expansion. Further expansion took place in Central America and South America during the 1990s with the opening of establishments in Costa Rica (1990), Nicaragua (1993), Venezuela (1997), and Mexico (1999). In 1999, the company expanded into Turkey with the incorporation of various establishments in the Bodrum region. This strong expansion has continued in recent years with the opening of hotels in the Philippines (2000), Ecuador (2000), Uruguay (2000), El Salvador (2001), Panama (2001), and Cape Verde (2001).

During the 1990s, the company also entered the city hotel sector, opening a hotel in Prague (1993) and Barcelona (1995). In 1992, the company entered the US hotel market with two establishments, in Washington D.C. and Orlando. Further expansion in the United States has taken place in recent years: in 2002, Barceló launched a friendly takeover bid for the US hotel operator Crestline Capital. As a result, Barceló, as well as being the Spanish pioneer in this market, is today the top Spanish hotel company in the United States.

Although the Barceló Group is a vertically integrated company in itself, the company has undertaken even more vertical integration. In 1996, Barceló Viajes became the representative in the Spanish territories of the British tour operator First Choice Holidays. In 2000, Barceló strengthened its position in the international issuing market by incorporating its Travel Division by First Choice Holidays, becoming in exchange the principal shareholder in this integrated travel and tourism group.

Barceló has doubled the number of its hotels in the last three years and has plans for further expansion. Historically, Barceló has been a hotel chain specializing in holiday products. From its classic portfolio based on low to middle income "sun and beach" products, the company has developed a wide range of vacation products, moving toward upmarket sectors. However, from this specialization, the company has also moved to the urban product, mainly aimed at tourists, but increasingly trying to catch the business traveler, especially the conference and convention market. Today, the company has a diverse portfolio of hotels catering to both individual and group business travel. Thus, the company is trying to widen its market coverage in terms of market sectors and geographic markets.

Riu Hotels & Resorts

Riu was founded in 1953 by Juan Riu, who started running a small hotel near Palma, in Majorca. As in the other cases, the impressive development of tourism in the Balearic Islands allowed the company to grow. After increasing its number of hotels in Majorca and consolidating itself as a company, Riu expanded its activity to the Canary Islands in the 1980s. During the 1990s, following its solid expansion in the Canary Islands where it is now the leading supplier of accommodation, Riu Hotels began its international expansion with the opening of a hotel in Punta Cana. From this island, the chain expanded into the Caribbean: Cuba, Florida, Mexico, and Jamaica. In 1999, Riu started its expansion in North Africa and the Eastern Mediterranean. Through management contracts or franchising, twelve hotels were incorporated into the chain in Morocco (8), Bulgaria (2,) and Cyprus (1).

The company, run by the third generation, had 110 hotels at the end of 2004, with categories ranging from three to five stars, offering globally more than 34,000 rooms and more than 60,000 beds. It accounts for more than 1.5 million customers and 12,500 employees. It has become the twenty-sixth biggest hotel company in the world, specializing in sun and beach vacations. Its guests come mainly from Spain and Central Europe but with an incipient American clientele (from the United States, Canada, and Argentina).

The chain had a turnover of €697 million in 2001, making it the second largest chain in Spain in terms of turnover. Riu establishments are located in the Balearic Islands (16), the Canary Islands (34), Portugal (3), Andalusia (8), Girona (1), the Dominican Republic (8), Cuba (2), Florida (2), Mexico (11), Jamaica (3), Tunisia (11), Bulgaria (5), Cyprus (1), and the Bahamas (1). The company plans to open new hotels in Croatia and Rumania in the next few years. All hotels in the chain are managed by Riusa II, a company created in 1993 with its German partner TUI, the largest tour operator not only in Europe but in the world: 50 percent of the company belongs to the Riu family, the other 50 percent are being held by TUI.

Since its creation in 1953, RIU hotels have never distributed profits: they have been totally reinvested in the expansion of the company. Thus, the company has basically self-financed its growth and has, currently, a low debt level. Riu is, therefore, another Majorcan case of a small family-operated business turned into an international hotel chain in four decades of mass tourism: a chain that is still strongly expanding while remaining specialized exclusively in sun and beach vacation destinations.

Iberostar Hotels & Resorts

As in the case of Barceló, Iberostar Hotels & Resorts is the hotel division company of the Iberostar Group, a vertically integrated company that covers nearly all aspects of the value chain in tourism. The company operates in three sectors: tour operators (Iberojet, Solplan, and Iberojet Internacional), travel agency (Viajes Iberia and Iberoservice, the incoming brand), and airlines (Iberworld).

The origins of the Iberostar Group go back to 1930 when the Viajes Iberia was founded in Majorca, as a small family business. In 1973 the company set up the tour operator Iberojet. It was not until 1986 that the hotel division of the group, Iberostar Hotels & Resorts, was created, since then rapid international expansion has taken place. In 1992 the company opened its first hotel in the Caribbean and in 1998 reached an agreement with Neckermann (now Thomas Cook) to manage their hotel establishments in Spain, Greece, and Tunisia.

Today, the company has ninety-one establishments, offering more than 50,000 beds in more than ten countries: Spain, Greece, Tunisia, Bulgaria, Croatia, Turkey, Mexico, Dominican Republic, Cuba, and Brazil. It has more than 10 million customers and a turnover of €2.197 million in 2003.

The International Expansion

The tourism industry is becoming global, especially in the case of those products/offers aimed at large market sectors. We are currently witnessing the creation of large conglomerates of tourism companies, which are seeking economies of scale and economies of scope and increased negotiation power over their suppliers.

It is evident from the above historical review that the four most important Majorcan hotel chains have also been actively seeking to expand outside their original base in the Balearics. In that sense we can call them the "pioneers," whose movements have more recently been imitated by other Majorcan hotel chains, smaller in size, that we can call "the followers."

Reasons for Expanding Outside the Balearic Islands

The first question we could ask ourselves is about the reasons for this expansion. Generally speaking, it can be said that as international tourism has grown, and as the companies that serve these markets have become larger themselves, so the opportunities and the reasons for international growth and expansion have become more complex.

It was Levitt[5] who first argued that we are progressively moving toward a "global village." By this he meant that consumer needs in many previously separate national markets were becoming increasingly similar throughout the world. But it is not only markets that are becoming more global. Industries are also becoming more global. An increasing number of organizations tend to concentrate their activities in locations where they hope to obtain cost, quality, or other advantages. The spread of an organization's value-adding activities around the world also means that there are important advantages to be gained from the effective integration and coordination of activities.

There has been sustained industry and academic interest in the process of internationalization of hotel groups. Dunning and McQueen's[6] study of transnational corporations in international tourism on behalf of the United Nations is one of the most widely quoted empirical studies. Since this seminal work, numerous studies have contributed to a better understanding of the international hotel expansion process.

There are several models that explain the basis for global strategy in generic terms.[7] There is also a large amount of literature on globalization and its impacts on the travel and tourism industry.[8] Yip (1992) argued that "to achieve the benefits of globalization, managers of worldwide businesses need to recognize when industry conditions provide the opportunity to use global strategy levers." He identified four drivers that determine the nature and extent of globalization in an industry, most of which are present in the specific case of Majorcan hotel chains:

1. Market drivers (common customer needs, global customers, global distribution channels, transferable marketing techniques).
2. Cost drivers (global scale economies, sourcing efficiencies, differences in country costs, steep experience curve effect).
3. Government drivers (favorable trade or investment policies, host government concerns, common marketing regulations).
4. Competitive drivers (competitors from different continents, high exports and imports, interdependence of countries, competitors globalized).

The main reasons for big Majorcan hotel chains to expand outside the Balearics could be summarized as follows (some of them are closely interrelated):

1. To exploit the opportunities derived from the expansion of travel demand in the main generating markets and the consequent tremendous growth of the tourism industry.

2. To take advantage of the opportunity to expand a "business model," know-how in catering for large numbers of holiday tourists in which they were, and still are, leaders in the world. They have acquired this know-how after years of holiday tourism expansion in their home base, the Balearic Islands. I will return to this point later.
3. To diversify strategic risk, by being in different destinations (not locked into the fate of the Balearics) and being in emerging tourism destinations. Because tourism development is a relatively easy way to achieve economic growth, it was quite clear that new countries and regions would try to foster tourism development and that competition among tourism destinations would increase in the future. This represented a threat insofar as it might constrain activity in the Balearics, but an opportunity if these companies were among the first to establish themselves in these new potential destinations.
4. Increased restrictions on hotel capacity in the Balearics due to administrative regulations or simply, to scarcity of suitable plots of land.
5. Higher costs (labor, buildings, land) in their home base, together with much lower costs in some of the destinations into which they expanded. In some cases, fiscal incentives offered by the new destination's government were important as well.
6. Last, and in some specific cases, to take advantage of "good deals," that is, the opportunity to buy at very advantageous prices. The acquisition of Hotasa by Sol Meliá in 1984 is one such example.

Areas Where They Expanded

Tables 7.2–7.5 show the four chains' geographic coverage.[9] If we exclude the urban hotels sections, in the cases of Barceló and Sol Meliá, and consider just the vacation hotels, there is a discernible geographic pattern of expansion, although there are some notable exceptions. The four chains have followed a similar sequence in their geographic expansion.

The pattern has been, roughly, as follows: first Majorca, where they started activity; they then moved to the other Balearic Islands (Minorca and Ibiza); later, they started operations in the Canary Islands and on mainland Spain (Mediterranean coast, mainly in Andalusia); next, they moved to the Caribbean and Central America; North Africa was the next step; later they began operating in Eastern Mediterranean tourism destinations (Greece, Cyprus, Turkey); and, finally, they have progressively penetrated new emerging tourism destinations (Bulgaria, Cape Verde, Croatia).

Therefore, we are talking about holiday tourism destinations, either consolidated or emerging ones. *Majorcan chains have moved to those countries where*

Table 7.2 Riu hotels and resorts, 2002

Country	Number
EUROPE	69
Spain	60
Portugal	3
Bulgaria	5
Cyprus	1
AMRICA	18
Dominican Republic	8
United States (Florida)	2
Mexico	5
Jamaica	1
Cuba	2
FRICA	11
Tunisia	11
TOTAL	98

Source: Reed Business Information, *Hotels Corporate 300 Ranking* (New York: Reed Elsevier, 2004).

Table 7.3 Barceló hotels and resorts, 2002

Country	Number
EUROPE	35
Spain	31
Czech Republic	1
Turkey	3
AMERICAS	64
Costa Rica	7
El Salvador	1
Ecuador	1
United States	18
Mexico	6
Nicaragua	1
Panama	2
Dominican Republic	19
Uruguay	3
Venezuela	5
Honduras	1
AFRICA	5
Cape Verde	5
ASIA-PACIFIC	2
Philippines	2
TOTAL	106

Source: Reed Business Information, *Hotels Corporate 300 Ranking* (New York: Reed Elsevier, 2004).

Table 7.4 Iberostar hotels and resorts, 2002

Country	Number
EUROPE	37
Spain	30
Greece	3
Turkey	1
Bulgaria	3
AMERICAS	14
Dominican Republic	5
Cuba	3
Mexico	6
AFRICA	8
Tunisia	8
TOTAL	59

Source: Reed Business Information, *Hotels Corporate 300 Ranking* (New York: Reed Elsevier, 2004).

Table 7.5 Sol Meliá hotels and resorts, 2002

Country	Number	Country	Number
EUROPE	249	Dominican Republic	4
Andorra	1	Guatemala	1
Belgium	1	Mexico	11
Croatia	27	Panama	1
Italy	3	Peru	1
France	8	Venezuela	2
Malta	1	Uruguay	1
Germany	12	AFRICA	22
Portugal	12	Egypt	1
Spain	180	Morocco	4
United Kingdom	2	Tunisia	17
Turkey	2	ASIA-PACIFIC	10
AMERICAS	75	Indonesia	6
Argentina	1	Malaysia	2
Brazil	20	Thailand	1
Colombia	7	Vietnam	1
Costa Rica	4	TOTAL	356
Cuba	22		

Source: Reed Business Information, *Hotels Corporate 300 Ranking* (New York: Reed Elsevier, 2004).

vacation tourism was emerging. However, to some extent, one could say that they have contributed to the creation of some of these destinations, especially in the case of the Caribbean region and Central America. The important role of the Majorcan chains in the development of tourism in the Canary Islands and the Caribbean region cannot be denied.

This leads us to the first important feature of the Majorcan hotel chains' expansion strategy: *specialization in vacation tourism.* This is particularly the case with Riu and Iberostar. Barceló and, especially, Sol Meliá, as previously stated, have entered the urban hotels sector. This relative specialization in holiday tourism also concentrates these chains, in general terms, in fewer countries. In other words, *Majorcan hotel chains tend to be more geographically concentrated* in comparison with other international major hotel chains.

Table 7.6 shows the international coverage, in terms of number of countries represented, of a sample of hotel chains. Obviously, chains that are at the top of the international ranking tend to be present in more different countries. But if, for example, we look at the Hilton Group, which ranks tenth, we can see that it is present in sixty-eight countries. Sol Meliá, which is of similar size (ranks twelfth), is present in no more than thirty countries. Geographic concentration is much higher in the cases of Riu and Iberostar, which have stronger specialization in the vacation tourism sector (with no urban division).

Table 7.6 Hotel company distribution

Rank 2001	Hotel Company	Countries
2	Six Continents Hotels	98
4	Accor	84
8	Starwood Hotels & Resorts Worldwide	82
10	Hilton Group PLC	68
3	Marriott International	65
9	Carlson Hospitality Worldwide	64
23	Le Méridien Hotels & Resorts	55
22	Golden TulipHotels, Inns & Resorts	46
5	Choice Hotels International	43
12	Sol	30
39	Barceló	15
32	Riu	10
47	Iberostar	8

Source: Reed Business Information, *Hotels Corporate 300 Ranking* (New York: Reed Elsevier, 2004).

Expansion Strategies

If the objective is expansion and growth, companies can achieve this through external or internal growth or through mergers or acquisitions pursuing vertical or horizontal integration. Strategic alliances or joint ventures are alternative ways of expanding. Hotel companies seeking internal growth can make use of different strategies, including the following:

1. *Ownership*, which consists of the total or partial acquisition of a hotel. Its main advantages are that total hotel profits are kept by the owners and there is greater control over the quality of the hotel product than with franchises or management contracts. Conversely, ownership is the slowest and most operationally and financially risky of all the different strategies aimed at expansion.
2. *Franchising*, which is a form of cooperation between companies in which one company, the *franchiser*, grants other companies, the *franchisees*, the right to commercialize certain types of products and/or services in exchange for some kind of financial compensation. The hotel industry was one of the pioneers in the introduction of the franchise system. With a hotel franchise contract, the franchisee operates under the same brand image and with the same production methods as its parent hotel chain, the franchiser. The franchiser company must be a prestigious hotel chain, with a reputation for the quality of the service its hotels provide and, as a result, a good corporate image. In recent decades, it has been particularly North American hotel chains that have invested most heavily in the franchise system (for example, Cendant Corporation is the world's biggest franchising chain). Franchise contracts involve a lower investment risk and a reduced cyclical risk for businesses in comparison with property ownership. As Tse and West (1992) and Go and Pine (1995) point out, the strategic popularity of franchising is largely due to the proficient manner in which geographical coverage can be achieved directly and without its customary high parent costs.[10]
3. *Leasehold contracts*, which can be defined as renting a hotel for a certain period of time, normally no less than three years and subject to automatic renewal. Usually, the leaseholder is a hotel group and so the leasehold tends to involve the hotel's assumption of the corporate image and production process of the hotel chain acting as leaseholder. The lessee tends to be responsible for the maintenance and conservation of the building in optimum condition.
4. *Management contracts*, which constitute an agreement between a hotel management company and the company owning the hotel, under the terms of which the management company runs the hotel. The owner does not make any operational decisions but is responsible for supplying the necessary capital and for meeting the payment of expenses and debts. The management company receives a fee for its services and the owner

receives the remaining profits after all costs have been deducted. In the United States, management contracts came to the forefront during the 1970s, with Hyatt in the vanguard.[11]

Ownership as a Feature of Majorcan Chains' Expansion

The hotel chains that have shown the greatest international growth are those that have concentrated most heavily on the franchising system. Indeed, the world's seven biggest franchisers are also the world's seven biggest hotel chains in terms of rooms. In general terms, it can be said that European chains have concentrated more on leasehold contracts and hotel ownership than the American ones.

In contrast, it has to be said that Majorcan chains have traditionally based their growth strategies mainly on hotel ownership. Reinvestment of profits obtained from this activity has been the basic way of funding expansion that is, initially, the large profits obtained in their home base, Majorca or the Balearics. The second phase involved the impressive benefits obtained in some of the new destinations to which they have moved. This is particularly the case of Barceló, the first chain to invest in the Caribbean where extremely high returns on investment encouraged the chain to foster further expansion in the area.

But there was a clear shift in their strategies during the second half of the 1990s. This shift has coincided with their major expansion and has led to a more intense use of management, franchising and leasing contracts. This is particularly the case with Sol Meliá and Barceló. Sol Meliá, for example, is currently one of the European hotel chains that have focused strongly on management contracts and this is currently its main growth strategy, accounting for 48 percent of its portfolio.[12] It was between 1993 and 1996 that Sol Meliá expanded most heavily into management and franchise contracts. In 1996, the group separated its hotel ownership business (based on Hoteles Meliá, which later changed its name to Inmotel Inversiones) from its management and franchise operations (centered on Sol Meliá). In July 1996, Sol Meliá was launched on the stock exchange. The 1996 the total revenue from the company's stock market launch was invested in Inmotel Inversiones. With these funds, a large part of Inmotel Inversiones' outstanding debt was written off, allowing the group to rectify its financial situation, renovate hotels, and continue its expansion by acquiring new ones. Since then Inmotel has focused its energies on real estate management. Since 1997, the Majorcan chain has focused its activities on management contracts, gradually incorporating new Spanish and international hotels. In the same year Sol Meliá and Inmotel founded Meliá Inversiones Americanas (MIA) to speed up the chain's Latin American growth: a priority area for the group's expansion strategy. Given MIA's lack of stock market success, Sol Meliá made a takeover bid for MIA's entire share capital, leading to a final shareholding of 97.12 percent. In the cases of Riu and Iberostar, their management contracts are closely linked to their partnerships or strategic alliances with major tour operators.

Strategic Alliances

As a consequence of the context in which they were created (a point explained at the beginning of this chapter), strategic alliances or partnerships with major European tour operators are basic to understanding the expansion of the Majorcan hotel chains.

With the exception of Sol Meliá, the other three chains have had traditional strategic alliances with major European tour operators: Riu with TUI, Iberostar with Thomas Cook (former C&N), and Barceló with First Choice Holidays (in the case of Barceló this partnership has evolved into genuine vertical integration). Due to these partnerships, Riu and Iberostar have been involved in the management of hotels, which were under the control of their partner operators. In some cases, tour operators have also funded expansion.

Joint Ventures

Joint ventures have also recently been used as a means of expansion by some of the four chains. Sol Meliá and Iberia subscribed to a joint venture that constituted a landmark in the history of Spanish tourism, because both were the leaders in their respective business sectors. As a result of this strategy, the tour operator Viva Tours was created, with effective synergies that mutually benefited both companies.

In 1998, Grupo Barceló, FCC, and Argentaria initiated a joint venture, leading to the creation of Grubarges. Two divisions were created within Grubarges: (1) Grubarges Inversión, responsible for channeling investments and for the ownership of the hotels, and (2) *Grubarges Gestión*, in charge of the hotels' management. As part of the project, eleven hotels were acquired by Grubarges Inversión, nine of which had previously been owned by Argentaria and two by Barceló. The objective was to create a hotel chain within a period of one and a half years with over forty hotels in Europe and America. All the companies benefited from the joint venture: FCC achieved a long-standing ambition, to enter the tourist industry; the Barceló Group formed a partnership with two important suppliers of financial support so as to accelerate the growth of its hotel division; and Argentaria managed to "relocate" part of its real estate assets acquired during the 1990s crisis.

Sol Meliá, Barceló, Iberostar, and Telefónica created Hotelnet, a B2B Internet portal for the hotel industry. Sol Meliá and Telefónica each own 24.5 percent of the shareholding; Barceló owns 10 percent and Iberostar 8 percent. The remaining share capital was left open for possible new investors, which took the form of AC Hoteles, Fiesta, H10, Grupo Husa, Grupo Piñero, Hesperia, Catalonia, Mac and Med Playa. Hotelnet's goal is to create a virtual marketplace for hotel owners and their suppliers in order to make their commercial relations less costly and more efficient.

Horizontal Integration

Horizontal integration has been used, particularly by Sol Meliá and Barceló. The most recent cases are the acquisition by Sol Meliá of the Spanish city hotel chain, Tryp, and the takeover of US hotel operator Crestline by Barceló.

Accelerating Expansion Rate

If we look at the evolution of the hotel and rooms portfolio of major international hotel corporations, we see tremendous growth. In addition, we find out that the growth rate has speeded up since 1999, as is the case with the expansion of the Majorcan hotel chains.

Specialization in the Hotel Business

In comparison with some of the major international hotel corporations, we can state that Majorcan hotel chains have a less diversified activity. Instead of getting involved in diversification strategies, which obviously have advantages but also risks, they have preferred to "export" the "business model" they really know in depth: how to care for and provide hospitality services to the tourists. They have not gone into the cruise-line business, like Carlson, the American multinational, that used its Radisson brand name to create Radisson Seven Seas Cruisers and is considered to be the world's biggest supplier of luxury cruises. They have not been engaged in the restaurant business like Six Continents.

Sol Meliá, Riu, Barceló and Iberostar have opted for the specialization strategy. Therefore, they mainly "have stuck to what they knew," offering the same core product (with different brands aimed at different market sectors in terms of spending power) but to the same major sector of the travel market: the tourist. This is particularly the case with Riu and Ibersotar. Barceló and, especially Sol Meliá, have entered into the city hotels sector, offering products aimed at catching the business traveler, still remaining in the hotel business. If they have entered into new business, this movement has taken the form of vertical integration or strategic alliances with other companies that are part of the value chain in travel and tourism. This has been a way of guaranteeing that they would be supplied with customers.

In the literature on organizational learning,[13] it is argued that when a firm obtains good results derived from an effective choice of actions, it tends to repeat its previous actions in order to maintain its favorable situation. On the contrary, if negative results are obtained, that often generates pressures for a strategic change. Morck et al. (1990)[14] concluded that firms that diversify are those that show profitability levels below average before undertaking diversification, which in turn indicates that diversified firms do not have lower profitability levels due to their increased diversification. The ecology of populations also supports the view that organizational profitability is positively related to inertia and that explains why firms are reluctant to introduce changes when they obtain good results. Chandler (1962)[15] showed that changes took place in large corporations when they detected bad results. Therefore, companies with high profitability levels seek strategic change to a lesser extent and therefore undertake less risky strategies. This seems to be the case for our "Big Majorcan Hotel Players": *to remain concentrated on their core business where they have historically obtained very high levels of profitability.*

They are a good example of the sound implementation of some theoretical concepts. In that sense, Yip (1992) identified three stages in developing a "total global strategy": (1) *developing a core strategy* that involves building core competences that can potentially give global competitive advantage; (2) *internationalizing the core strategy*, stage at which the core competences and strategy are introduced to international markets and when the organization begins to locate its value-adding activities in locations where competitive advantages are available; and (3) *globalizing the international strategy*, which implies coordinating and integrating the core competences and strategy on a global basis and deciding which elements of the core strategy are to be standardized and which are to be locally adapted based on the strength of the globalization drivers in the industry and market.

Similarities and Differences among the Four Big Players

After reviewing the historical evolution of the four major Majorcan chains, some similarities can be identified:

1. Common geographic origin: Majorca.
2. Each began as a small family-operated business. Now they are large organizations but essentially remain family businesses. Although there is no consensus of opinion about the concept of the family business, there are

certain common elements in the definitions in the literature. Behind many of these conceptualizations, there is, either implicitly or explicitly, the idea of family influence or control over the business in two forms: ownership and management.[16] This is absolutely the case in the three of the hotel chains analyzed: Barceló, Riu, and Iberostar. In the case of Sol Meliá, although part of the company is quoted on the stock markets, the family's influence in ownership and management remains very important.

3. Mass tourism development and expansion in the Balearic Islands allowed them to consolidate. Reinvestment of these benefits made expansion outside the Balearics possible.
4. Relatively restrained international coverage (compared with major world chains of similar size).
5. None of them have hotels targeting the super "deluxe" sector. They are specialized in the mid-price sector with some hotels featured in the top range sector.
6. Three chains are either part of a vertically integrated group or have historical partnerships and strategic alliances with major European tour operators. Of the four protagonists of our story, Sol Meliá is the only one which is, essentially, a solely hotel chain, although it has recently entered the tour operator and travel agency sector as part of its diversification strategy.

At the same time, we can divide the major chains into two groups as differences in their growth strategies can be found in more recent years. In the first group, Sol Meliá and Barceló have determinedly entered the urban hotel sector and are trying to catch both the tourist and the business traveler. They are also making greater use of franchising or management contracts to support their expansion. In the second group, Riu and Iberostar remain concentrated on the tourist travel sector.

Conclusions

Despite the number of similarities, there is no unique expansion or growth strategy among the leading Majorcan hotel chains. Although, once commenced, there were basic reasons for expanding that were similar to all of them, in the first stages the reasons for getting involved in expansion were clearly different, ranging from the opportunity to take advantage of a "good deal" for horizontal integration (Sol Meliá) to some tour operators' partners request to manage some of their hotels.

As they have become larger, they have moved from more traditional ways of management and growth to more modern ones, taking advantage of all the options to foster growth (management, franchising and leasing contracts, horizontal integration, etc.). Riu and Iberostar have not moved outside the kind of product and market they started to serve many years ago. They have a high degree of specialization. To some extent, this also applies to Barceló and Sol Meliá, but they have introduced a higher level of market diversification in the hotel business sector.

Finally, it might be worth mentioning that this heavy investment outside the Balearic Islands has been the object of criticism by some of the Balearics' resident population. These critics complain that these hotel companies prefer to invest in other destinations instead of improving their hotels in the Balearic Islands and that, in doing so, they have learned from their mistakes and built better hotels in competitor destinations, with more respect for the environment. This is one point that, from the strictly private management point of view, cannot be a matter of criticism; on the contrary, it can be termed a wise management strategy of diversification risk and growth. But according to these critics, these chains should devote more effort in terms of quality and tourism product diversification to the islands where they were born. This is a concrete example of social controversy that has arisen in the home country of these hotel chains.

These four chains are examples of small family-operated businesses that, from very modest origins, have constantly expanded to the point of becoming global companies due to the development of mass tourism in the Mediterranean and by so doing, are stimulating tourism development in new destinations outside the Mediterranean.

Notes

1. For a comprehensive description of the air transport regulation, see Rigas Doganis, *Flying off Course. The Economics of International Airlines* (London: Harper Collins Academic, 1991), 24–42.
2. Conselleria de Turisme (Balearic Islands Tourism Ministry; several years): *El turisme a les Illes Balears. Dades informatives.* Govern de les Illes Balears, Palma de Majorca.
3. Extracted from the conclusions of the International Committee of Tourism Experts (document not published). This group was commissioned by the Balearic Islands' Tourism Ministry to discuss present and future tourism in the Balearic Islands and potential ways of introducing more sustainable practices into the development of tourism in the Balearic Islands. Among the members of this Committee were Victor Middleton, Jafar Jafari, Richard Buttler, Walter Freyer, Georges Cazes, Auliana Poon, and Miguel Santesmases. The author of this chapter had the pleasure of conducting and coordinating the group's meetings and discussions.

4. Many of the facts described in this section can be found in the annual reports of the companies analyzed: Riu, Sol Melià, Barceló, and Iberostar.
5. T. Levitt, "The Globalization of Markets," *Harvard Business Review* (May–June 1983).
6. J. Dunning and M. McQueen, "Multinational Corporations in the International Hotel Industry," *Annals of Tourism Research* 9, 69–90.
7. See, for example, M.E. Porter, *Competitive Strategy: Techniques for Analysing Industries and Competitors* (New York: Free Press, 1980); M.E. Porter, *Competitive Advantage* (New York: Free Press, 1985); M.E. Porter, *Competition in Global Business* (Cambridge: Harvard University Press, 1986); C. Bartlett and S. Ghoshal, *Managing Across Borders: The Transnational Solution* (Cambridge: Harvard Business School Press, 1989); G.S. Yip, *Total Global Strategy: Managing for Worldwide Competitive Advantage* (Englewood Cliffs, NJ: Prentice Hall, 1992); J. Ellis and D. Williams, *International Business Strategy* (London: Pitman, 1995), G.H. Stonehouse, J. Hamill, D. Campbell, and A. Purdue, *Global and Transnational Business: Strategy and Management* (London: John Wiley, 1999).
8. See, for example, F. Go and R. Pine, *Globalization Strategy in the Hotel Industry* (London: Routledge, 1995); F. Go, S.S. Pyo, M. Uysal, and B.J. Mihalik, "Decision Criteria for Transnational Hotel Expansion," *Tourism Management* 11, no. 4 (1990): 297–304; P. Hanlon, *Global Airlines. Competition in a Trans-National Industry* (Oxford: Butterworth-Heinemann, 1996); P. Keller, *Globalization and Tourism* (Saint Gallen, Switzerland: Editions AIEST, 1996); S. Wahab and C. Cooper, *Tourism in the Age of Globalization* (London: Routledge, 2001).
9. Figures may not be completely accurate due to constant changes in the hotels managed. Data come from the companies' reports.
10. F. Go and R. Pine, *Globalization Strategy in the Hotel Industry* (London: Routledge, 1995); E.C. Tse and J.J. West, "Development Strategies for International Hospitality Markets," in *International Hospitality Management: Corporate Strategy in Practice*, ed. R. Teare and M.D. Olsen (London and New York: Pitman and John Wiley), 118–34.
11. Onofre Martorell Cunill, *Cadenas Hoteleras. Análisis del Top 10* (Barcelona: Editorial Ariel, 2002).
12. Its last big acquisition, the Spanish city hotel chain, *Tryp Hoteles*, was solely made up of hotels run under management contracts.
13. See, for example, R.M. Cyert and J.G. Mach, *Teoría de las Decisiones Económicas de la Empresa* (Mexico City: Prentice-Hall, 1965); J.G. March and H.A. Simon, *Teoría de la Organización*, 2nd ed. (Barcelona: Ariel, 1969); J.G. March and J.P. Olsen, *Ambiguity and Choice in Organizations*, 2nd ed. (Bergen: Universitetsforlaget, 1979).
14. R. Morck, A. Shleifer, and R.W. Vishny, "Do Managerial Objectives Drive Bad Acquisitions?" *Journal of Finance* 46, no. 1 (1990): 31–48.
15. A.D. Chandler, Jr., *Strategy and Structure: Chapters in the History of the American Industrial Enterprise* (Cambridge, MA: MIT Press, 1962).
16. F. Neubauer and A.G. Lank, *The Family Business: Its Governance for Sustainability* (Houndmills: McMillan Press, 1998).

Chapter 8

The French Group Accor and Tourism since 1967

Business Tourism without a Mass Tourism Strategy

Hubert Bonin

"The Accor paradox" provides a key argument in the study of the history of the services industry as Accor is deeply involved in tourism through a wide range of tourist activities without actually having a clear business tourism strategy. If we consider tourism not only as leisure time enjoyed by businessmen/women after their working day but also as activities dedicated to entertainment, vacation time of any duration, tour operating, and so on, the Accor Group lacks any real power in that market segment in the face of huge British and German competition. If hotel tourism means entertainment, journeys and stays abroad, tourist resorts, high life capitals, here the Accor Group also lacks the presence of American hotel groups. Even in 1991, of the top twenty hotel groups, only seven European ones could compete with twelve American. Of these, only the Accor and Taittinger groups were French. The Accor Group, therefore, deserves special study within the tourism economy. Its paradoxical profile underlines the strength of the Accor Group in the hotel business, which allowed it to become a first rank transnational group; it defines the tourism strategy followed by the Group, but then determines the weaknesses that hindered its emergence as a real tourism group.

Although the firm came into being recently, compared with the Hilton or the Marriott, which were created as early as 1927, it has played a part in tourism

---

Notes for this chapter begin on page 171.

history for decades,[1] having been itself an actor in that history. This "business story" case study is scrutinized in this chapter along classical "business history" lines, assessing the constitution and the evolution of the portfolio of strategic activities and market segments, first of the Novotel Group, then of the Accor Group, then the portfolio of management skills of the firm, before assessing its diversification strategy toward tourism, where successively business tourism, mass tourism, and elite tourism are gauged in order to determine which kind became the core activity of the Group. Such issues are raised alongside the chronological evolution of the company from a strategy focused on a single product of middle-range hotels to a strategy enlarged to a diversified ability to provide facilities for every segment of the market, alongside revenues and business or leisure profiles.

Toward a Transnational Group

A brief survey of the history of the Accor Group[2] provides clues about the "non-tourism" culture of the company as a transnational enterprise. It was based on a strategy earmarked for services to businessmen from all professional levels and not to satisfy consumers' entertainment requirements.

The Assertion of a French Specialty: Economy-Class Hotel Business

In 1967 the founders of the Accor Group, Paul Dubrulle and Jean-Pierre Pélisson, set up a new hotel concept, the budget and standard class hotel.[3] At that time, the hotel economy included either magnificent palaces and high class hotels in capitals and resorts, or basic hotels in tourist areas of capitals or resorts and in business areas of regional towns, in the center or near the railway station; these low-cost hotels were family owned and managed, ill-equipped and provided a low level of comfort.

The Novotel Saga. The Accor Group heroes thus launched the concept of Novotel, in the suburbs of Lille, in northern France: a middle level hotel with comfortable rooms and a restaurant, which could be reproduced all over the country, as a way of convincing customers that the same quality of service could be expected everywhere. Novotel was more than a hotel: it became a brand name, key to the creditworthiness of a hotel chain where standards of service were available to managerial and professional people traveling around the country on business trips. Commercial managers, sales representatives, or groups of executives could gather there for training or meetings in special suites or function rooms integrated within the building itself. The standards for nomadic business people were therefore revolutionized from Balzacian boarding-house to Novotel modern lifestyle. Far from tourism concerns, P. Dubrulle and G. Pélisson then built a chain of Novotels all around France, each hotel standing near a road junction in order to ease access and visibility.

The Ibis Breakthrough and Its Results. In the meantime, the company devised a less expensive type of hotel, the Ibis chain, for middle executives and businessmen. Started in 1974 through a special subsidiary (Sphere, co-financed by the Suez financial group through its subsidiary Compagnie La Hénin), it spread rapidly in every town suburb (one new hotel a month), and as early as 1988 the Ibis chain numbered 182 hotels in France. The drift toward the economy hotel concept led, in 1985, to a far more attractive type, the Formule 1, and high life standard but conversely low key lodging: small rooms, cheap furniture and equipment, collective commodities, no on-site restaurant; but this concept flourished too. These successes spurred the Group to acquire in the United States, in 1990, a similar low-range chain – Motel 6 – equipped with 540 hotels in forty-two states, which was refurbished in order to reach the quality standards required by the Group. By May 1993 the Group included about a thousand low-range hotels (750 Motel 6 and 277 Formule 1). With no thought of tourism, the Accor Group asserted itself as the world leader in economy-class business hotels, which became a kind of "French concept," with as a few other groups following the path in setting up their own chains, especially the Taittinger-Envergure Group (with Campanile). Whereas American and British groups developed their quality hotel chains, the French established strong positions on the lower levels.

A Wave of External Growth. The leading position of the Novotel Group (the predecessor of the Accor Group) was reinforced in two stages. First it bought a competitor that had tried to challenge its leadership on the Novotel segment (three stars) without being so efficient: the Mercure chain joined the Group in 1975 and became one complement to Novotel in the middle upper-class range as its hotels could be less standardized than the Novotel ones and thus more adapted to the inner city environment where they generally stood. Second and more important, the Novotel Group succeeded in 1990–1991 in taking control of Compagnie Internationale des wagons-lits (CIWL).[4] Whilst managing restaurants on board trains in France and all over Europe and a very few sleeping-cars (thus "wagons-lits") – the remnants of its glorious past as the provider of luxurious sleeping-cars to traveling bourgeoisie since the end of the nineteenth century – CIWL had extended its activities portfolio to the hotel business through several chains the Novotel Group took over. To the Novotel and Mercure chains it added the PLM and Frantel chains, which had just been grouped under the Altea brand name; to Sofitel were joined the high level hotels Pullman; to the Ibis chain it added the Arcade, which disappeared, paving the way for a new hotel concept located downtown, Etap Hotel, which gave the Novotel Group a firm footing within inner cities. All in all, CIWL brought the Novotel Group's 288 hotels[5] in 1991; and access to a firm specializing in lunchtime catering for companies or institutions in communal restaurants for employees.

Toward Some Hints of Glamour

Far from suffering from an inferiority complex vis-à-vis large palaces or quality hotel groups, the Novotel Group began to consider the segment of top businessmen and executives traveling from one market place to another to build the multinational economy. The Novotel or even the Mercure concepts were incapable of attracting such high purchasing power. Fortunately the Novotel Group got control – in several stages – of a failing company set up by a dictatorial tycoon, Jacques Borel, the self-styled (French) king of glamorous hotels: since 1972 the firm Jacques Borel International had established numerous Borel hotels and he hoped that this name would equal that of the Ritz or the Hilton. In 1975 it had purchased the Sofitel, a failing but prestigious chain, the management of which was beyond Jacques Borel International; it became choked by massive debt and its bankers blamed Borel, himself, who had to cede his group to its creditors.[6]

The Novotel Group got the opportunity[7] to buy a majority in Sofitel in 1980, to manage the Jacques Borel International Group between 1980 and 1983, and to get total control in 1983. It therefore acquired access to the upper level of the hotel range through a unified brand name, Sofitel, which became the flagship of the Group, as it had to assert itself internationally with a prestigious brand to compete with groups such as the Marriott or TrustHouse Forte, which had already built large networks of such hotels. It immediately attracted the high-spending businessmen and chief executive class and hoped to capitalize on the reputation of Sofitel to appeal to a new and profitable clientele. Even if the Group failed to purchase the Méridien chain in 1994, the Sofitel chain provided the top fifth world network of high class hotels: 37 in France, 68 in the rest of Europe, and a total of 150 in fifty countries in 2001, complemented by hotels managed by the Accor Group with the Sofitel brand but belonging to other companies.

Such a conglomerate of brands confused the image of the Group, which had to adopt a new financial trademark under the Accor label in 1983 when Jacques Borel International and Novotel-SIEH merged. Under that label, Accor was floated on the Paris stock exchange in the same year. In just two decades, G.

Dubrulle and P. Pélisson had succeeded in establishing a large group in accommodation facilities, and moreover, in introducing France to the new concept of "hotel standards and franchise," which provided strong leverage for the new type of "business model" structuring the sector during the 1970s and 1980s.

The Worldwide Reproduction of the French Process

The strategic scenario reached a new stage as the Novotel Group, then the Accor Group, followed a strategy of duplication of the French model and the diffusion of the French hotel concepts in foreign markets from the end of the 1970s. The Ibis, Novotel (and Mercure), and Sofitel trade names appeared in suburbs or highway junctions all over industrialized Europe: Germany, Italy, Spain, the Netherlands, Belgium, and the United Kingdom. Asia welcomed the Group too as Ibis and Novotel conquered several cities. The Sofitel flag was raised in affluent districts of international cities and was used as a key to promote the creditworthiness of the entire Group in competition with well-known competitors. Roots in the United States deepened as the Motel 6 was joined by the Red Roofs Inns chain of two-star hotels similar to Ibis, which provided the Group with a two-pronged network there. Even if success was achieved in the Netherlands where the Accor Group became the leader, observers noted that during the 1970s and 1980s the Novotel concept had failed badly first in Great Britain, Switzerland, Italy, Spain and – for a time – in Belgium in the 1970s, then also in the United States where high class consumers were more used to the semi-luxury chains (e.g., Hilton), which appeared more adapted to their taste than semi-standardized hotels like Novotel. In the United States 90 percent of hotel rooms still belonged to local US chains in the 1990s.

It appeared that the "Novotel model" was not perfect or easily transferable, even in the neighboring countries like Italy and Spain. This led to the use of the Mercure brand to short-circuit that corporate image deficit: this brand surpassed Novotel abroad, with a boom from 14 units in 1975 to 655 in 2001 (73,000 rooms), more than the Novotel chain (341 units and 58,000 rooms). The Group thus proved its resilience as it avoided stubbornly sticking to a policy and instead chose ways of diversifying its service offer. This diversification brought new life to the concept of the "residential hotel," with small apartments equipped with a kitchen, as this formula had met with some success among executives staying for several days in the same location and wishing to have access to individual apartment-like accommodation. The same policy was adopted in Brazil where the Accor Group emerged as the leader in that segment with the Parthenon chain (75 units in 2001).

In the 1980s the strategy of European and African development was clearly a success with top ranking in Africa, Western Germany, Belgium, and the

Netherlands. It was followed by a move into Asia: a subsidiary appeared in 1982 and was equipped with 81 hotels in 1995. Even if in 1986 the Novotel Group had already reached the eighth place among hotel groups and second in continental Europe and Africa, it remained mainly a French concern as 334 out of 534 hotels were still located in France, where it offered 33,000 rooms as opposed to 29,000 abroad. The internationalization policy gained more momentum through successive moves in the second half of the 1980s, for instance, in the United States and in Asia with a first hotel in Singapore in 1982; China was penetrated in 1986 with a management contract in Beijing but acute management problems at the beginning of the 1990s necessitated a pull-out. The strategy in Asia then evolved rapidly: whereas the low-range chains were the key axis of growth in North America, Asia welcomed a multifaceted strategy as several brand names were transferred there (Novotel, Ibis, Mercure) through a subsidiary created in 1993, the Accor Asia Pacific Corporation, which adopted a flexible policy in each country through local partnerships (see table 8.1).

Table 8.1 The internationalized Accor hotel business

	1999 (%)	2001 (%)
France	30	49
Europe	19	
North America	36	32
Asia and Pacific area	7	11
Africa and Middle East	5	4
Latin America	3	4

A Strategy of Rapid Growth and Profitability

Such easy development from scratch always raises questions about the skills, charisma, leadership, and stamina of the managers of such rapid upward movers. Were Dubrulle and Pélisson exceptional tycoons able to build a multinational and diversified group in a quarter of a century?

A Successful Strategy

The figures prove the perceptiveness of both founders of the Group and the validity of their strategy. The upsurge of the Group's hotels and number of rooms was spectacular as growth gathered momentum in the 1970s and 1980s. In the second half of the 1980s, for instance, the group opened between 50 and 60 hotels a year; however, the hotel business provided only 40 percent of the global turnover as restaurant, catering, and *Le Ticket Restaurant* activities fostered their own developments. The growth rhythm kept its force in the 1990s owing to the multinationalization of the hotel business; in 2001 organic growth provided 58 percent of global growth and 42 percent of external growth (see table 8.2).

Table 8.2 The development of the Accor Group

Year	Hotels	Rooms	Turnover (thousands of FFs or euros)	Net Profit (thousands of FFs or euros)
1970	7			
1976	130			
1980	283			
1983	414			
1986	534 (334 in France)	33,000 in France; 29,000 abroad		
1983	406 managed (40,000 employees) 47 Sofitel 175 Novotel 50 Mercure 116 Ibis			
1984	445	50,000		
1987	713			
1988	812		FRF 14.9	FRF 450
1989	856 2,712 restaurants 80,000 employees		FRF 18	FRF 575
1990			FRF 22.8	FRF 1,004 (consolidated)
1991				FRF 949
1992				FRF 802
1993				FRF 615
May 1993	750 Motel 6 277 Formule 1			
1995	81 hotels in Asia	14,500 in Asia		
1997			€4,843	€230
1998	2,577	288,000	€5,623	€297
1999	129,000 employees		€6,105	€352
September 2000	168 hotels in 16 Asian countries (20,000 employees)	29,000 in Asia		
2000		389,000	€7,007 billion	€447
2001	150 Sofitel in 50 countries (37 France; 68 elsewhere in Europe) 341 Novotel hotels 655 Mercure hotels 3,700 147,000 employees	 58,000 73,000 416,000 in 90 countries	€7,290 billion	€474

Various Means of Financing

The development strategy of the Novotel Group or Accor Group has clearly been a dual one with organic growth owing to the spreading of the various hotel concepts and trademarks, on the one hand, and with external growth owing to the purchase of several hotel chains in diverse business segments, on the other hand.

Partnership in Financing. That very growth and the purchasing policy had to be financially sustained. One path was financial partnership with financial groups, which accompanied the Novotel Group through a specific project: the Compagnie financière de Suez;[8] thus became the partner of the Novotel Group in Sphere, the subsidiary in charge of the building of the Ibis chain. The costs were then shared between the partners, as were the profits; it allowed the Novotel Group to alleviate the load of initial investments and, through the hallmark of quality provided by the Suez connection, to get easier and better access to bank credit. The Novotel Group had indeed to convince the Paris market of its creditworthiness as its hotel business project might have appeared audacious and revolutionary.

On a larger scale, the Novotel Group or the Accor Group looked for alliances in order to create financial partnerships and acquire an entrance into foreign markets. Partnerships were thus set up to establish the Groups in Western Europe: alliances were reached in Portugal with the Amorim Group, in Italy with the Agnelli Group (through the Sifalberghi subsidiary, created in 1990), both initially for economy-class hotels (Ibis). In Asia, investors from Australia joined the Accor Group, which spread hotels all over Asia: the Accor Asia Pacific Corporation was set up in 1993 after the purchase of the majority stake in an Australian company, Quality Pacific Corporation. The Accor Group, then owning only 23 percent in the Accor Asia Pacific Corporation, which was quoted on the Sydney and Hong Kong stock exchanges in 1993–94, was able to raise $600 million, thus avoiding excessive debt, particularly as local investors co-financed the new buildings in some places. A parallel policy was followed in the Middle East through association with a hotel subsidiary of Pakistan Airlines, the Minhal Group. The acquisition of Motel 6, in fact, was completed through a new financial subsidiary, IBL, with 40 percent to the Accor Group, with 60 percent of whose capital provided by banks (Société Générale, Caisse des Dépôts, Indosuez, etc.), which afterward promoted the issue of bonds to finance the operation.

On a day-to-day level, numerous hotels were, in fact, financed by financial investors through real estate leasing systems with specialized banks, or more generally, entrepreneurs who invested their own funds and managed one or several hotels using first the franchising of the Novotel Group then the Accor Group. This arrangement was followed for numerous Novotel units as the high return on investment attracted investors who owned only about half of the buildings of its hotel chains in the 1980s and barely a quarter in 2001: that is, 23 percent, whereas 42 percent were rented units and 35 percent managed units from franchising or subcontracting.

Table 8.3 Hotel management, 1983

Total	Owned by the Group	Managed through Franchising	Under Management Contract Only
406 hotels	207 hotels	101 hotels	98 hotels

Externalized Financing. Eventually, the Group found sources of funding apart from its own cash flow: the Novotel Group joined the Paris stock exchange in 1983; the founders chose a brave policy, which avoided confusing their personal financial interests with the fate of their company: they resolved to float the capital of their firm. It drew in several financial and banking investors, among them respected, original partners such as the Société Générale and Suez. The capital structure became increasingly jointly owned as it attracted large blocks of investors, both institutional and individual. That capital basis served as leverage to raise its debt ceiling either through bank credit or through bond issuing. The balance between a rapid growth strategy and the requirement of sensible financial balances had to be respected, which was in fact the main obstacle to growth: on several occasions opportunities had to be rejected as the Group pursued some hotel firms that were for sale as too expensive; the Hilton International chain[9] in 1987 and 1988, the Méridien chain in 1994, bought by Forte. Although the latter was sold by the French state-owned company Air France, leading observers to imagine that the Accor Group's mission was to acquire the Méridien to preserve French national interests, Air France was only trying to get a better price for its assets. Disappointment could therefore be perceived here and there among group executives or newsmen; but the survival of the Group was at stake, and required that brakes be applied to expensive external growth, all the more as some purchases appeared a posteriori overpriced (Motel 6: US$1.3 billion; FRF 7 billion, or €1 billion as it had been bought at the apex of an economic boom just before the 1993 slump; CIWL: FRF 5 billion).

In the middle of the 1990s heated arguments took place about the fate of the Accor Group: could it financially bear such money-consuming growth (for instance, FRF 1 to 1.2 billion a year for investment in the second half of the 1980s), resist competition and worldwide development? The debt load reached FRF 13.9 billion in 1993 and equaled 94 percent of the permanent funds; servicing the debt absorbed a heavy chunk of current profits; net profits crumbled from FRF 800 million in 1992 to 615 in 1993. The ability of the aging founders to manage the Group was also questioned; in fact the transition was achieved smoothly; the main stock-holders did not give up the company;[10] both founders semi-retired as co-chairmen of the board and managers were promoted to the executive committee with Jean-Marc Espalioux as CEO in January 1997. He held that position until 2005. As a financier,[11] Espalioux reassured the Paris market and defined the strategic priorities of the activities portfolio: the catering branch Eurest was sold to the British Compass Group in 1995; numerous hotel buildings were transferred to investors and thus their ownership externalized; and the Group followed the path of drastic economizing policies. Banks brought fresh credit lines in the 1990s; bonds were issued (FRF 2 billion in 1990, convertible into shares); and the debt burden in proportion to the permanent funds decreased from 70–75 percent to 55–60 percent. The Accor Group could thus plan a new phase of growth in the second half of the 1990s as investments had to follow a careful rhythm especially in Asia; the burden of debt had been curbed.[12]

The Assertion of Specific Skills in the Hotel Business

Business history has to cope with specific immaterial factors, which in fact constitute the unquantifiable capital of each firm. In the case of Accor, at first some kind of commando spirit propelled the team of founders and early managers toward both personal and company achievements. As every branch of the Group had to be set up from scratch it needed to spur some entrepreneurship at whatever level of the executive staff.

Slowly, a portfolio of skills and techniques were defined and duplicated. As neither founder had links with the hotel business, they tackled it simply from marketing and finance points of view: Dubrulle had studied commercial skills in Dayton in 1962–63, as a research assistant to Bernardo Trujillo, the "king" of new mass marketing and sales methods; Pélisson's first career was as an executive with IBM Europe.

- The initial logic of the chains set up the basic principles: each building was to be designed on the principles of industrial architecture in order to lower the costs; hotels were planned more by engineers than by architects with an aesthetic interest; room volumes (24 sq. meters for the first Novotel hotels), layout, equipment had to be standardized;

cost-consciousness was thus the key device of the development policy so as to reduce amortization costs, debt, and even management costs. Most hotels were established in suburban areas, the real estate costs were considerably lower than for hotels in town centers, which allowed a more rapid amortization of the expense.

- Precise lists itemized the details of the day-to-day management, from the catering to integrated restaurants to room service. For example, for Novotel a ratio was established of one employee for every three rooms – as the room cleaning service constitutes about 6 to 7 percent of the customer's bill. Everything was to be measured, evaluated, standardized, and translated into codes of daily action; every experience was to be shared between hotels within the chain so as to accelerate the transferal of little successes.
- The new marketing techniques were employed from the start, as they emerged in the 1960s. Customers had to be lured toward the chains by numerous methods of enticement. Institutions had to be investigated in order to offer them relevant packages (seminar rooms, restaurant services, room accommodation).
- A centralized booking system, Resinter, was set up early on within each chain so as to ease the relocation of business customers.
- Meanwhile, in 1993–94, a centralized wholesale purchase system was developed on several levels (worldwide, national, regional) in order to improve economies of scale and reduce buying costs; Scapa, a dedicated subsidiary was set up, as a purchasing unit, while another subsidiary, Devimco, managed the purchasing and even the selection of hotel equipment.
- The professional standards of the staff were defined and standardized in order to set up an internal employment market, to find and promote executives to the differing hotels and tasks; the Accor Academy was founded near Paris to train recruits and executives.
- To achieve decentralized management more adapted to the requirements of the local environment, executives were responsible for their area of expertise (bartender, restaurant manager, hotel manager, etc.). This modus operandi was accompanied by a thorough system of analytical accounting.
- There were serious problems with the management of basic labor resources with side-effects on social relations and recruitment, as (legal) immigrant workers were often employed in developed countries, which explained the recurrent argument about the social policy of the Group; but the outsourcing of room service, which had been systematized in France in the 1990s, had to be given up here and there as the quality of the service had deteriorated because of bad employment and salary conditions among subcontracting firms; and in 2001–2 these did not seem able to provide

acceptable working conditions for most of their employees, which led the Accor Group to negotiate a common social policy with French subcontractors in December 2002 as Accor wished to announce its commitment to a recognized policy with respect to ethical and social matters.

- All in all these now commonplace practices helped the Group to achieve higher returns on each room, a better occupancy ratio. One maxim – underpinned by a variety of procedures – was the *revpar* (rev*enu* par *chambre*), the financial net return by room; this naturally required the use of very detailed, critical modes of reporting and the close involvement of financiers in the management of the Group.

This modus operandi explains not only the managerial success but also the attractiveness of the Group for investors in hotel buildings or hotel ownership: they trusted the Group more and more. The management of their units had been transferred from the Sheraton hotel in Yaoundé (Cameroon) in 1976, which had joined Novotel, to numerous hotels all over the world, even to communist Vietnam.

The Emergence of a Leader Group

The initial strategy had therefore been successful: massive investment led to a massive European network of several chains of mostly standardized hotels. It is important to note that the economy range provided the Group with constant revenue and thus the necessary cash flow, as such hotels depend less on economic cycles than luxury and high class hotels, which have to respond to the whims and tastes of the rich and to the fluctuations of company budgets earmarked for top executives, which are reduced during slumps. It is estimated that Accor's low- and middle-range hotels provided a global return on investment of 15 percent, in comparison with a mere 2 percent from the luxury sector. However, should there be a change of ownership, the goodwill value of the luxury and high class hotels far outweighed that of the cheaper ones.

The "Novotel saga," which started modestly in 1967, was crowned with tremendous success and in 2001 the Accor Group was managing 416,000 rooms.

Table 8.4 Types of hotels within the Accor Group, 2001

Hotel Type	%
High class and luxury	7
Middle class	35
Economy class	58

Accor's stock exchange quotation was impressive: FRF 20 billion in 1990; €9.3 billion in March 2002. The number of shareholders grew as a sign of trust in this French flagship.[13] Despite this, the predominance of Anglo-American groups continued, as new competitors appeared at the end of the 1990s with British Bass buying Intercontinental in 1998 and Granada buying Forte in 1997, while in the United States groups like the Marriott bought Renaissance in 1997. Among the 200 leading hotel chains in 1997, 65 were owned by 35 American groups and provided 56 percent of the available room space. Even France did not escape their clutches: in the 1990s the Choice Group, for instance, purchased the Primevère chain of 145 hotels in the economy-class segment favored by Accor.[14] Despite this, the Accor Group was the fourth largest hotel group in 2001, far ahead of other continental European groups, the German TUI being only thirteenth with 75,000 rooms in 284 hotels, the Spanish Sol Meliá twelfth with 86,000 rooms in 347 hotels and the other French group, Envergure, fourteenth with 69,000 rooms in 940 hotels;[15] only two other European groups were able to compete with the American ones, the British Six Continents and the Hilton Group (see tables 8.5–8.7).

Table 8.5 Comparison of the leaders in the hotel business, 1998 and 2001

	1998		2001		
	Hotels	Rooms	Hotels	Rooms	
Cendant US	5,623	504,000	6,624	554,000	Cendant
Bass	2,606	453,000	3,234	507,000	Six Continents (ex-Bass) (with *Holiday Inn*)
Marriott	1,443	303,000	427,000	2,333	Marriott
Choice	3,474	292,000	416,000	3,654	Accor
Accor	2,577	288,000	363,000	4,545	Choice (*Comfort Inns*)
Starwood	552	189,000	320,000	1,934	Hilton US
Promus US	1,118	165,000	312,000	4,109	Best Western US
Hilton US	254	102,000	226,000	751	Starwood
Carlson US	487	96,000	135,000	795	Carlson Hospitality Worldwide
Hyatt US	173	77,000	94,000	385	Hilton UK
			92,000	214	Hyatt

Table 8.6 The leaders in the hotel business, 1998

	Hotels	Rooms
Holiday Inns	1,645	327,000
Hospitality franchise systems	2,298	289,000
Best Western International	3,370	266,000
Choice Hotel International	2,295	214,000
Accor	1,875	213,000
Marriott	698	161,000
ITT Sheraton	423	131,000
Hilton	257	94,000
Forte	853	76,000
Hyatt	159	75,000

Table 8.7 Chronological landmarks

1957	Creation of the Borel company in the restaurant business
1963	Creation of Sofitel (with the support of the financial group Paribas)
August 1967	The first Novotel hotel in Lille
1968	Second Novotel, in Colmar
1970	Seven Novotel in action
1970	Creation of the Jacques Borel (three stars) hotels
1972	A dissident executive launched the Mercure chain; first Mercure in 1973
1972	The Jacques Borel Group entered the hotel business
1972–73	First Novotel in Belgium, Switzerland and Great-Britain
1973	The first huge Novotel hotel in Bagnolet, a Paris Eastern suburb (600 rooms)
1973	Creation of the Ibis chain; the first one in Bordeaux in 1974
1973	Purchase of the Courte-Paille grill-restaurant chain
1975	Novotel bought the ill-managed Mercure chain
1975	CIWL launched the Arcade chain
1976	Jacques Borel International purchased Sofitel
1976	First hotel in the Netherlands
1977	Jacques Borel ousted by bankers
1980	Novotel Group bought Sofitel and managed Jacques Borel International
1982	First hotel in Asia, in Singapore
1982	CIWL bought the PLM chain
1982–83	Struggle between Novotel and Sodhexo for the control of Jacques Borel International
1983	Merger between the Novotel Group and Jacques Borel International
1984	The first step toward the thalassotherapy strategy: purchase of the Quiberon unit
1985	CIWL bought the Frantel chain
1985	Purchase of the high class restaurant group Lenôtre
1985	The Formule 1 chain
1986	First bridgehead in China
1987	CIWL federated its hotels under the brands Pulman and Altea

(*Continued*)

Table 8.7 Chronological landmarks (*cont.*)

1987–88	The Novotel Group missed the opportunity to purchase Hilton International
1990	Acquisition of Motel 6 (created in 1962)
July 1990	Stake holding in CIWL
1990	Joint venture in Italy with the IFIL
1990	Partnership with Viajes Ecuador in Spain
1991	CIWL under the control of the Novotel Group
1991	The Mercure chain absorbed the Altea (inherited from CIWL, with 200 hotels)
July 1993	Purchase of a majority stake in Quality Pacific Corporation (Quality Inn) absorbed by the freshly created Accor Asia Pacific Corporation
1995	Sale of Eurest to Compass (communal dining and food catering)
1999	Acquisition of the Libertel chain (45 two-star hotels and 2,600 rooms in France and Belgium)
1999	Acquisition of Red Roofs Inns (created in 1972 in the Midwest)

A Strategy Dedicated to Tourism

As its history shows, the company was not interested in jet-setting and glamour: firm economic control, exacting, self-critical reporting, economies of scale, a positioning in the economy and middle-range segments of the hotel sector for businessmen and professionals are a far cry from tourism. Most Accor hotels do not create a festive mood during the working week. What part could tourism thus play within the strategy of the Accor Group?

Tourism as a Second-String Policy

In the early decades of the Group's history, tourism was only a side-effect of the core business, providing extra clients when professionals and businessmen went back home during the weekend. It was welcome as it improved the average rate of room occupation, but was in no way a key activity of the strategic portfolio. Numerous hotels, particularly the Ibis Etap Hotels, attracted people going on or coming from sun or skiing vacations as a stopover opportunity. Since the 1980s the Group has launched a systematic policy to attract such customers during the weekends or for short vacation stays through attractive tariff ranges for families – but always in order to reduce the room vacancy rate. As modern life allows more opportunities for short vacations, this market segment now has a dedicated sales program with a marketing policy[16] and the use of the centralized booking system. The results are impressive with hotel bookings fairly equally balanced between business and leisure (see tables 8.8 and 8.9).

Table 8.8 The clientele at the economy-class hotels of the Accor Group, 2001

	Number of Hotels	Number of Rooms	Percent of business overnights	Percent of leisure overnights
IN EUROPE				
Ibis	583	61,000	55	45
Etap	236	18,000	50	50
Formule 1	363	27,000	50	50
IN THE USA				
Red Roofs	360	40,000	55	45
Motel 6	814	85,000	40	60
WORLDWIDE				
Novotel			65	35
Mercure	655	73,00	55	45

Table 8.9 Types of clientele at the Accor hotels in Africa, 2002

Total number of rooms in 68 hotels	6,600
Customers from Africa itself	48%
Customers from outside Africa	52%
Business individual customers	76%
Business customer groups	15%
Individual tourists	5%
Tourists groups	4%

Tourism as a Global Strategy to Gain Middle- and Upper-Class Customers

The patchy knowledge drawn from these experiences led to a slow but steady move toward a formalized tourism strategy. Three factors were paramount: the room occupancy rate; the higher return margin on services to leisure customers; glamour added to the corporate brand image, which had been a concern since the flotation of the equity: it helped to improve "brand awareness" as assessed by opinion surveys.[17]

Sofitel as a Key Leverage to Brand Image. The Accor Group continued promoting the Mercure and Novotel brands as core business in the middle- and upper-market segments, especially in foreign cities; their restaurants became instruments to promote "the French touch" abroad and the architecture and services of some of these units provided customers with a more relaxed atmosphere to balance the business focus of the majority of these customers, as in the Novotel units in Beijing and Shanghai or those newly opened in Turin, Wellington (New Zealand), Moscow, and Osaka (the first Novotel established in Japan) in 2002. In the meantime the Sofitel brand became the key leverage factor in sustaining the corporate image abroad: "new émotions" became the motto around the Sofitel brand in 2002–3 to accompany the rebuilding and the strengthening of the brand reputation in competition with luxury and high-class brands, all the more as most of these were being reshaped after their incorporation into newly restructured groups created through mergers. Sofitel hotels were redesigned or opened in major world cities (Cologne), in 2002 targeted initially at business customers but also as high class leisure venues when some Sofitel units appeared in Cancun, Marrakech, and Venice (February 2003). The Sofitel brand allowed the Accor Group to start a new offensive in the United States, no longer offering economy-class hotels after it had failed to develop the Novotel concept there: Sofitel units in Washington DC, and Chicago thus became the beacon of the Group in the United States.

After the Work Day. One strategy followed by Accor was to pursue its core customers after their day-to-day business activities; it is a classical case study to show how companies extend their strategic portfolio to new activities either linked to their core ones or to new services provided for the same customer base. The Group thus discovered fresh outlets in leisure services addressed to its core customers as the latter wished to alleviate the psychological and physical stresses imposed by their way of life. New pieces of the jigsaw of services appeared intended to satisfy the needs of business people and professionals. Accor reaches further into their lives. Five key elements were set up.

1. The Accor Group combined its core business activity with its leisure strategy to form its *incentive services* as it prospected a fast growing market. Ever more firms were gathering their executive or sales employees during weekend or short vacation stays as a reward for the best or as a way to consolidate corporate culture through a mix of seminars and collective leisure time (sometimes with husbands and wives). The Accor Group therefore started "Incentive House" as a trademark for that activity offering both group accommodation and services or providing firms with individual leisure vouchers to be distributed to deserving employees.
2. The Accor Group developed another core activity, *congress management*, which became a key means of filling up hotels beyond mere seminars or daily meetings. Such congresses, especially the international ones,[18]

brought together high-powered, sometimes very large groups of up to several thousand; the hotels complemented the meetings with a whole range of support facilities: sightseeing tours, catering, restaurants, travel management, and so on. Being itself no longer a mere complementary activity, the congress segment asserted itself as a high-profit margin outlet. A "ploughing back" policy also emerged in 1998 when a specialized network was established within the Accor Group to promote its hotels and these incentive or congress services among corporations worldwide: an "elite" sales force, 550 strong, was grouped in twenty-two offices (twelve abroad, ten in France) in order to centralize the administration of the various ranges of travel, accommodation and leisure services of the Group: business accommodation, meeting incentives, congress and exhibition support services, leisure for groups, air flight booking.

3. The Accor Group established hotels at *ski resorts.* The tourism strategy went far beyond services linked to business activities and Accor wished to join its wealthy customers in their leisure activities as well, in order to get a foothold in that accommodation market.
4. The Accor Group's rapid rise as one of the French specialists in *thalassotherapy* and *balneotherapy* (seawater spa treatments). The purchase of the Quiberon thalasso therapy unit in 1984 paved the way for the development of a successful strategy as it became fashionable for executives and their partners and the aging or rather eternally youthful middle- and upper-classes to undergo heath therapies. Hotels were linked with health services in seaside resorts, first in Novotel Carnac (in Brittany), a model which has since been duplicated. A subsidiary, Thalassa International, dedicated to this activity, extended its scope by the takeover of hotels in traditional spa resorts, under the Thermale de France chain, with investment to reshape hotels joining the group so as to maintain its quality and management standards. This activity was promoted to being a core business at the beginning of the twenty-first century under the name Accor Thalassa, with several spheres of operation: spa centers; fitness, beauty and health services; thalassotherapy and aqua therapy – all linked to hotels, which increasingly added such services to their previous offerings. At the same time, tour-operating was expanded to complement the health and fitness business in the "package" program, through a separately available "welfare offer." The Accor health and fitness business grew from 90,000 customers in 1998 to 150,000 in 2002 (80 percent of them originating from France),[19] with a network of forty sites in 2004 after twenty years of development.
5. Finally Accor entered the *gambling and casinos* market, where much of the power was already in the hands of international groups all over

> the world, especially in the Anglo-Saxon areas where betting and gambling activities provided the Hilton International Group (outside the United States) with 40 percent of its turnover in 2003, or of specialized French groups like the Barrière Group (from Deauville) or the Partouche Group. With regards to legality it was necessary to avoid criminal money laundering, fixed gambling, and racketeering. This explains the low key approach adopted by the Accor Group: it first chose to be a partner of the Barrière Group (of the Barrière family) through a minority stake holding and to develop its own casinos only slowly. It then purchased the Société de participation et d'investissement de casinos (SPIC) in 1997 and developed it thereafter, in fact alongside its traditional policy of enlarging the potential customer base of its hotels as it linked its casinos to its hotels, as in Bordeaux since 2002. Overall, almost twenty casinos were thus available in 2003, mainly in France but with three abroad (Malta, Dinant in Belgium, Courrendlin Délémont in Switzerland); but the Group remained prudent, refusing to get bitten by the gambling bug! It refused to outbid the Partouche Group for the purchase of an important French casino chain[20] in 2002 and decided to get out of the Barrière Group in 2002 as it could not acquire effective control of the family firm: the partnership had taught them a great deal in a sensitive area, but had not produced a durable attachment to the Group.

The Accor Group returned to its traditional customer base to offer support in all areas of professional and (individual or collective) leisure life. The outcome of this systematic approach to these various market segments was of course to fill up the hotels of the Group; the famous *revpar* was dependent primarily on revenue, which in turn depended on the room occupancy rate. But the side effects of that room-filling policy became more and more important: first the restaurant and bar use; second, the development of higher margin activities (health, gambling, touring services). One clear result of that evolution was that the range of operations was greatly extended during the 1980s and 1990s owing to the expansion into different kinds of tourism.

Accor toward Mass Tourism

This expertise could then be applied to tourism management and even mass tourism, but always with Accor's traditional concern, "room occupancy first!"

The Management of Tourism and Travel Agencies. The purchase of CIWL in the early 1990s established the Accor group in a specialized tourism segment – travel agencies. CIWL had developed a network of outlets first to promote and sell its railway services (mainly sleeping cars), second to become a travel agency. It had 1,700 shops and 7,000 employees in 1993, mainly in France but some in other European countries. Its competitors, among others, were Havas Voyages and Thomas Cook. This sphere of activity was ideally suited to Accor's core business dedicated to corporate institutions and professionals, as 70 percent of CIWL turnover was fostered by orders from these very market segments, especially from companies (about 50,000 were customers) arranging their employees' travel.

The CIWL agency network merged with that of Carlson in 1993. The Carlson Company,[21] solidly established in the United States, chose this alliance in Europe to enlarge its base in continental Europe where CIWL was much stronger: a sales force of 4,000 outlets in 140 countries with 14,500 employees was thus constituted with the trademark Carlson Wagonlit Travel. The Accor Group had therefore inherited half of that joint subsidiary; its strategy then consisted in extending that business to leisure activities, especially for individual customers. There was a policy of external growth: an ex-SNCF French railways subsidiary, Frantour, was purchased; a systematic policy of alliances was concluded with several franchised networks of independent agencies, one important one, Selectour, and several smaller ones with origins in networks set up by regional newspaper groups. These various initiatives led to a network of about 300 travel agencies all around France itself. In the meantime a partnership was established with the Spanish agencies' network Viaje Ecuador in 1999, before another with the main Italian one – CIT (highly profitable with four million customers) in 2000: joint subsidiaries were set up to manage specialized agencies in France, Italy, Spain, Belgium, and Switzerland.

These networks could be usefully mobilized to promote Accor Group services and brands as it is well known that air flight, tour operating, and hotel companies are given preferential locations on software booking programs through the links they maintain with the centralized access system. Accor Group's printed and digitized catalogs, booking forms, and promotion or discount campaigns could thus be favored by that network without monopolizing it as each member of the network had their own business to pursue. The cohesiveness of this informal group partnership, franchising, and separate agencies was proven when the trademark Accor Travel appeared in 2001 as an "umbrella brand" to label every product of that segment of business and develop synergies with the tour-operating activities of the Group (Accor Vacances and Frantour).

Toward a Large and Specialized Tourism Business. In the 1990s the Accor Group seemed committed to establishing a structured strategy in the tourism business, signaled by the creation of Accor Tourisme in 1990 as a parent entity to various developments in the field of tourism. It was a multifaceted tourism strategy. The Accor Group launched bridgeheads in the *leisure hotel business* through a residential hotel formula: it took control of Marine Hotels for stays in tropical countries; of Pan Sea for stays in Asia. A brand new residential hotel chain called Coralia was created to offer the "club concept" (hotel and entertainment). A stake was purchased in Croisières Paquet in 1988, as mass tourism developed outside the United States, the *cruise* formula having already met with huge success there. The partnership with Paquet entailed joint management of the cruise vessel Mermoz, a flagship of the small French cruise flotilla. Acquiring *tour operating* skills became a priority; several medium-sized companies were purchased with the aim of either fulfilling the traditional objectives of the Group – raising the occupancy rate of the Group's hotels, or of fostering the recently developed residential hotels. Africatours, Asietours, and Directours thus became subsidiaries of the Group and joined Frantour and a new one, Accor Tours. The medium-sized tour operator GO Voyages was also purchased (for 60 percent) after it had suffered financial difficulties and had been restructured in 2002.

Accor began to angle for the customers of other tour operators as they could fill its hotels with whole groups. This required new skills, including marketing for each of the "business segments," the management of differentiated tariff lists and of yield management, linking the booking systems of tour operators, air flight, or railway companies,[22] as well as Accor's own. The Osaka Novotel was an example of a hotel established according to Accor's traditional principles as it "benefits from simple and speedy access to Osaka two airports," which conforms to the "convenience concern first" of the Accor Group; but "it also offers an ideal location for travelers wishing to visit the recent theme park built by Universal Studios or the famous port of Kobe,"[23] which indicates the new trend toward responding to mass tourism. Since 2000 a sub-strategy has been discernable, dedicated to tour operating linked with residency at Accor hotels or clubs (Coralia): packages with tours around the local area or attendance at cultural events and festivals have been offered, targeted at up-market clients (Tunisia, Morocco, Malta, Maurice, Cuba, French Polynesia, and the West Indies, etc.). The marketing of other tour operators' products and managing its own tour operating business were developed in parallel with the following profits: in 2000 tour operating (FRF 330 million), tourist products and retail distribution (FRF 1,100 million); combined leisure and residential hotel business (FRF 549 million) delivering a very respectable turnover; the Accor Group was also active in the "sun markets" in Maghreb (Tunisia and Morocco) and southern Europe (Portugal, Italy, Greece).

The whole range of activities in the tourism business was finally grouped under the management of a specialized division, Accor Loisirs & Tourisme, oriented toward collective and individual tourism and leisure, a department different from the one in charge of entertainment activities targeted at businesses, the Affaires Loisir division. These initiatives in tourism were intended to reorient the Group from large towns in industrialized or emerging countries, where most of the hotel chains were established, to sunny country and coastal areas such as Spain, Morocco, and Tunisia, as they offer accessible and easily manageable markets for a beginner.

Table 8.10 Chronological landmarks about tourism at the Accor Group

1962	The first Motel 6 opened in Santa Barbara
1974	Creation of the Ibis chain
1993	Project of merger of CIWL agencies and Carlson into Carlson Wagonlit; achieved in 1997
1988	Partnership with Croisières Paquet
1989	Stake purchased in Lucien Barrière group
1990	2% acquired in Club Méditerranée
1990	Partnership with Viajes Ecuador in Spain
1990	Accor Tourisme to promote leisure hotel business in resorts
1997	Purchase of the Société de participation et d'investissement de casinos SPIC
1998	The subsidiary Accor Casinos
1998	A taskforce of multibrand units dedicated to worldwide companies
2000	Partnership with CIT
2000	Creation of the Coralia chain concept
2001	The Accor Travel umbrella brand name
2001–2003	Global promotion of the Sofitel chain
2002–2003	The Accor group affirmed its commitment to direct tourism products
June 2004	Accor purchased the Agnelli stake in Club Méditerranée

Disappointment in Failed Strategies or Requirements in Terms of Financial Resources Selection. Retrospectively all these ventures look like mere tokens in order to gain a foothold in every market. Of course one must be aware that the Accor Group went through severe financial crises in the 1990s and an ambitious tourism policy could not have taken off because of the lack of funds, and so a stake of 2 percent was purchased in Club Méditerranée in 1990; but no money would have been available if the Group had dreamt of becoming the main stockholder and manager of Club Med, a responsibility that was transferred from institutional investor Caisse des dépôts to the Agnelli IFIL Group without an ultimately clear-cut choice by Accor Group. Nevertheless, Accor was tempted to go into residential hotel management but without the security of knowing how best to proceed: a takeover of an existing large group, possibly? The creation of a new group as they did with Thalassa International and Coralia?

No robust strategy emerged in contrast to the one firmly chosen by their German competitors Preussag-TUI and Thomas Cook. Did the hotel group fail to integrate a new "corporate culture," to diversify its skills while evolving from a mere hotel business to a more general tourism business? Or should we recognize that the requirements in terms of the selection of financial resources imposed a drastic strategic line that condemned vast and rapid diversification? Too many service groups crumbled in the years between 1997 and 2002 as they had grown too rapidly and taken over too many companies without acquiring enough long-term resources and structuring balance sheets able to resist slumps and fiscal changes. The Accor Group management had been so affected by its own financial and strategic crisis in the mid-1990s that it had at that time set up some lasting rules about its evolution: it had to be aware of its financial limits in order to anticipate market recessions and fiscal problems. For instance, in the residential hotels and clubs segment, the Accor Group failed to move above 191 units in 2000 or even in 2003, as compared with 3,900 hotels for the whole Group. To reach a leading position it ought to have purchased Club Méditerranée or some other entity like Jet Tours (residence clubs), which Air France had to sell to Club Méditerranée, or Maeva (a residence chain, without the club formula), which Club Méditerranée resold to Pierre & Vacances in 2001. In each sector – casinos, residence clubs, residence hotels, and cruise business – the Accor Group ought to have promoted intense external growth to reach competitive positions as was proven in each segment between 1999 and 2003.[24] Theoretical strategies produced by academic specialists in case studies intended to reshape the business world in terms of their wishes or by financial analysts and investment bankers attracted by large fees in M&A operations have to be seen in relationship to financial realities in order to gauge their actual feasibility. Mass tourism was excluded from the core strategic portfolio of the Accor Group.

Severe strategic pruning was the consequence of the arguments that took place on the board in 2000 and 2003; it was in fact decided to reef in the sails of growth: partnerships were prioritized over direct developments. For instance, the partner CIT was given the tour operating activities of Frantour in Belgium and Switzerland; the stake in GO Voyages was resold in 2003; Frantour stopped delivering its own short-term travel products. Whereas the staff of the tour operation business in France itself was severely reduced in 2003, a strategy was proposed whereby the integrated travel agencies of the Accor Group were to be devoted solely to the distribution of tourism products for other companies while continuing as a priority to sell hotel rooms of the Group. Partnerships were privileged in several segments of the tourism business, especially tour operations and the distribution of products; for instance, through the links established with CIT and Viajes Ecuador in Italy and Spain, which led to a kind of network expressively called "the alliance."

Current Moves toward a Refreshed Tourism Strategy

After this strategic and financial scrutiny of expansion into the tourism business, the Accor Group finally decided how it should develop: outside its core hotel business where skills and modus operandi are efficient and productive, the Group had to rely on specialized entities for its other activities; each one has to acquire skills, enterprise culture, well-explicated, perceived, and practiced methods so as to be competitive; and it acquires the market share, which will provide it with economies of scale and purchasing power in competition with service suppliers. Having proved that the Group was able to cut costs and to sharpen the finance management, Chairman Jean-Marc Espalioux regained some margin for maneuver and restarted moves toward external growth.

Two targets were chosen. First, because the Agnelli families had to trim their assets, Accor purchased their stake (a little less than 30 percent) in Club Méditerranée.[25] This long-dreamed-of business finally joined the Group in June 2004 and sounded the signal for a renewed strategy in tourism; but mass-tourism was still rejected as Club Méditerranée itself had changed its strategy for some years and decided to specialize in middle- and high-range clientele, so as to rebuild its profitability and to refurbish its brand image by distinguishing it from mass-tourism brands (e.g., Fram). A second target was the CIT; Accor took a little stake into this Italian group in 2004 as a signal that it was interested in the rescue of this ailing company, which had suffered severely from mismanagement and from the crisis of entities structured around networks of agencies controlled by the CIT. But both attempts failed in 2005 after the reshuffling of the Group's management led to the sale of the stake in Club Méditerranée, and the collapse of the CIT marked an end to the alliance; the company refocused on its core business model and the strategy of reinforcing the tourism sector was strictly contained within severe financial limits.

Conclusion: What Kind of Hotel and Tourism Group?

The business history of the Accor Group was undoubtedly a success story: it ranked fourth in the world for well-equipped hotel rooms and had become genuinely transnational (see table 8.11).

After Accor's restaurant activities had fallen from 35.2 percent in 1992 to 8 percent in 2001 owing to the sale of Eurest communal restaurants to Compass, its core business remained staunchly hotels: the tourism strategy had produced interesting additional areas of activity with new customers in order to boost room occupancy, and a few profitable niches or even segments; but nothing emerged as the basis for a two-pronged strategy for the whole Group. Globally

Table 8.11 Gross profit of the Accor Group, 2001

Country	%
France	30
Europe	31
North America	29
Latin America	6

tourism is calculated to account for about 40 percent of Accor turnover: apart from the casinos (3 percent), it is thought that rather less than half (40 to 50 percent) of each activity is tourism-oriented, which explains my estimate: 18 percent from business and leisure hotels, 14 to 15 percent from economy-class hotels, 4 percent from the half of the travel agency business, which is dedicated to tourism rather than to business travel management. All of this leads to the final 40 percent assessment.

Table 8.12 The part of each activity in the Accor Group turnover

	2000	2001
Business and leisure hotels	36.00%	37.09%
Economy-class hotels outside the United States	13.50%	32.20%
Economy-class hotels in the United States	18.50%	
Travel agencies	8.00%	6.86%
Restaurants (outside hotels)	8.00%	6.47%
Services in railway transports (CIWL)	5.00%	3.80%
Casinos	3.00%	4.10%

Tourism business regained its key role in the Group's strategy – to contribute to the raising of the hotel room occupancy rate – but it also fulfilled a more exciting role, that of refurbishing the corporate image of the Group as several fresh activities provided it with some glamour: the new Sofitel strategy, the positioning of Mercure as a less standardized concept than Novotel, the gradual evolution of the Novotel concept abroad too; the casinos and thalassotherapy activities. The travel agencies themselves assumed a triple mission: to favor the Group's hotel business and occupancy rate; to spread feelers to detect market moves among corporate practices and mass tourism; to provide global facility services to institutions in search of various means of easing and stimulating the business life of their employees.

At the end of all this, we might consider the Accor Group to have reneged on its plans to be involved in the mass leisure tourism market – to have yielded to German or British groups and been satisfied with partnerships and the mere distribution of externalized tour operating products. But what actually happened was that Accor adopted the strategy of mixing its excellent knowledge of corporate needs, its own managerial expertise, and its tourism ambitions: the Accor Group emerged from the 1990s as a key "business tourism" specialist. It clearly rejected the Anglo-Saxon model of mass tourism (e.g., Thomas Cook-C&N, TUI, MyTravel) as the largest groups stood to gain most benefit from the massive transfer of people (60 million Germans and 26 million British traveled abroad in 1999 compared with only 15 million French tourists), instead reaching profitable economies of scale in tour operating, hotel renting, and air charter. Because 400 tour operators were competing in France, the four leaders gathered only 35 percent of the customers, whereas the two German leaders together attracted 60 percent of customers. The Accor Group therefore did not take part in the huge reshaping of the European tourism business between 1997 and 2003.[26] It also rejected the entertainment club formula (Center Parc, Disneyland Paris), the residences for rent (Pierre & Vacances) and stuck to promoting its own "business model," which continues to be successful at the beginning of the twenty-first century, whatever tentative developmental research it has tried in the last decade. In addition to the activity of hotels for business and professional customers, it defined a tourism strategy mainly dedicated to middle- and upper-class customers in health and fitness activities, expensive tourism and gambling; profitability and "French chic" prevailed on mass tourism (see table 8.13).

A company's strategy might seem rational and clear-cut ex post facto, because of precise and durable business models. In reality the opposite is often the case and randomness often predominates in the story of each enterprise: opportunities have to be seized; competition imposes the need to explore new market segments to determine whether they are promising, commercial, or financial deadlocks may be met. While enlarging its scope throughout the business customer range, the Accor Group considered whether or not those businesspeople and their families could use the Accor products for their leisure; or whether leisure could be inserted within business activities through incentives or congresses. The results of such policies were the reinforcement of the attendance rate and high-margin revenues. But the systematization of this strategy of leisure toward a tourism strategy was obviously neither a success nor a long-term choice; a few trials were undertaken, and retrospectively, it seems to have been mere experimentation. The major event that contributed to the suspending of a move toward the tourism business seems to have been the emergence of the Asian market, which required huge priority investment in hotel equipment in

Table 8.13 The strategic portfolio

	Accor Group	Pierre & Vacances[1]	Club Med	Nouvelles-Frontières	FRAM	Look Voyages	Envergure (Taittinger Group)	Disney-land Paris
Hotels	Yes	No	No	Yes	Yes	No	Yes	Yes
Clubs	A little[2]	No	Yes	No	Yes	No	No	No
Cruises	No more	No	A little	No	No	No	No	No
Property development	No	Yes		No	No	No	No	Business only
Residences for flat renting	No	Yes	No more	No	No	No	No	No
Entertainment parks	No[3]	Yes[4]	No	No	No	No	No	Yes
Tour operating	Somehow	No	For its own products	For its own products	For its own products	Yes	No	Partner-ships
Travel agencies	Yes	No	For its own products	For its own products	For its own products	No	No	No
Air charter company	No	No	No more	Yes	No	Yes	No	No
Casinos	Yes	No	No	No	No	No	No	No
Thalassotherapy	Yes	No	No	No	No	No	No	No
Incentives tour operator	Yes	No	Yes	No	No	No	No	No

[1] Pierre & Vacances gathered in 2002: 170,000 beds in France; 50,000 in Italy and North Europe; a total of 50,000 apartments.
[2] Club Méditerranée in 2004–2005.
[3] The Accor group resold its stake in Parc Astérix, now a member of the mini-group built by a subsidiary (up to 2004) of Caisse des dépôts, Compagnie des Alpes, with Musée Grévin.
[4] Center Parcs.

order to be able to compete effectively there as mass markets developed. After having established solid bridgeheads in the United States, the Accor Group had to move eastward and thus to dedicate its available finances to this market at the expense of the tourism business model. It did not become the leverage for a huge and robust French tourism group as hoped for by experts and the State, and French tourism companies kept their over-specialization (Pierre & Vacances, Club Méditerranée) with the result that French tourism still relies for the most part on small- and middle-sized family business.

Notes

1. Nacina Baron-Yellès, *Le tourisme en France. Territoires et stratégies* (Paris: Armand Colin, 1999); Fred Inglis, *The Delicious Story of the Holiday* (London: Routledge, 2000); John Walton, *The British Seaside: Holidays and Resorts in the Twentieth Century* (Manchester: Manchester University Press, 2000); Harold Vogel, *Travel Industry Economics: A Guide for Financial Analysis* (Cambridge and New York: Cambridge University Press, 2001); Rémy Knafou, ed., and MIT Team, *Tourismes. Lieux communs*, vol. 1 (Paris: Belin, 2002).
2. This study does not intend to pose as a pioneering business history sketch; it is only a historical case study presenting facts and determining both skills portfolio and strategy portfolio with arguments about dilemmas between growth and diversification on one side and finance balance on the other side, while assessing the margin of maneuver left by competitors. It is mainly derived from press articles, the official annual reports of the company and internal or personal documents, without access to historical archives. An actual "business history" of the Novotel-Accor group is still waiting to be written.
3. Both founders have sponsored the book retracing their business saga: Virginie Luc, *Impossible n'est pas français. L'histoire inconnue d'Accor, leader mondial de l'hôtellerie* (Paris: Albin Michel, 1998).
4. In 1988 CIWL had concluded an alliance with a competitor to Novotel group for catering, Sodhexo, which intended to get control of the catering subsidiary of CIWL, Eurest. But the Belgian and French interests (Caisse des dépôts, with 28 percent) involved in CIWL turned their back on Novotel group; it launched a takeover bid in 1990: first it got a stake holding in CIWL in July 1990 through a direct purchase on the stock exchange and the finance group Bruxelles-Lambert; then its partners welcomed it into their holding company Cobefin, which raised its equity capital so as to allow Novotel group to control 55 percent of its capital while *Société générale de Belgique*, its ally, kept 25 percent, at the same time directly owning shares in CIWL. Third Cobefin launched the bid over CIWL. Sodhexo had to sell its holdings (20 percent of CIWL) to the investors' group and was thus defeated. The French company Sodhexo Alliance is now a world leader in the catering and collective restaurants business, having given up its hotel dreams to assert its core activities through important purchases in Great Britain and the United States.
5. CIWL had launched Arcade in 1975; bought PLM in 1982 (from the Rothschild group) and Frantel in 1985 (from the railway company SNCF), which constituted a group of 183 hotels in 1987. Two brand names were destined to unify the three-star units: *Pullman* (three stars high level) and *Altea*.
6. Jacques Borel had started his firm as early as 1957 in the restaurant business; it had developed a chain of fast-food restaurants and a company dedicated to selling restaurant tickets to firms for their employees; in 1968 the US group Grace contributed capital in order to sustain its development; but excessive growth occurred as the capital-consuming hotel activity was entered in 1972; for instance, the group doubled its turnover from 1975 to 1976 (from one to two billion FRF) because of the purchase of Sofitel, a hotel firm created in 1963.

7. There was some competition between the Novotel group and Sodexho in 1982, but the stock exchange struggle was won by the former in 1983.
8. H. Bonin, *Suez, du canal à la finance, 1858–1987* (Paris: Economica, 1987).
9. The Hilton International chain was sold by the United Airlines to KLM in 1987 as it offered $950 millions to the Novotel group's offer of $905 million. As LMM resold it as soon as 1988, the Novotel group then proposed $1,000 million but Ladbroke won the bid with $1,070 million. When the Intercontinental chain was also for sale in 1998, the Accor group did not consider the case because of budgetary considerations and the Bass group bought it, after the Marriott had bought Renaissance and the Granada group Forte in 1997.
10. In 1987 the main stockholders were: Suez (10.5 percent), Société générale (4.7 percent), Caisse centrale des mutuelles agricoles (8.9 percent), along with some main members of the board and the founders, their families and their own associates (7 percent). But the individual and institutional members of the board together held only a third of the equity and the executives 5 percent, as the capital was largely spread among stockholders, which could have paved the way for an easy takeover bid.
11. J.M. Espalioux had been the financial chief executive of the Compagnie générale des eaux, a huge utility service group.
12. The debt load against permanent funds was contained: 87 percent in 1997, 60 percent in 1998, 77 percent in 1999, 64 percent in 2000, and 67 percent in 2001. Development investments reached FRF 2,680 million in 1999 for instance; but sales of activities (FRF 3,306 million in 1998 and 1999 altogether) alleviated the financial balance sheet.
13. The number of shareholders grew from 65,000 in 1997 and 64,000 in 1998 to 177,000 in 1999, 205,000 in 2000 and 195,000 in 2001. International institutional investors held 49.3 percent of the equity in 2001 versus 25.1 percent for French institutional investors and 15.1 percent for individual investors.
14. The Six Continents group, with 3,325 hotels (Inter-Continental, Holiday Inn, Crowne Plaza, Express by Holiday Inn) and 515,000 rooms in 2001–2 had only 69 hotels in France and therefore planned to extend its stake there, especially through the three-star brand Express by Holiday Inn, able to compete with Novotel. The group changed its brand name to InterContinental Hotels Group in the middle of 2003 and sold its 2,000 pubs and restaurants inherited from Bass.
15. The Envergure hotel group was a subsidiary of the financial family group Société du Louvre, owned by the Taittinger family (champagne, luxury entities, etc.). Its main brand names were Campanile and Kyriad. This group joined an investment fund in 2006.
16. "Give yourself a treat with Ibis weekend rates. At Ibis, weekend rates per night and per room are valid for Friday, Saturday or Sunday. Make the most of *Ibis* weekend rates to get away from it all in one of almost 580 Ibis hotels in Europe for a weekend escapade with the one you love or with friends, to see the sights or just to relax." (an *Ibis* flyer, 2002).
17. The Accor group used indicators set up by the Taylor-Nelson SOFRES research institute; samples were consulted in 1997, 2000, and 2002 and "the results have

revealed further improvement in the group's reputation and its brand image" (*Accor News*, December 2002–January 2003).

18. France (6,5 percent of the market share) is the third location of international congresses in 2002 behind the United States (12.9 percent of market share) and the United Kingdom (6.6 percent) and before Germany (5.9 percent), Italy, and Spain. In France, Paris has drawn the majority of that type of congresses far ahead of Strasbourg, Lyon, Montpellier, and Nice.
19. Accor Thalassa resorts are located in Morocco, Tunisia, Portugal, Sardinia, Jordan, and France (Dax, Aix-Les-Bains, Arcachon, Carnac, etc.).
20. The Partouche Group succeeded in 2002 in purchasing the Compagnie européenne de casinos and thus asserted itself as the leader in that activity in France (with a €372 millions turnover in 2002) ahead of the Barrière group, the Accor group (Accor casinos), and the Moliflor Loisirs group.
21. The Carlson Hospitality group was in fact a competitor of the CIWL hotel business and then the Accor group as it managed a hotel chain equipped with 69,000 rooms and 315 hotels (Carlson, Radisson, etc.) in 1991. But it also controlled about 2,330 travel agencies as number two in that business all over the world.
22. The Accor group and the French railway company thus concluded a pact, Train+Hôtel, to entice customers to book their railway ticket and a hotel room at the Accor group all at once, at the attractive discount prices.
23. *Accor News*, December 2002–January 2003.
24. Cf. the harsh financial fight to form important cruise groups in 2002–2003 with Carnival as a winner.
25. Accor purchased the stake of the Agnelli and of Caisse des dépôts, through an exchange with its own equity, for about €252 million.
26. Two companies emerged as leaders in Germany: the ex-metallurgy group Preussag, a major conversion to tourism, bought TUI in Germany in 1997, then Hapag-Lloyd in 1998, Thomson Travel in England in 2000 (which had just bought the Norwegian Via Gruppen in 1999), before purchasing Nouvelles Frontières in France in 1999–2002. Its competitor Condor & Neckermann, owned by Lufthansa and the retailer Karstadt-Quelle, developed its activities in Germany under the name C&N, then bought Thomas Cook in England and Havas Voyages in France, united under the brand Thomas Cook in 2003, the brand already adopted in Germany as early as 2000.

Chapter 9

Club Méditerranée, 1950–2002

Ellen Furlough

In early 1950, posters in Paris advertised a new vacation experience: "For 15,000 Francs: Vacation in the Balearic Islands with Club Méditerranée ... a new and friendly vacation program, a comfortable tent village, the most beautiful sites in the Mediterranean, a large and devoted staff, all Mediterranean sports, fast and comfortable journey, quality entertainment." Club Med's founder, Gérard Blitz, was astonished by the response to his advertisements. Attracted by the innovation of paying a single, low cost (around $40) for transportation, food, accommodations, sports, and entertainment in a Mediterranean locale, some 2,400 people signed up for the two-week vacation adventure in Majorca. Blitz believed in the sensual and restorative pleasures of nature, and the new organization's name was meant to invoke the blue skies, light, and warmth of the Mediterranean.[1] Apparently the poster's description and the name Club Méditerranée struck a responsive chord. Club Med was a success from the start, despite the first village's makeshift atmosphere, inadequate facilities and water supply, accommodation in US army surplus tents, and a thirty-six-hour trip by train and boat. Vacationers enjoyed frolicking on the beach, playing sports, eating at group tables, and dancing under the stars to a small orchestra. The casual camaraderie was such that guests, dubbed *gentils membres* (GMs) by Blitz, gladly pitched in with food preparation and general tasks.

After the first successful year, the number of members increased and Club Med villages proliferated along the sunny Mediterranean coast and the Adriatic Sea. This pattern of growth and expansion persisted for forty years. Eager consumers embraced Club Med's hassle-free all-inclusive vacations in exotic

---

Notes for this chapter begin on page 191.

locations, and for the most part the Club's management met the challenges of growth and international expansion by adapting its offerings to provide greater differentiation by market segments. By 1990, with over 100 villages in thirty-three countries, Club Med was one of the most successful enterprises in the international tourism sector and a leader in the concept of all-inclusive vacation villages. Although Club Med remains a prominent multinational tourist organization, its growth and profitability declined from the early 1990s as the firm faltered in the face of significant internal and external challenges.

This chapter explores the history of Club Med in three parts: the Club's "heroic years" during the 1950s and 1960s when its core concept was created and refined; the years of growth and international expansion during the 1970s and 1980s; and the spiral of economic decline, growing competition, and an aging image that have challenged the firm's core concepts and seriously diminished its profits since the 1990s.

Creating Club Méditerranée: 1950s–1960s

Three key elements fueled Club Med's development as a successful business selling a particular product and vacation experience: the nature of consumer demand; the visions and personalities of its founders; and the business decisions of the firm's management. During the 1950s and 1960s Club Med's vacation concept (called at the time its *esprit club*) was well suited to post-war consumer desires and to the development of post-war tourism options that would reach a broader social clientele. In other words, Club Med's social inclusiveness and its all-inclusive, relatively standardized, vacation village format was an example of post-war mass tourism. For people who had recently experienced the horrors and privations of the war, Club Med vacation villages offered low cost and self-indulgent sensual pleasures, abundant food and wine, and liberation from social and cultural constraints – all in exquisite Mediterranean landscapes of light, beauty, warm sand, and good weather. Club Med's all-inclusive formula and its casual village format obviated a large part of the effort involved in taking a vacation and encouraged physical and social relaxation.[2] Even the employees of Club Med villages, the *gentils organisateurs* (GOs) seemed hardly to be working, as they ate, played, danced, and slept with the GMs.

The demand for Club Med vacations was extraordinary in the early years, and the team assembled by Gérard Blitz struggled to create and finance new vacation villages. In the early 1950s Blitz established an office in Paris and instituted a membership fee for GMs. These fees, and the GM's advance deposits on their vacations, were the Club's only sources of revenue for the subsequent leasing and provisioning of its tent villages on the shores of the Golfo di Baratti in Italy (1952), Yugoslavia, and the Greek island of Corfu (1953), Djerba in Tunisia (1954), and in Tahiti (1955). After five years, Club Med had approximately 10,000 members. How did Club Med's product evolve, and what was the nature of its appeal?[3]

The most fundamental and persistent element of Club Med's concept in the 1950s and 1960s was its all-inclusive village format. Designed to be different from everyday life and provide "mental and physical detoxification," Club Med villages were isolated from their surroundings.[4] Intrusions from "civilization," including telephones, radios, newspapers, televisions, and clocks were strictly prohibited or discouraged. By the early 1950s, the explicit model for this "counter-society" was a mythologized Polynesia; GMs wore flowered Tahitian sarongs and aging tents were gradually replaced by grass-roofed Polynesian-style huts. In addition, each village acquired its own "personality," with a village song and the strong imprint of the village manager (*chef de village*). GMs were loyal to particular villages, and when they signed up for the following summer's vacation, many requested specific villages and/or villages managed by their favorite *chef de village.*

A second element of the Club's concept was the stated objective of erasing social distinctions by abolishing their most visible signs, in essence peeling away social conventions to reveal people's "authentic" selves. People in the villages, from workers to managers, addressed each other in the familiar "tu" form, called each other by their first names, and avoided discussing their occupations. The relaxed dress code was cast as a "rupture with daily life," proof that "there are no social differences when everyone is in a bathing suit." Club publications explained that the policy of replacing cash with colored beads muted external signs of status.[5]

A third element was the emphasis on leisure activities and sensual pleasures in a convivial group setting. All villages provided a wide range of sport activities such as sailing, water-skiing, volleyball, fishing, tennis, ping-pong, and scuba diving. Club Med vacations celebrated the beautiful, active body and endorsed an erotically charged climate in the villages, and Club Med became known for its tolerant attitude toward casual sexual encounters. This perception, satirized in the well-known 1970s film *Les Bronzés*, depicted Club Med as the epitome of a "sea, sun, and sex" vacation.[6]

Although these concepts expressed and responded to the desires of the GMs who vacationed there, the originality of Club Med also rested on the productive synergy between the Clubs' evolving concept and the creative imprint of its two founders: Gérard Blitz and Gilbert Trigano. Despite Trigano often being seen as the major force behind Club Med, Blitz was its founder and his impact in its early years was the most significant.

Gérard Blitz (1912–1990) was born in Antwerp, Belgium, the son of a prosperous Jewish diamond merchant.[7] Blitz left school at sixteen and was apprenticed as a diamond cutter. He also became a champion water-polo player. During the war, he was a member of the Belgian resistance network in Switzerland. After the war, three experiences profoundly influenced both Blitz's life and the future direction of Club Med. The first was his involvement with a rehabilitation center in the Haute-Savoie for Belgian survivors of the Nazi concentration and death camps. There Blitz discovered the recuperative power of a tranquil and beautiful natural environment, with sports and plentiful food, which would later resurface in his construction of Club Med. The second was Claudine Coindeau (later Blitz's second wife), a Frenchwoman from Tahiti who introduced Blitz to Eastern mysticism and yoga. Her invocation of Tahiti as a place of authenticity and calming beauty would have a strong impact on the future ethos of Club Med. The third experience was Blitz's visit in the summer of 1949 to Club Olympique, a tent resort on Corsica where he became an aquatics instructor. When Blitz later decided to create his own vacation village on the Mediterranean he largely replicated Club Olympique's minimal material comforts, dining in common, emphasis on sports, dancing under the stars, nightly impromptu performances put on by the staff, and its all-inclusive format with wine included in the overall price (people received coupons to exchange for drinks at the bar). Deciding to turn his passions into a job, Blitz formed his own enterprise, Club Méditerranée, and registered it as a non-profit association in Paris on 27 April 1950. Blitz was now in a position to realize his vision of vacations as a time and space for people to find "interior peace, equilibrium, and a profound happiness" in vacation villages along the Mediterranean.[8]

There were, of course, practical matters to be dealt with first. Prior to the opening of the Majorca resort, Blitz had to equip the site, arrange transportation from Paris, and obtain the tents necessary to accommodate the first vacationers. It was in his pursuit of tents that Blitz first encountered Gilbert Trigano, the man whose business skills would later result in his appointment as Club Med's president and chief executive officer.

Gilbert Trigano (1920–2001) was born in Paris, the son of Algerian Jews who had settled in France after World War I.[9] His father owned grocery stores and a company that manufactured tents and canvas covers. Trigano left school at 16, and during the war he was a factory worker and member of a communist resistance group in the Ariège. After the liberation in 1944, he returned to Paris, got married, and worked in the family business. It was the Trigano's wholesale distribution of US army surplus tents, used largely to supply the growing taste for camping in France that brought Gérard Blitz into his life in 1949. After their first meeting, the Triganos supplied tents to Club Med.

Although Gilbert Trigano was initially involved with Club Med as a supplier, over the next decade his influence within the organization grew. In large part this was due to Blitz's relative inability to manage Club Med's phenomenal growth in its early years. The number of villages kept growing, as did the number of members. Club Med's clientele expanded beyond France to include more Belgian, German, and British GMs. Former GMs loved the experience so much that they signed on as GOs for the following summers, and were willing to accept relatively low wages.[10] The irony was that as Club Med expanded its membership and operations, it kept losing money. Blitz's main concern was for people to find tranquility and sensual pleasures in the villages; he saw little need for Club Med to make profits so long as it covered costs. Blitz's limited sources of revenue did not keep up with the pace of growth and the need for capital. Blitz himself later recalled that his management of the Club was "disastrous." He often could not pay employees or suppliers, and was never sure if each summer would be the last. Blitz's father advised bringing in an associate who "knew how to count" and Blitz chose the Triganos. Not only were the Trigano family's business skills sorely needed, but Club Med was indebted to them for tents and camping equipment. After the Trigano family became partners in Club Med, Gilbert Trigano was appointed treasurer of the Club in 1953.

Club Med continued to extend and refine its operations. In 1956–57, the Club absorbed its principle competition, the Villages-Magiques (partly owned by *Elle* magazine), doubled the number of its villages, and diversified its offerings by opening its first winter ski village in Leysin, Switzerland. By 1959 there were twelve Club Med villages and 45,000 members. The Club's financial affairs stabilized somewhat after 1957, when the Club changed its legal status from a non-profit association to a limited liability company (*société anonyme à capital variable*), but its debts kept mounting. By 1961 Club Med was millions of francs in debt, and creditors threatened to call in their loans. Club Med was on the brink of bankruptcy and desperately in need of an infusion of capital. Blitz and Trigano elected to seek out Baron Edmond de Rothschild, who agreed to invest 10 million francs and took a controlling interest in return (he was hence known within Club Med as the *gentil capitaliste*).[11]

Rothschild's entry into the Club signaled a shift in emphasis as well as the onset of much needed financial and managerial stability. While Rothschild was not directly involved in managing the Club, he restructured the administrative council, brought in several new people at the top levels of the organization (including Jacques Giraud, a graduate of the Harvard Business School), modernized operations with an up-to-date computer system, and made sure that his accountants closely scrutinized the Club's financial affairs. The Club henceforth operated on a sound financial basis, and in 1966 it became a public corporation with its stock listed on the Paris Bourse. Club Med's subsequent growth and financial stability provided Trigano with an opportunity to streamline operations and adopt a different management style.

The 1960s were an era of expansion and change for Club Med; four or five new villages opened annually and memberships mounted. The tone of the villages began changing with the opening in 1965 of the first "luxury" village at Agadir in Morocco. This village, with its permanent concrete buildings along prime beachfront property, presaged the future shift from grass huts to more comfortable and durable accommodations, and it was the first Club Med village to remain open all year round. The GMs of the 1960s tended to be older and wealthier than those of the 1950s, and the newer notions of comfort had a certain appeal. Club Med also continued to diversify its offerings. By 1963 there were nine ski villages, five in Switzerland and four in France. The Club opened its first village in the Americas, Fort Royale in Guadeloupe, in 1968.[12] That same year, Blitz persuaded American Express to purchase around 15 percent of Club Med for a new cash infusion of 2.7 million dollars. This allowed Club Med access to American Express's sales outlets and computerized reservation services, and American Express became the booking agent for the Club in the United States.[13] Club Med was poised for its robust expansion in the 1970s and 1980s.

Administratively the "era of the technicians" arrived, implementing more managerial rationalization. Trigano, an aggressive, energetic, and motivated person, embraced these changes. For a short time, Trigano and Blitz alternated the presidency of the Club, until 1963 when Blitz declined and Trigano was henceforth the permanent president. The Club's management became more hierarchical. Plans for and decisions concerning the villages were largely created in the Parisian corporate offices and replicated in selected environments. As the first generation of village managers retired, subsequent managers not only lost the power and autonomy to select their own team of GOs, but began to receive more formal training, as did the GOs. Activities became more structured; for example, the nightly animations were no longer spontaneous engagements between GMs and GOs, but staged performances.[14]

By the late 1960s, Club Med had become a large, multinational corporation, one of the major players in the commercial leisure and tourism industry. For Trigano, there was little difficulty reconciling his values with the growth-oriented corporate character of the Club. He believed the Club could be an avant-garde business within a new leisure-oriented economy and society.[15] For Blitz, the Club's balance between continuity and change was more complicated. Following his decision to decline the presidency of Club Med in 1963, Blitz had distanced himself from its operations. Although he had played an important role in opening up the American market (Blitz spoke excellent English) and negotiating the relationship with American Express, Blitz's interests in Eastern mysticism and yoga increasingly became the major focus of his life. Blitz recognized that Trigano was better suited to guide the Club in the direction of an international corporate enterprise. After problems emerged during Blitz's handling of construction for a new village in Martinique, Edmond de Rothschild concurred. One morning in 1969, Blitz arrived at the Club's Parisian headquarters, resigned his position, and liquidated his assets in the company. Blitz remained the Club's honorary president, his life henceforth focused on his quest for spiritual growth.[16] It was the end of an era for Club Méditerranée.

Growth, Expansion, and Challenges: 1970s–1980s

In October 1978, Gilbert Trigano's picture was on the cover of *Le Nouvel Economiste* as "Manager of the Year." The accompanying article saluted Trigano's leadership in Club Med's international expansion. It declared that "the sun never sets on its empire" of 100 villages staffed by 6,000 GOs of fifty different nationalities. *Le Nouvel Economiste* also applauded Club Med's commercial success and adaptation to new technologies (noting there were "computers hidden behind the palm trees"). Blitz, who was interviewed for the article, commended Trigano as "the prototype of an entrepreneur and manager who identifies 100 percent with his enterprise."[17]

Club Med did indeed enjoy phenomenal growth and financial success during the 1970s and 1980s, growth that extended far beyond its Mediterranean beginnings. By the mid-1980s, it was the world's largest vacation-village operator. Club Med's financial performance was outstanding; from 1974 to 1981 profits increased by around 500 percent.[18] Membership rose 380 percent in the twenty years from 1970 to 1990. The number of villages grew to ninety-seven in 1988–89, up from fifty-five in 1972–73. On the eve of its fortieth anniversary, Club Med operated villages in fifty-four countries: twenty-five villages and five villas (inns) in North America, the Caribbean, Asia, the South Pacific, and Indian Ocean Basin; and seventy-two vacation villages and six villas in Europe, Africa, and South America.[19]

Trigano later noted that by the 1970s he and the Club's management felt increasing pressure from both the GMs and the Club's investors, as well as from a seemingly ineluctable internal logic, that "The Club must always be growing. It must prepare itself for the conquest of the world."[20] Aside from its initial but limited growth beyond the Mediterranean in the 1950s and early 1960s, most Club Med villages in the mid-1960s were in Europe and dotted along the Mediterranean. The clientele was predominately European. Club Med continued to attract Europeans (50.7 percent of the GMs were French in 1975), and to augment its holdings within France and Europe.[21]

The Club accelerated the expansion of its operations beyond Europe to new locations, continents, and markets in the 1970s. For example, in 1971, Club Med extended its presence in Africa with the opening of a new village in the Ivory Coast, followed a few years later by one in Senegal. New villages opened on the island of Réunion (1973) and in Central and South America (Mexico [1974] and Brazil [1979]). Club Med opened its Chateau Royal village in New Caledonia in 1978, intended primarily for Japanese guests. The first village in Asia, Cherating, debuted in Malaysia in 1980, the same year that Club Med established its Copper Mountain ski village in the United States. The push into the Americas continued in the Bahamas and the Caribbean during the 1980s. Trigano's friendly relationship with the Mexican government, and the latter's own commitment to building a tourist industry, resulted in a major expansion of Club Med into Mexico, with nine villages built there under particularly favorable financial conditions by 1986.

Several factors contributed to Club Med's generally successful financial growth and geographical expansion in this period. One was that Club Med's labor costs remained low for employees in its villages. Club Med also enjoyed the important competitive advantage of selling a well-known, clearly defined, and appealing product with certain predictable elements. At Club Med locations around the globe, Club Med's consumers could be assured of an all-inclusive vacation at villages with lavish meals, a vast array of activities and entertainment possibilities, exquisitely beautiful locations, comfortable accommodation, and the individual freedom to participate, or not, in group activities. The all-inclusive structure obviated concerns about prices, tipping, and so forth, and the friendly staff of GOs played a crucial role in the Club's dynamic of sociable camaraderie. Further, the Club's historic traditions – the special terms and songs, rituals, and so forth – meant that GMs could subsequently vacation at another Club Med and experience a different locale while knowing what to expect. This predictability continued Club Med's position as a major purveyor of post-war package tourism. Whereas the lingua franca of the early villages was French, the range of "official" languages spoken in the villages expanded as the Club became more international.

Club Med's other operational advantages included its ability to negotiate substantial airline discounts due to its large passenger carrying capacity. This kept transportation costs relatively low (and profits high). Club Med either purchased blocks of seats on existing flights or used charters. Because of its all-inclusive packages, Club Med stood to profit from sales of vacations that included transportation. (It also sold land packages only.) Beginning in 1970, the entry of the larger capacity Boeing 747s lowered the cost of air travel, and Club Med's long-time relationship with Air France became more financially advantageous.[22] It was also in partnership with UTA (and hence its parent company Chargeur

Réunis) for villages in Tahiti, New Caledonia, and Réunion. In 1989 Club Med signed a joint marketing agreement with American Airlines for transportation to and within the Americas. It also acquired a 34 percent holding in the French air-travel firm Nouvelles Frontières, a move designed to strengthen their position when dealing with airlines.[23] Another operational advantage was that Club Med saved money by minimizing sales of its vacations through travel agents. With two-thirds of its sales made directly to customers, and only one-third by agencies, Club Med's distribution costs were around 8 percent as opposed to the 23 percent costs for tour operators.[24]

Furthermore, Club frequently leased rather than owned its villages, and when new villages were built the Club sought financially advantageous concessions from the host countries. These might include low leasing fees, special immigration arrangements, direct construction subsidies, or payment by the host country for any necessary infrastructure (airport, roads, electricity, and so forth), and favorable tax concessions.[25] In addition, Club Med benefited from its successful collaboration with important French and international financial groups. Its board of directors consisted of powerful people and financial interests, both private sector and French government controlled. Although Edmond de Rothschild's group continued to hold shares and play an important role, during the 1980s he began to distance himself from Club Med and divest stock. Giovanni Agnelli's IFINT became a shareholder in the early 1970s and by the late 1980s it was Club Med's majority shareholder.[26]

Club Med's successful growth also resulted from its aggressive acquisition of competitors. For example, in 1970 Club Med absorbed the Club Européen du Tourisme (CET). Founded in 1958 by François Huet and Marcel Lesur, CET was initially a non-profit association providing inexpensive bus tours. It later became a commercial corporation that overtly adopted Club Med's village format. However, the CET anticipated consumer demand for more comfortable and durable accommodation before Club Med. In 1962 the CET opened a village on a superb site near Tangier and launched an ad campaign meant to challenge Club Med: "No More Straw Huts!" Also, as Club Med would open a new Mediterranean village the CET would open one nearby. After fierce price wars and complex negotiations, Club Med absorbed CET hoping to contain the competition. This merger brought Club Med 100,000 new clients and thirteen vacation villages. Club Med neutralized another European rival in 1976, when it acquired 45 percent of Valtur Servizzi, an Italian vacation group similar to Club Med.[27] These and other acquisitions helped position Club Med as one of the largest tourist organizations in Europe.

The extraordinary international expansion of the 1970s and 1980s called for administrative innovation. In 1981, Trigano began dividing the company into four administrative zones in order to streamline operations and enhance efficiency within regional operations. The zones, which included all villages and sales offices, were delimited as: Europe, Africa, and the Middle East; America; South America; and Asia. The Europe, Africa, and the Middle East zone was the most important one in the mid-1980s. With its seventy villages, it had over 70 percent of the Club's bed capacity and close to 65 percent of the Club's total guests, the majority of whom were European. The second most important zone was the American, with close to one-third of all guests. Both the South American and Asian zones in the mid-1980s were small, although the latter was considered to be poised for extensive growth.[28]

In 1984, Club Med created a new administrative and financial entity, Club Med Inc., specifically to administer the growing American and Asian zones. With its corporate offices in New York, the company operated sixteen villages, managed four others, and directed sales offices in its North American, Caribbean, Mexican, Pacific, and Asian markets. Its parent company, Club Méditerranée S.A., located in Paris, operated seventy resorts and all sales offices in Europe, Africa, the Middle East, and South America. The new company's stock was listed on the New York Stock Exchange, with new capital targeted both for debt repayment and for expansion. The stock sold represented only 22 percent of Club Med Inc.'s stock, with 78 percent retained by the parent company in Paris.[29] Gilbert Trigano was named chairman of the board of both companies, with his son Serge appointed as Club Med Inc.'s first president.

By the late 1980s, Club Med's expansion slowed and its profits stagnated.[30] To a certain extent, Club Med encountered the same difficulties as other firms within the international tourism market: terrorist attacks in the 1970s; the drop in Mediterranean tourism during the Gulf War; economic recessions; political unrest and monetary instability within developing countries; and natural disasters such as hurricanes. But there were also issues that were of particular import to Club Med. In essence, the Club was faced with the challenges of maintaining an identifiable product while adapting to a changing clientele, new consumer tastes, and intense competition. The Club's directors realized that Club Med would need to adapt to its market and to changing times, and rethink at least some of its business strategies.

Club Med's vacationers in its early years were relatively young (67 percent were under thirty in 1961), largely French and European, and for the most part, although not exclusively, broadly middle class. While young "swinging singles" were prevalent during the 1960s, from the 1970s the GMs were generally older, wealthier, and more international. Their expectations were often different from those of earlier members who brought their youthful exuberance, spontaneity, and acceptance of straw hut villages with minimal sanitation. As Gilbert Trigano put it: "At the beginning of the 1970s, everything was changing: the size of the Club, the expectations of the clientele, the behavior of the G.O." According to

Trigano, the new clients were "attracted by a higher level of comfort, and became more exacting," and amateurism and spontaneity gave way to "those who created ambiance."[31] The emphasis on singles gave way progressively to married couples with families. By 1989, the average GM was thirty-five and almost half were married with children. Many of them were also in tune with the changing consumer tastes for more individualism and autonomy within the villages. Club Med needed to adapt its product to more flexible forms of tourism.[32]

The Club attempted to anticipate and meet the needs of its changing clientele as well as diversify and upgrade its villages. Although Club Med began to accommodate families with children in the 1950s, it was only in the 1970s that it cautiously committed to the growing family vacation market.[33] The major strategy was to cater to families: in selected villages, GOs supervised children of various ages during the day, with special activities at Baby (4–23 months), Petit (2–3 years), Mini (4–7 years), and Kids (8–11 years) Clubs on site. To some extent, the family vacation strategy successfully broadened Club Med's appeal; one adult participant noted happily that "Club Med has perfected the carefree vacation that pampers the modern two-paycheck family."[34] Although the Club's older reputation for sexual liberty and hedonism persisted, it became associated primarily with villages that were for "adults" only. Buccaneer's Creek in Martinique, for example, had this profile.

The Club also adapted to older GMs desires for more comfort, higher quality services, more privacy, and individual choices. Straw huts have been gradually replaced by durable and more comfortable accommodation (although several straw hut villages remain to this day). The new villages built in the 1970s and 1980s were decidedly more upscale, with architecturally sophisticated designs and air-conditioned private rooms with modern bathrooms. During the 1980s, Club Med aggressively sought a wealthier clientele as it constructed luxury full-service clubs in the Caribbean, the Americas, and Southeast Asia. In these new villages, and to some extent in older ones, Club Med also responded to the growing social inclination for greater personal privacy and individualism, neither of which had been particularly emphasized at the early Club Med villages. Villages began to provide keys for doors, safes in the rooms, tables for two in dining areas in addition to the Club's traditional group tables for eight, and different choices of restaurants in the same village. The near-mandatory use of the familiar "tu" form of address in the early years of the Club was largely abandoned by the 1980s. Club Med also turned its attention to the changing interests of its GMs. For example, as tennis and golf increased in popularity in the 1980s, villages added tennis courts and golf courses. These transformations helped keep Club Med competitive within a more socially segregated tourist industry that increasingly catered to individual choice. They also risked altering the Club's core concept in favor of a more conventional resort experience.

The Opio village was the model for Club Med's new generation of high-end resort villages catering to older and wealthier clients. Completed in 1989 and located on the French Riviera in the hills behind Cannes, the 1,000-bed village had air-conditioned private rooms with telephones, clocks, and a fax machine in every room, door keys, and safety deposit boxes. Rooms even had televisions, a telling departure from the Club's earlier emphasis on sociability and group activities. Opio was one of several places by the late 1980s where the beaded necklaces were phased out and replaced with a special credit card. Emphasizing both luxury and service, Opio was constructed with a corporate conference center, and offered large meeting rooms, a theater with state of the art audio-visual facilities, sports such as golf and tennis, a new health and fitness center, and five restaurants.

Club Med continued to diversify its offerings for vacation experiences with ski resorts, time-shares, honeymoon and weekend packages, specialized activities at particular villages, more villages open all year round as well as the option to choose a village with activities for children. In 1975, for example, Club Med created Maeva, a subsidiary of apartment resorts, most on the Riviera, available for time shares and rentals. A year later the Club obtained a 55 percent interest in Club Nature, a small chain of nudist resorts as well as another vacation chain, Clubhotel. The cruise ship Club Med 1, introduced in 1990, was meant to position Club Med within the rapidly growing cruise market. It was luxuriously outfitted, more expensive for GMs than the villages, and touted as the world's largest sailboat. The continuing quest for leisure-oriented diversification also resulted in the opening of "city clubs," urban vacation complexes meant for business travelers and tourists seeking a cold-weather alternative to a tropical getaway. The one in Vienna, Austria, opened in 1986 and consisted of a luxury five-star hotel linked to a large glass pyramid containing palm trees and a swimming pool undulating with electronically powered waves.[35] These were not very successful, perhaps because consumer's expectations in terms of the Club Med concept did not readily translate into urban areas.

Club Med also renewed its commitment to lower cost villages when it acquired Club Aquarius in 1991. Its founder, Lotfi Belhacine, had portrayed his villages as "the other Club" – like Club Med but less expensive (prices were around 40 percent cheaper). This acquisition had mixed results. The intention was to offer market diversification within the Club Med brand, that is, villages that were more expensive and up-scale, and others that were less expensive. The result, however, was to blur rather than differentiate Club Med's product, creating a perception that a Club Med vacation was less expensive than it really was. As one study put it, "The studies showed quickly that Aquarius had cannibalized Club Med."[36] Nonetheless, Club Med gained fifteen villages, a network of travel agencies, and a charter airline, Air Liberté, with this acquisition.

Although Club Aquarius proved relatively profitable, Trigano made a costly mistake. In 1989 Club Med had purchased a controlling stake in Minerve, another charter airline, and decided to merge it with Air Liberté for transporting GMs to its far-flung destinations. Within six months, however, Club Med lost money when the planes lost 50 percent of their value due to overcapacity in the airline industry.[37]

As Club Med sought to diversify its product and broaden its appeal, there were signs that its image was not only aging, but becoming increasingly muddy. The French press noted that while television showings of *Les Bronzés* perpetuated the "sea, sun, and sex" image of Club Med, the high prices and upscale villages confused some consumers who expected an "antidote to civilization" in grass hut villages.[38] Another serious challenge Club Med faced during the 1980s was the intense competition from various "copy cat" companies, particularly in the American sector. These enterprises copied Club Med's all-inclusive village format, offered a more consistent and luxurious product, directly targeted singles and couples without children, and lowered the prices for similar amenities in exotic locales. Some of the most successful, such as the Hedonism, Couples, and Sandals resorts, were in the Caribbean, and appealed to the US market. Several large hotel chains, including Hyatt, Holiday Inn, Hilton, and Marriott, also launched resort-like accommodation with child care that competed with Club Med's foray into the family market.[39]

Club Med thus generally met the challenges of growth and expansion by innovating in order to stay competitive during the 1970s and most of the 1980s. The Club's ambitious program of building new resorts and refurbishing older ones was very costly, however, and prices for Club Med vacations rose steadily during the late 1980s. The Club's profits slowed even as its sales remained high. Club Med Inc.'s stock, which hit a high of $32.00 a share following its introduction on the NYSE at $17.00, was priced at around $14.00 in 1988. In 1990/91 the Club posted a net loss of just over 17 million francs.[40] By the early 1990s, it was becoming evident that Club Med was in financial trouble.

Trouble in Paradise: From the 1990s to 2002

On 2 September 1993 Gilbert Trigano announced in *Le Figaro* that he planned to retire by the end of the year and turn his position as president and chief executive of Club Med over to his son, Serge Trigano. Most of Club Med's shareholders and employees were thunderstruck by the surprising news, especially given the Trigano family's ownership of less than 1 percent of the firm's stock. Trigano's announcement came the day after the Club reported a fall of 89 percent in net profit in the first half of the fiscal year, from 20.3 million to

2.15 million francs – the worst financial result in the Club's history. Club Med had also predicted losses for the close of the fiscal year, which would end on 31 October 1993.[41]

Serge Trigano inherited a business beset by both external and internal difficulties. Since the early 1990s Club Med had faced a tough economic climate. Recession, wars in the Persian Gulf and in Yugoslavia, combined with price wars among tour operators and the financial losses of the Minerve/Air Liberté charter airline troubles, all resulted in falling profits. Unstable political situations had required Club Med to close villages in Israel, Senegal, Turkey, Yugoslavia, and Egypt. Internally, only the American and Asian sectors were showing a profit, a situation that continued for the 1990s. The Club's aggressive program of growth and expansion had been expensive, and it faced a high level of fixed costs with lower revenues. The quality of the villages was uneven, with many needing renovation, which would require still more capital for a company burdened with high long-term debt. The Club's attempts to diversify its offerings, which had some success in attracting a more varied clientele, called for refocusing its image and its product.[42] Serge Trigano addressed the Club's problems by economizing and reducing costs and by emphasizing key aspects of the Club Med's core concepts rather than a strategy based on diversification. Over the next few years, Trigano reduced prices at selected villages (not at all villages), laid off 300 employees and cut operating costs. Club Med also sold several villages and put the construction of new villages in China and Vietnam on hold. At the same time, Club Med accelerated its program of renovating older villages, an expensive task involving 50 to 100 million francs per village. This strategy was meant to keep Club Med villages competitive and to attract corporate business to its villages with conference facilities.[43]

These measures failed to turn the tide. Europeans reeling from recession sought less expensive vacations, and Club Med's sales dropped every year except one from 1994 to 1997. This decline prompted Harvard Business School to use the firm as a case study illustrating "the death of a brand." The Club's choice to go up-scale and cultivate families had not been attracting younger GMs, and again the Club raised prices in response to lower revenues and high fixed costs. In February 1997, Serge Trigano announced a colossal loss of 743 million francs, more than double the 1993 deficit, instead of an expected profit. This was enough for Club Med's shareholders, and especially for its largest shareholder, the Agnelli family. The board of directors, many of whom had never fully accepted Gilbert Trigano's fait accompli of appointing his son in 1993, then ousted Serge Trigano on 21 February and appointed Philippe Bourguignon, head of Euro Disney, as chief executive effective 1 March 1997. The board also announced that it would close seven villages (six in Europe and one in North America), and recenter its offerings around two levels of villages: the low-cost Aquarius villages and the traditional Club Med villages. This would involve upgrading and renovating fifteen villages, and transferring four villages to Club Aquarius. It would also divest itself the Vienna "city club" as well its shares in the Italian group Valtur.[44]

The choice of Bourguignon, an executive from outside the Club, signaled a major transformation in management priorities and style. Serge Trigano was himself a product of the Club's history and its accumulated business culture, and for the board of directors this was precisely the problem. They counted on Bourguignon's experience with turning around the faltering Euro Disney, and his American-style commitment to "brand marketing" to rejuvenate Club Med's image and financial health.[45]

Bourguignon began by acknowledging the importance of Club Med's original concept: all-inclusive villages with a convivial, sporty, and festive ambiance animated by GOs. He traveled around the world to view Club Med's villages first hand. On his tour he saw aging facilities (peeling paint at Djerba, dark and dank rooms at Cancun) and poor management decisions (in Turkey the Club Aquarius villages were gaining GMs from the Club Med villages). In 1998 he started implementing a recovery plan: revamp the brand with an advertising campaign aimed at families and young couples; lower prices with off-season rates and more air-included packages; reduce overheads; and close unprofitable outdated villages and refurbish the rest. A new share issue, additional bond debt, and bank loans were to finance this plan. Shortly thereafter Europeans saw ads targeting young couples and smiling children, a far cry from Club Med advertising in the 1980s depicting a topless woman in a bikini. Bourguignon assembled a new management team after firing twenty-four of seventy middle managers and offering early retirement to around 100 employees at Club Med headquarters. Twenty-eight villages were refurbished and eight closed.[46]

Club Med slowly returned to profitability, with a net income of €59 million in 2000. Yet although profits had risen slightly in Europe, they languished in the Americas. Bourguignon then shifted from focusing on Club Med's core product to diversification and marketing the Club Med brand. As stated in the Club's *Annual Report, 2000,* the new "strategic vision" involved adopting "a brand-based strategy rather than a mass market strategy … We want to make Club Méditerranée a world leader in all leisure activities." In early 2001 Club Med launched its first "Oyyo" village to try and attract young people and to create a new concept under the Club Med brand. Located in Tunisia, it was geared toward eighteen- to thirty-year-olds. Prices were low, accommodation minimalist, and the focus was on round the clock music, dancing, and sports. Oyyo's advertising campaign claimed "If you sleep, you're dead." Bourguignon also attempted to associate the Club Med brand with broader lifestyle offerings, and expanded into urban leisure offerings (Club Med World), sports clubs (Club Med Gym), online bookings (Club Med OnLine), and Club Med branded products (including suntan lotion, luggage, and sportswear).[47]

These initiatives failed to find markets and profits. Bourguignon's troubles were compounded by the weak demand and fall in profits in the tourism sector following the terrorist attacks in the United States on 11 September 2001. Club Med's stock prices on the Paris Bourse oscillated between 30 and 38 euros in October, a sharp drop from 107.4 euros in February 2001, and Club Med began closing villages. By January 2002, seventeen villages in over a dozen countries had closed with six more to follow, and Bourguignon announced that Club Med had lost €70 million in its last exercise.[48] The financial situation did not improve in 2002. Stock prices fell 46 percent and the company reported a loss of €62 million for the year ending 31 October. Bourguignon's expansion program had been costly, and he failed to turn around the American sector. Philippe Bourguignon resigned on 16 December 2002. As *The Economist* put it, Club Med's largest shareholder, the Agnellis, "were no longer backing Mr. Bourguignon's expensive drive to transform Club Med into a diversified leisure group."[49] Henri Giscard d'Estaing, son of the former French president and managing director of Club Med under Bourguignon, succeeded him shortly thereafter.[50]

Conclusion

Club Med's concept in its early years was not entirely original, but it was certainly novel and it proved to be extraordinarily successful financially. Business historians have recognized that success is most likely when firms perceive the forces of change and embrace them. For most of its history, Club Med has done just that. In its early years, it profited from the desires of war-weary Europeans to leave their cares behind, relax, and bask in the warm sunshine along the Mediterranean shores. Gérard Blitz and Gilbert Trigano both understood the recuperative power of vacations in beautiful, scenic places with warm seas and plentiful sun. Club Med's all-inclusive vacation villages devoted to pleasure and easy-going sociability with abundant food and drinks, friendly GOs, and a relaxed egalitarian ambiance were a fresh and exciting concept with strong appeal. Even as the actual locations of its villages expanded beyond the Mediterranean, its name evoked the region's exquisite beauty, light, and blue skies to signify a special Club Med ambiance.

Club Med exemplified early "mass" tourism, with its low cost, broad social access, relative degree of standardization, and all-inclusive package format. Its growth from the 1950s through the 1980s was linked to rising incomes, paid vacations, economic growth and recovery, and the rise of mass consumption societies. When Christiane Peyre and Yves Raynouard called Club Med the "*prisunic* of vacations," they implicitly acknowledged Club Med's historical location within both early mass tourism and the growth of a consumer society.[51] For much of the twentieth century, Club Med was a distinctive product within a socially expansive market. Demand derived from widespread desires for relaxation and escape, and from the cultural construction of Mediterranean tourism as the epitome of sea, sun, sand (and sex) vacations. Its novelty came from the vision of its founders, its particular rituals, the GO/GM dynamic, and its accent on liberation from daily life and its constraints, social hierarchies, and conformist behavior.

But as consumer demand for its vacations accelerated, Club Med's finances were in disarray. From the 1960s, with Edmond Rothschild's help, Trigano turned Club Med into a profitable business committed to international growth and expansion. Trigano embodied crucial aspects of the ethos of Club Med's past and forged its commercial future. Blitz, who incarnated its early ethic of personal and social liberation and its non-commercial past, withdrew from active management by the end of the 1960s.[52]

Club Med's growth and expansion in the 1960s and 1970s was part of a new geography of tourist development that accompanied the growth of mass tourism. It realized and expressed changing consumer desires for more comfort, privacy, and individual choice. Club Med built more durable and comfortable villages first around the Mediterranean in Europe and North Africa, and then on other continents. The Club diversified its offerings as it expanded into ski resorts. Both of these initiatives anticipated its later shift into more upscale villages in international markets. More durable villages and winter ski options had the advantage of extending the Club's periods of revenue production. The changing demographic profile of GMs, and the growing internationalism of the villages, coupled with a wealthier clientele, meant that newer villages went even more upscale and offered more individual choices.

The Club's accelerating economic success required the modification of its organization to fit new markets and circumstances. Its clientele was becoming older, and GMs wanted more autonomy, comfort, and vacation options for families. Club Med responded by offering full-service luxury villages scattered across the globe, and diversified its offerings with apartments, city clubs, cruises, and "family villages." As profits and membership rose, Club Med appeared to have wide appeal as a stylish and affordable vacation option for the growing middle class.

Trigano brought quality to mass tourism, and for many years Club Med was financially successful. But from the late 1980s it was beset by troubles, both external and internal. Its image had become unfocused as it sought to adapt to changing consumer demand, growing competition, and the diversification of tastes and markets while at the same time maintaining selected elements of its core concept. Older regimes of mass tourism and mass consumption were eroding as new forms of tourism and vacations (which some analysts call "post-modern" or "post-Fordist") emphasized more individualism and flexibility and less standardization. In addition, the Club's rapid expansion had postponed much-needed refurbishments of older villages and caused major financial strains. Instabilities within the larger economic and political climate also had deleterious effects. Gilbert Trigano, and later his son Serge Trigano, were unable to stem the Club's downward financial spiral and to appeal to a new generation of consumers. As profits stagnated and later plummeted in the early 1990s, the shareholders brought in Philippe Bourguignon from Euro Disney, and later Henri Giscard d'Estaing.[53] It remains to be seen whether Club Med can again successfully perceive and embrace the forces of change in the twenty-first century as it once did so successfully.

Notes

1. Christiane Peyre and Yves Raynouard, *Histoire et Légendes du Club Méditerranée* (Paris: SEUIL, 1971), 28–33. One of Gérard Blitz's children initially suggested the name "Club Méditerranée." The scholarly treatment of tourism along the French Mediterranean is quite extensive. For examples in English, see E. Furlough, "Packaging Pleasures: Club Méditerranée and Consumer Culture in France, 1950–1968," *French Historical Studies* 18, no. 1 (Spring 1993): 65–81; E. Furlough and Rosemary Wakeman, "Composing a Landscape: Coastal Mass Tourism and Regional Development in the Languedoc, 1960s–1980s," *International Journal of Maritime History* 9, no. 1 (June 1997): 187–211; B. Gordon, "The Mediterranean as a Tourist Destination from Classical Antiquity to Club Med," *Mediterranean Studies* 12 (March 2004): 203–19; and R. Kanigel, *High Season: How One French Rivera Town Has Seduced Travelers for Two Thousand Years* (New York, 2004).
2. When Club Med's in-house newsletter, the *Trident*, first appeared in December 1950, its opening editorial summed up Club Med's early *ésprit:* "To depart, leave it all … not open a newspaper or listen to the radio, to say goodbye to the weight of convention, leave everything and become another person for two weeks … to finally live in the sun, by the sea, in the wind, and to laugh and sing, and fish and swim."
3. Peyre and Raynouard, *Histoire*, 49–83. Alain Faujas has observed that the key elements of "the principles and rites that distinguished the Club" came together between 1950 and 1955. Alain Faujas, *Trigano: L'aventure du Club Med* (Paris: Flammarion 1994), 53.
4. As such, elaborate rituals evolved in the early 1950s so that people would both symbolically and physically enter and leave its "closed" world. Henri Raymond,

"L'Utopie concrète: Recherches sur un village de vacances," *Revue française de sociologie* 1 (July–September 1960): 323–33.

5. Raymond, "L'Utopie concrète," 327; "Low-Cost High-Old-Time Holiday," *Life* (25 February 1966): 75–86; *Le Trident* (Summer 1969). Prior to 1957, when the first bar-beads were created, the Club used pre-purchased "tickets" to buy drinks at the bar.
6. Jean-François Held, "Le Bonheur en Confection–II: Des filles, du soleil, des garçons," *Le Nouvel Observateur,* 3 August 1966.
7. This discussion of Gérard Blitz is derived primarily from Gérard Blitz, *La Vacance* (Croissy-Beauborug: Dervy, 1990); Alain Ehrenberg, "Le Club Méditerranée, 1935–1960" in *Les Vacances*, ed. Brigitte Ouvry-Vial et al., *Autrement* (January 1990); Patrick Blednick, *Another Day in Paradise? The Real Club Med Story* (Toronto: Macmillan of Canada, 1988) and Faujas, *Trigano*.
8. Blitz, *La Vacance*, 39–40. Because of his Belgian nationality, Blitz was legally unable to found a French association, so Tony Hatot, a former French swimming champion, was officially listed as president.
9. Material on Gilbert Trigano largely derived from Faujas, *Trigano*; Ehrenberg, "Le Club Méditerranée"; Blednick, *Another Day in Paradise?* and "Les Cent Villages de M. Gilbert Trigano," *Le Nouvel Economiste* 53 (16 October 1978): 44–49.
10. Béatrice Gartenberg recalled her experience in Corfu in the mid-1950s as a "miracle … an earthly paradise." André Regad, who had been deported to Buchenwald during the war, felt his time at Club Med was "an adventure." Quoted in Ehrenberg, "Le Club Méditerranée," 124 and 127.
11. At the time of its listing on the Bourse, Club Med was operating twenty-nine vacation villages. Baron Rothschild's Paris-based *La Compagnie Financière*, held 34.13 percent of the company's stock. Blednick, *Another Day in Paradise?* 50.
12. New villages were listed each season in the *Trident*. By the late 1960s, it essentially served as a sales catalog. For example, the summer 1969 *Trident* (no. 100) had 186 pages and detailed descriptions of each of Club Med's twenty-eight villages. Gilbert Trigano provides useful statistics on GMs in his "Consommation de Loisir et Nouvelle Convivialité," *Temps Libre* 1 (1980): 73–80. See also Raymond, "L'Utopie concrète" and Alain Ehrenberg, "C'est au Club et nulle part ailleurs …," *Le Débat* 34 (March 1985): 130–45.
13. Laurence Olivier, "Le Club Méditerranée: De l'Utopie à l'Internationalisation, 1950–1990" (Maîtrise (Master Thesis), Université Paris I, 1992), 64.
14. Ehrenberg, "Le Club Méditerranée," 129 and Gilbert and Serge Trigano, *La Saga du Club* (Paris: Grasset, 1998), 149.
15. During the events of May 1968, protesters believed otherwise. They shattered the windows of Club Med's Paris headquarters, seeing the Club as the epitome of all they despised and rejected in consumer society – idle bronzed bodies in the midst of underdeveloped countries and a commitment to narcissistic hedonism. On 1968 at Club Med, see Peyre and Raynouard, *Histoire,* 223–33 and Faujas, *Trigano,* 118–26.
16. Blitz, *La Vacance,* 49–70; and Triganos, *Saga*, 144–45.
17. "Les Cent Villages," 44–49. Trigano was chosen by the readers of *Le Nouvel Economiste.*

18. "Does Club Med's Chief Have an Antidote for Unemployment?" *Business Week*, 14 January 1985, 45. See Faujas, "Évolution du chiffre d'affaires" from 1966/67 to 1991/92 in *Trigano*, 260.
19. Membership: 55,000 GMs in 1969/70; 700,900 in 1979/80; and 1,226,000 in 1989/90. Faujas, *Trigano*, 259–60 and "The World of Club Med, Inc.," *1989 Club Med Inc., Annual Report*, 2. The ninety-seven villages do not include the thirteen villas. France, with fifteen villages, had the largest number of villages of any country.
20. Triganos, *La Saga*, 161.
21. Gilbert Trigano, "Consommation de loisir et nouvelle convivialité," *Temps Libre* 1 (1980): 79.
22. The Club's connection with Air France began in 1954, when it contracted for the transportation of GMs to its Djerba village in Tunisia. Club Med and later formed Tourisme France International for foreign tourists traveling to villages in France. In the late 1970s, Trigano opened negotiations with two air charter companies, Aérotour and Air Florida, and Air France countered with more attractive rates. Peyre and Raynouard, *Histoire*, p. 82; Club Méditerranée, *Exercice 1972–73* (Paris, 1973); Faujas, *Trigano*, 163.
23. The Club Med/Nouvelles Frontières agreement was short-lived, only four months. See Faujas, *Trigano*, 222–223, for Jacques Maillot's version of events.
24. "Les Cent Villages," 44–49.
25. See, for example, the tax concessions listed on page 39 in *1989 Club Med, Inc. Annual Report*.
26. In the mid-1980s, members of the board of directors included Baron Edmond de Rothschild, Ghaith Pharaon, Gianluigi Gabetti, representing Giovanni Agnelli's IFINT, and representatives of the Berliner Handels und Frankfurter Bank, the Banque de Gestion Privée, Banque Paribas, the Union des Assurances de Paris, Crédit Lyonnais, and the Caisse des Dépôts et Consignations. Blednick, *Another Day in Paradise?* 4. The Agnelli's interest grew from 11.4 percent in the mid-1970s, to 19 percent in 1997 and 33 percent in 2003. Triganos *Saga*, 157; "Former Club Med Chief Executive to Testify in Suit against Boston-Based Firm," Boston Globe (28 January 2003); and "Club Med Seeks a New Cure" *Chief Executive* (March 2003).
27. On CET, see Faujas, *Trigano*, 139–45 and Triganos, *Saga*, 151–52. On Valtur, see Blednick, *Another Day in Paradise?* 81 and "The Economist Comments on Club Méditerranée of France, the Largest European Tour Operator," *The Economist* (13 July 1986).
28. Blednick, *Another Day in Paradise?* 4–5, and Triganos, *Saga*, 271–72.
29. Club Med, Inc. was legally a Cayman Islands corporation. (The Cayman Islands are a tax haven in the British West Indies.) By 1989, Club Med, Inc. operated twenty-five villages and seven villas.
30. Club Med saw only a modest 0.8 percent rise in earnings in 1985/86, and a near stagnation of profits for 1988/89. See "Comment," *The Economist* (13 July 1986) and Pascal Lietout, "Club Med would Welcome More Foreign Holders," *Reuters News* (10 February 1980).
31. Triganos, *Saga*, 148–49.
32. On new forms of tourism that have been called "post-Fordist," see John Urry, *Consuming Places* (London: Routledge, 1995).

33. In 1952 at Baratti, GMs could bring children over six years of age. The children were guarded by what were called *des hostesses speciales*. In 1957 Club Med opened its first "Junior Village." See "Une expérience passionnante: Notre premier village junior," *Le Trident* 50 (1957).
34. Judson Culbreth, "Club Med Magic," *Working Mother* (December 1991): 78–81.
35. Trigano, "Consommation de Loisir," 80; Blednick, *Another Day in Paradise?* 81 and 202–3; and *1989 Club Med Inc., Annual Report*, 20.
36. Jean-Noël Kapferer, "Le Club Med: Déclin vieillissement et revitalisation d'une marque," *Cahiers Espace* 59 (1998): 39.
37. Triganos, *Saga*, 304–5 and Tom Nash, "Club Med's Creative Family," *Director* (October 1992): 78–80.
38. Claude Soula, "Club Med: Le bonheur n'est plus ce qu'il était," *Le Nouvel Observateur Economie* (9–15 September 1993), 35–38.
39. See A. Poon, "All-Inclusive Resorts," *Travel and Tourism Analyst* 6 (1998): 62–77; and J.J. Issa and C. Jayewardene, "The 'All Inclusive' Concept in the Caribbean," *International Journal of Contemporary Hospitality Management* 15, no. 3 (2003): 167–71. The head of the Hyatt hotel group, Mr. Pritzker (described by Serge Trigano as a "faithful G. M.") copied Club Med's program for children under the name "Camp Hyatt." Triganos, *Saga*, 276.
40. Faujas, *Trigano*, "Évolution du chiffre d'affaires" 1966/67–1991/2," 260; and Richard Phalon, "Trouble in Paradise," *Forbes* (19 September 1988).
41. John Ridding, "Club Med Sails Close to the Red" (London) *Financial Times* (2 September 1993), 19; and three articles by Éric Lecort in *Le Figaro* (2 September 1993): "Club Med: Gilbert Trigano passe la main," 29; "Club Med: De l'abondance à la crise," 30; and "Né sous le signe du Trident," 30.
42. Nash, "Club Med's Creative Family," 80; and Lecort, "Club Med: de l'abondance à la crise," 30.
43. Serge Trigano, "Les conditions pour un second soufflé," *Espaces*, no. 140 (1996): 16–18; and Sharon Waxman, "Club Med Resorts to Tough Measures," *Washington Post* (6 January 1994), 10 (Financial Section).
44. Serge Trigano was appointed chairman of a new entity, the Supervisory Board (Conseil de surveillance), but he resigned shortly thereafter. Natacha Tatu, "Ne contez pas sur moi pour tuer le père," *Le Nouvel Observateur* (30 July–5 August 1998): 46–49; Philippe Chevilley, "Serge Trigano est constraint de passer la main au patron d'Euro Disney," *Les Echos* (24 February 1997), and "Le Club Med va entrer dans l'après Trigano," *La Tribune* (24 February 1997). In January 2003 Serge Trigano lost a \$70 million lawsuit against Boston-based Bain & Co. consulting firm. Trigano alleged that Bain's Paris-based director conspired with members of Club Med's board of directors, in particular the Agnelli group, to have him removed. He also accused them of ruining his reputation. See Christopher Rowland, "Lawsuit of Former Club Med Executive Dismissed," *Boston Globe* (7 February 2003).
45. Tatu, "Ne contez pas," 44 and 49. Tatu compared the "five favorite words" of Trigano and of Bourguignon, stating that Trigano favored "*Product:* the village, always the village, only the village" whereas Bourguignon preferred "*Brand*: or better yet *brand marketing* as the heart of his strategy." On tourism and the branding of

unique experiences, see Nancy F. Koehn, *Brand New: How Entrepreneurs Earned Consumers' Trust from Wedgwood to Dell* (Boston, MA: Harvard Business School Press, 2001).

46. Cecile Daurat, "Paradise Regained?" *Forbes* (22 March 1999): 102–4; and Patrick Frances, "Les habits neufs du Club Med" *Le Monde* (24 September 1998). Club Med also acquired Jet Tours, France's fourth-largest tour operator, in June 1999.
47. Club Méditerranée, *Annual Report, 2000*, 5; and Marc Coutty, "Au Club Med jeunes, Si tu dors, t'es mort," *Le Monde* (2 March 2001).
48. "Laure Belot, "Le Club Med ferme des villages," *Le Monde* (20 October 2001) and "Le Club Med en difficulté," *Le Monde* (9 January 2002).
49. Losses in the American sector, which had been Club Med's most profitable sector in the early 1990s, were €40 million. Arnaud Frerault of Société Générale Securities in Paris noted that Americans preferred Sandals, the all-inclusive Caribbean holiday chain that provides free drinks, unlike Club Med. "Club Méditerranée: Beached," *The Economist* (21 December 2002), 94. The London *Times* reported that the Agnellis held 23.8 percent of Club Med's shares and 32.9 percent of the voting rights in the Club at this time. Adam Sage, "Unlikely Heir Seeks Rebirth of Club Med," *Times* (12 December 2000), 24 (Business Section).
50. Henri Giscard d'Estaing was expected to focus on Club Med's core business of vacation villages. For a discussion of "HGE's" background and program for Club Med, see Mohammed Aissaoui, "Le nouveau visage du club med," *Le Figaro* (28 April 2003).
51. Peyre and Raynouard, *Histoire*, 263. Prisunic was, and is, a French chain of low-cost variety stores. For mass tourism and consumption, see E. Furlough, "Making Mass Vacations: Tourism and Consumer Culture in France, 1930s to 1970s," *Comparative Studies in Society and History* 40, no. 3 (April 1998): 247–86.
52. It is indicative of Gilbert Trigano's dual embrace of Club Med's avant-garde and non-conventional origins, and of its subsequent corporate and transnational character, that he dedicates his (and his son's) memoirs, *La Saga du Club*, to both Blitz and Rothschild: "*A Gérard. A Edmond.*"
53. In 2004, the large hotel group Accor acquired almost 30 percent (28.90 percent) of the firm's shares, replacing the Agnelli family as Club Med's largest shareholder.

Chapter 10

Tourism on the French Riviera

Philippe Mioche

Mass tourism has been one of the main economic successes of the French economy since World War II. An increasing number of French citizens were traveling within the country; and an increasing number of foreigners were coming to visit. Inside France, the Provençal region, which comprised six departments from 1972 on,[1] became the second most popular tourist destination after Paris. In Provence, a large proportion of mass tourism was concentrated on the French Riviera, a thin strip of territory of 250 kilometers long by 30 wide. The French Riviera, partly the old county of Nice, is mainly situated in two French departments, Var and Alpes Maritimes. Provence benefited from 7 million stays in the 1980s. In 1983, tourists spent 18 million nights in Provence.[2] This number has increased almost continuously over the past twenty years.

The impacts of mass tourism were numerous, including on employment, transport, the environment, and so on. Tourist operators and local politicians were confident faced with such success. This chapter measures the scope of the phenomenon; then goes on to explain and to analyze its impacts on local areas. The chapter addresses two main questions: Why was there such a sustainable success? Is it really a success? That is, more an inherited success than a dynamic development? I am not going to follow those who have described the French Riviera as the "California of Europe." I am wondering about the real economic success of mass tourism on the French Riviera and about a possible decline.

Notes for this chapter begin on page 203.

The Growth of Mass Tourism on the French Riviera

The starting point of French mass tourism on the French Riviera was the introduction of vacation legislation by the Popular Front in 1936, but the real increase came during the 1950s. The growth in national mass tourism was faster than the decrease in legal working hours in France (from forty hours per week in 1936 to forty-eight in 1938, and two weeks of vacation; 1956: three weeks of vacation; 1968: four weeks; 1981: five weeks and thirty-nine hours; 1999: thirty-five hours per week with variations among employment sectors).

The success of the French Riviera increasingly owed to foreigners. By the end of the twentieth century, France welcomed 60 million visitors annually; the numbers were even higher in some years, for example, nearly 70 million in 1998. These visitors were mostly Europeans – 90 percent came from eight countries: Germany, United Kingdom, Belgium, the Netherlands, Italy, Spain, Switzerland, and the United States. Some became the owners of second homes, and sometimes they became naturalized citizens.[3]

Beyond the success, we may ask where the future lies. The increase in foreign travelers to Provence may have been concealing a decrease in French visitors. Was one decrease to be followed by another?

For a long time many authors have proclaimed the end of mass tourism on the French Riviera: too much pollution ("En été, les corps des baigneurs se touchent sur les plages et les germes pathogènes pullulent" [In summer, the bathers' bodies touch one another on the beaches, and pathogenic germs are pullulating everywhere]),[4] too many fires,[5] not enough water, not enough land.

Tourism and Culture on the French Riviera: The Power of Presentation

The success of mass tourism on the French Riviera was supported by some obvious natural factors like landscape, climate (2,800 hours of sun per year on the coast) and the sea. The name "French Riviera" was coined by Stéphane Liégard in 1887. This was very important because it influenced the way the area was presented from one tourist guidebook to another.[6]

The history of tourism on the French Riviera is well known. For a long time Provence was just a stop-over on the way to Italy. The first tourists did not like this area where people did not speak good French and where the roads were too narrow.[7] Then some British tourists made Nice and French Riviera the "winter capital" (the slogan of R. de Souza in 1913). For instance, these included Smollett in Nice and Lord Bougham, who made the reputation of Cannes in 1834. Among the first visitors were also "medical tourists." "A Nice, le phtisique et le scrofuleux choisiront le bord de mer, le tuberculeux et l'asthmatique, le Vallon des Fleurs, tandis que les vieillards et les diabétiques éliront domicile dans les quartiers du Cimiez ou de Saint-Barthelemy" (At Nice, the phthisic and the scrofulous will choose the seashore, the consumptive and the asthmatic the Vallon des Fleurs, while the aged and the diabetic will choose to stay in the quarters of Cimiez or Saint-Barthelemy).[8]

Early twentieth-century painters like Matisse in Saint-Tropez, as well as authors like Stendhal, Mérimée, Nietzsche, or Hugo also played an important part in the history of the French Riviera. Moreover, famous tourists, including Scott and Zelda Fitzgerald, John Dos Passos, and Henry Miller, created the fashion of spending the "summer in the Mediterranean" during the 1920s. This history determined the future of mass tourism. When holidays were enforced by legislation in 1936, the administration asked for priority in the hotels on the French Riviera. It seemed natural that people wanted to spend their vacation time there.

The real success of mass tourism came later, during the 1950s and 1960s, when France and Western Europe became part of the mass consumption society. Some tourism managers consider this history as something that is permanent, even under present-day conditions, thinking that because it was like that in the past, it will always be like this. They are betting on an increase in tourism. I quote one of them: "World arrivals in 2000: 660 million; 2010: 937 million. In 35 years, tourists will be multiplied by 10; the income from tourism will be multiplied by 30." The wishful thinking is that for Provence, the future is great: "new records in tourism!"[9]

Sometimes, the mode of presentation seems to be very active. Let us quote the example of the Cannes Festival. It was founded against the background of the success of the Venice Festival created during the Mussolini era in 1932. The French, British, and Americans wanted to organize a competing festival in 1939, but it did not take off until September 1946. It is not the purpose of this chapter to discuss cinema as art or propose an artistic assessment; nor is it the place to speak about the exceptional nature of French culture. Nevertheless, it seems appropriate to note that at present the Cannes Festival is still a part of a dream for the French and the Europeans. It became a dream for a lot of people to go to the French Riviera and be like the stars. Some presentations have recently made a "comeback." This is the case with "la petite Russie" in Nice. This area was frequented by anti-Soviet Russians after the October Revolution and became a popular vacationing spot for the nouveau riche Russians since the downfall of communism.

Some people have tried to explore relatively new paths for mass tourism on the French Riviera. Here are some of the proposed expansions. Cruises looked like a new "frontier" for upper- or even middle-class tourism. This is interesting in terms of territory management, because Marseilles tried to welcome cruise tourism as the main port on the North Mediterranean coast. This might mean a "western expansion" of tourism on the French Riviera. Conferences are a challenge. The town of Nice has clearly organized a policy favoring conferences. In the competition between main Provençal towns, Marseilles and Nice, the latter appears to have been the winner in this respect. A new approach to tourist consumption was illustrated by the *Guide du routard*, published in 1979. This sort of guide was connected with new cultural products like contemporary music festivals. But when one considers the most frequented places, we might conclude that mass tourism was popular and not really oriented toward new forms of tourism (see table 10.1). The table gives some indication of the more frequented places on the French Riviera. Places linked with the representation of sea accounted for 45 percent of these visitors (the success of Marineland in Antibes owed to the famous dolphins).

One very important challenge is to remove the concentration of mass tourism from the coastal area. This includes numerous "green tourism" projects for people visiting rural landscapes behind the coast. I would like to stress the weakness of industrial tourism on the French Riviera and in Provence in general. This region was a land of industry: shipbuilding, perfumes, soaps, chemicals, coal mining, and so on. Many of these industries have disappeared, except

Table 10.1 Most frequented places on the French Riviera, 2000 (in thousands)

Parc Marineland, Antibes (06)	1,400,000
Verrerie, Biot (06)	732,000
Musée océanographique, Monaco	719,289
Jardin exotique, Monaco	258,264
Fondation Maeght, Saint Paul de Vence (06)	235,640
Eglise Russe, Nice (06)	227,500
Parc Aquatica, Fréjus (83)	204,000
Musée Chagall, Nice (06)	191,354
Musée Matisse, Nice (06)	174,964
Petit train express, Monaco	168,379
Jardin exotique, Eze (06)	155,319
Musée Picasso, Antibes (06)	153,429
Fondation Ephrusi de Rothschild, Saint Jean Cap Ferrat (06)	142,120
Musée d'art moderne et contemporain de Nice (06)	131,443
Parc Phoenix, Nice (06)	131,167
Hippodrome Cagnes du mer (06)	131,144

Note: Only places frequented by more than 100,000 people with tickets in the two departments of the French Riviera were selected.

Source: Office National du Tourisme, *Les sites touristiques en France métropolitaine. Fréquentations, 1994–2000*, May 2002.

for chemicals. Politicians and local government tried to claim that the future of the region was founded on tourism and agricultural success, and forgot the industrial past. More recently, some have tried to develop industrial heritage and industrial tourism. Let us consider two examples.

In Lalonde les Maures, near Hyères, on the coast in the Western part of the French Riviera – one of the most expensive real estate areas in France – there is a metallurgical factory built by the French firm Schneider in 1917. This plant produced bombs and was owned by the French Army. The Army is selling it and there is competition between tourism managers who are thinking about new marinas and people who are trying to develop industrial heritage activities. Even more interesting is the case of the bauxite mines. Provence and the Var department were the main producers of bauxite in the world before World War I. The mines have been closed since 1993. The town of Tourves is preparing a bauxite mine museum. It is a very interesting way to diversify tourism on the French Riviera.

These paths have not really been explored. To quote an official document by the European Commission about regional policy: "Tourism plays a main part in development. Housing accommodation in hotels, camps, and homes, is very important. The region welcomes 27 million tourists annually and tourism is the major economic activity. But potential activities have not been exploited in a rational way and the main flow of tourists is still going to the coast."[10] Agricultural life has disappeared as competition for water and for real estate has increased.

Tourism and Territory

Over time Provence has experienced an increase in population: 1.5 million in 1850, 2.5 million in 1950, 3 million in 1960, 4 million in 1980, and 4.5 million in 1999. This growth was double the national average because of international migration, the independence of Algeria, and tourism. Demographic growth does not depend on tourism in the Bouches du Rhône department. With regard to tourism, we are only going to consider Alpes-Maritimes and Var, where population growth was definitely the result of mass tourism.

Nice was the capital of the French Riviera with around 340,000 habitants in 1990, but 520,000 including surrounding urban areas. In 1913, there were 140,000 habitants in Nice with 150,000 tourists in the winter. Since World War II, most tourists came in the summer: 310,000 in 1939; 600,000 in 1956. Mass tourism meant seasonal tourism, probably more in France than other countries because of the concentration of vacations in July and August. According to a geography book, "la Côte d'Azur passe brutalement d'une nonchalance inquiètante à une agitation forcénée" (The Côte d'Azur moves brutally from disquieting nonchalance to frantic activity).[11]

It is important to consider the age structure of this population. Those over sixty accounted for 24.1 percent in 1999, compared with 20.4 percent nationally. At 27.6 percent, the department of Alpes-Maritimes had the most elderly people in France (26.6 percent in Var). The number of people over seventy-five increased in the region from 8.4 percent in 1990 to 9.2 percent in 1999. Forecasts for 2020 are as follows: if the population increase is 25 percent, the increase in elderly people will be 85 percent. That means 535,000 people over the age of seventy-five and 1,500,000 over the age of sixty.

Retirement to the French Riviera has become a major phenomenon. The average age is higher than in France as a whole. There were 16.2 percent over sixty-five-year-olds in 1982 compared with 12.8 percent in France generally. They come for quality of life, sun, and air, and because of the organization of medical facilities. The region had 385 doctors for 100,000 habitants in 1995. There are many conflicts between retirement and mass tourism.

A very interesting field for the economic history of tourism is the history of electricity. I touch on it briefly in this chapter because there has not been much research done on this topic and because when mass tourism emerged as a phenomenon after 1950, a great deal was done in connection with electrification.[12] The company Énergie Électrique du Littoral Méditerranéen (EELM) was created in 1900 by Compagnie Française Thomson Houston (52 percent of shares), the bank Société Marseillaise de Crédit (20 percent), Grands Travaux de Marseille (10 percent), and Omnium Lyonnais (8 percent). The chairman from 1900 to 1911 was Augustin Féraud, president of the Société Marseillaise de Crédit and president of the Marseilles Chamber of Commerce. The second chairman was Charles Burrell of Thomson Houston, the third was Gabriel Cordier (from 1915 to 1934), who was also a senior manager in the French aluminum industry.

EELM founded Sud Electrique for distribution in 1905. In 1924, EELM owned eleven hydroelectric plants and six steam plants producing 150,000 kWh. This power increased to 200,000 kWh in 1939. It was partially interconnected in 1932 and with the national network in 1936. Then the firm was nationalized in 1946. The initial project was clearly linked with the development of tourism on the French Riviera, especially in Nice. The idea was to light the towns of the French Riviera for upper class tourists. This small firm had great success and became a regional monopoly in production and distribution. Initially intended for tourism, this firm developed other strategies for industry and regional control.

In 2000, the transport used to access the French Riviera was as follows: 78 percent by car; 12 percent by train; 9 percent by air; 1 percent by boat. Here is the classic dialectic between supply and demand. It is clear that railways created some capacity for tourists; it is not so evident that tourism supported transport. The chronology of railway development was as follows: the railway came to Marseille in 1849 and to Nice in 1864. The company Paris Lyon Méditerranée obtained a second track to the East, from Gardanne to Var in 1881.[13] This was for military reasons: to move away from the seaside in the case of an Italian attack. This railroad was not used for war, but it was useful for transporting bauxite from the bauxite mines in Var to aluminum plants in Marseilles and its region.[14]

When the national company (SNCF) was setting up the high-speed train (TGV) in 1966–67, it did not pay a lot of attention to tourism.[15] After a lot of discussion, it seems that the high-speed track from Marseilles to Italy by Nice has been abandoned. The future track is intended go from Lyon to Milan, crossing the Alps. In fact, in 2003 the high-speed train took three hours from Paris to Marseilles, but will need three hours more to reach Nice. The main motorway from Paris to Marseilles was completed in 1970 and from Marseilles to Nice in 1979. France was late in developing motorways and the demand for mass tourism did not seem to accelerate this process. This situation contributed to the success of Nice airport, which became the second largest in France with 6 million passengers in 1993.

In 2002, Provence had 2,214 hotels (68,400 rooms), 715 camps (96,000 spaces), and 3,660 homes. The Var department contained half of the total camping spaces. The Alpes Maritimes department was more specialized in luxury hotels. The most significant figure is probably that for second homes: 415,000 in 2002 (125,000 only for the department of Alpes Maritimes). In 1979, there were 214,395 second homes, which meant 723,876 rooms.[16] Between 1968 and 1975, second home occupation increased from 49,000 to 83,000 in Alpes Maritimes; from 38,300 to 64,000 in Var. That was the second home boom, with of course a lot of consequences for the regional economy.

Incomes from tourism were estimated at about €5 billion per year in the 1990s. Half of this income came in the summer months. Spending by foreigners represented 25 percent of the total. There were 47,000 full-time jobs, and 70,000 summer-time jobs. With indirect employment the total estimate was 150,000, that is, 10 percent of regional employment, much more on the French Riviera.

Except for the research park of Sophia Antipolis, which was a success (2,000 direct jobs and 4,000 indirect) and some high tech firms (IBM, Texas Instruments) as well as some chemical industries like the new perfume industries around Grasse,[17] there was not a lot of employment diversification. Some people have talked about a dialectic between tourism and new activities. The author of this chapter believes it to be a myth of the "sun belt." Firms are not coming to Provence because of the sunshine. In fact there has been a great deal of competition between tourism and regional development: for water, for real estate. This dialectic is negative. The French Riviera is almost a one-activity area.

Table 10.2 Employment in the tourism sector in Provence, 1980 and 1990

	1980	1990
Restaurants	11,578	21,929
Bars	4,670	4,802
Hotels with restaurants	11,955	13,840
Hotels without restaurants	2,938	3,755
Various homes	3,885	3,741
Camps	1,448	1,373
Travel agencies	1,171	1,871
Thermalism and Thallaso	2,109	1,590
Tourism offices	479	860

Source: "Les emplois dans le tourisme, analyse régionale," *Analyses et perspectives du tourisme*, no. 33, 1992.

Conclusion

Mass tourism has reached its limits on the French Riviera. The coast was saturated; landscapes were destroyed as real estate prices continued to rise. The only path for growth is to organize new destinations in France and Europe, to promote new forms of tourism like "green tourism" or industrial tourism.

The French Riviera as the California of Europe is a myth and, what is worse, an error. In California, the melting pot and the youth of the population carried cultural and economic growth. In the French Riviera, the major demographic fact is the elderly. In real estate, the major fact is the growth of second home ownership. The elderly and second homes have generated a conservative culture that is far removed from San Francisco.

Tourist managers on the French Riviera have lived as if they were on a pension, on heritage, on purchased benefits. They believe in an unchanging situation. No historian believes in unchanging situations.

Notes

1. Corsica was constituted later as a separate region. The regional administration acquired new powers in 1982.
2. *Guide bleu Provence Alpes Côte d'Azur* (Paris: Hachette, 1985), 120.
3. Rachel Naud, *Les flux migratoires intra communautaires dans la région Provence Alpes Côte d'Azur des années 1959 à nos jours*. PhD diss., L'Université de Provence, Aix Marseille I, 1992, 161.

4. Roger Livet, *Atlas et géographie de Provence Côte d'Azur et Corse* (Paris: Flammarion, 1978), 161.
5. Links between fires and mass tourism are probably indirect, from competition for land and excessive visiting.
6. Bernard Toulier "L'influence des guides touristiques dans la représentation et la construction de l'espace balnéaire (1850–1950)," CNRS, UMR 22, 2002.
7. Marc Boyer, *Histoire de l'invention du tourisme, XVIe–XIXe siècles* (La Tour d'Aigues: Editions de l'Aube, 2000), 14ff.
8. Quoted in Toulier, "L'influence des guides touristiques dans la représentation et la construction de l'espace balnéaire (1850–1950)."
9. Françoise Martial and Xavier Monchois, on line INSEE regions, 23 April 2002, http://www.insee.fr/fr/themes/document.asp?ref_id=8408.
10. European Commission, DOCUP PACA, 2000–006.
11. Livet, *Atlas et géographie de Provence Côte d'Azur et Corse,* 152.
12. For more information on electricity, see Anonymous, *Alcatel Alsthom. Histoire de la Compagnie Générale d'Électricité* (Paris: Larousse, 1992); Dominique Barjot, "Le rôle des compagnies d'électricité dans l'industrialisation de la Provence: L'exemple de l'*Énergie Électrique du Littoral Méditerranéen* (1900–1946)," in *Histoire industrielle de la Provence*, ed. G. Chastagnaret and Ph. Mioche (Aix-en-Provence: Publications de l'Université de Provence, 1998), 194–216; François Caron and Fabienne Cardot, *Histoire de l'électricité en France,* tome premier 1881–1918 (Paris: Fayard, 1991); Henri Carvin, Gérard Chastagnaret, and Michel Lescure, "Les débuts de l'électricité à Marseille (1882–1906)," in *L'Électricité il y a cent ans,* ed. Jean Cazenove (Paris: Editions de l'Ecole des hautes études en sciences sociales, 1989), 139–50; Olivier Lambert, *Marseille entre tradition et modernité. Les espérances déçues (1919–1939), Histoire du commerce et de l'industrie de Marseille, XIXe–XXe siècles*, vol. X (Marseille: Chambre de Commerce et d'Industrie Marseille Provence, 1995); Maurice Lévy-Leboyer and Henri Morsel, eds., *Histoire de l'électricité en France*, vol. 2: *1919–1946* (Paris: Fayard, 1994); Philippe Mioche, "EELM: succès ou boulet pour l'économie régionale?" in XIIe colloque de l'AHEF, Paris les 3, 4, 5 February 1999; "Stratégies, gestion, management: Les compagnies électriques et leurs patrons 1895–1945," actes du/12e colloque de l'Association pour l'histoire de l'électricité en France les 3, 4 et 5 février 1999; sous la direction de Dominique Barjot, Henri Morsel et Sophie Coeuré; S. Mons and M.A. Pipito, *La société d'énergie électrique du littoral méditerranéen (EELM)* (Maîtrise, Université de Montpellier III, 1986); Henri Morsel, "L'hydroélectricité en France (1902–1946)," in *Le capitalisme français 19e–20e siècle. Blocages et dynamismes d'une croissance,* ed. Patrick Fridenson with André Strauss (Paris: Fayard, 1987), 382ff.
13. Olivier Bonniot, *La ligne de chemin de fer de Gardanne à Carnoules*, Mémoire de maîtrise (Paris: Université de Paris I), 1982.
14. Philippe Mioche, *L'alumine à Gardanne de 1893 à nos jours. Une traversée industrielle en Provence* (Grenoble: Presses Universitaires de Grenoble, 1994), 179.
15. Jean-Michel Fourniau, "Des grandes vitesses au TGV. Les transformations de la politique commerciale de la SNCF," in *Les chemins de fer l'Espace et la Société en*

France, Association pour l'Histoire des Chemins de fer en France, Actes du colloque mai 1988 (Paris: A.H.I.C.F., 1989), 339–57.

16. Philippe Langevin, *L'économie provençal: I – Les structures économiques* (Aix-en-Provence: Edisud, 1981).
17. Philippe Mioche and Xavier Daumalin, *Provence, terre de chimie. Cent ans de l'Union des Industries Chimiques en région Provence-Alpes-Côte d'Azur* (Marseille: UIC, 2002).

Chapter 11

Tourism on the Costa del Sol

Carmelo Pellejero Martínez

The aim of this chapter is to analyze the historical evolution of tourism on the Costa del Sol, on the Southern coast of Spain, since its origins at the end of the nineteenth century until the present day. There are several different opinions regarding the extent of the Costa del Sol. Initially, the Costa del Sol was the stretch of coastline between Torremolinos and Estepona, both towns in the province of Málaga. Later, but then its boundaries were extended. The Costa del Sol then included the entire coastline from Tarifa in Cádiz to Almería. However, as time went on, the Costa del Sol was gradually identified with the coastline of the province of Málaga, including the capital city. For the purposes of this chapter and to make the best use of the available statistics, the entity Costa del Sol includes the entire province of Málaga, both inland and coastal municipalities.

The choice of the province of Málaga as the geographical boundaries of this study is based on the following reasons. First, because this area located on the southern Mediterranean coast of Spain is a world-class tourist destination. And this distinction is recognized both in and outside of Spain. In my opinion, the following information from 2000 strongly endorses this statement: That year Málaga received eight million visitors, 59 percent of whom were foreigners. In addition to that, 3.3 million visitors stayed in hotels in Málaga. There were also 15 million overnight stays registered in those hotels, 70 percent of which were by foreign visitors. All this made Málaga the fifth most popular destination in Spain according to the number of travelers, staying at hotel accommodations; and the fourth destination according to overnight stays.

Notes for this chapter begin on page 231.

Málaga's shares of the national total were 5.5 and 6.6 percent, respectively. The Costa del Sol also stands out because of its wide offering of lodging facilities: approximately 820 establishments and 112,000 beds in its hotels, hostels, apartments, and campsites.

The second reason is the remarkable transformation underwent by the local economic structure due to the development of the tourism industry. It is a fact that today, or even during the last few decades, tourism is the main economic engine of the province. At the end of 2000, the tourism industry employed more than 60,000 people and its gross value added (GVA) in Málaga represented, including both direct and induced earnings, over 26 percent of the total gross domestic product (GDP). However, this was not always the case. Just half a century ago, Málaga had an economy based on agriculture. The primary sector employed 57 percent of the population and generated 24 percent of the GVA. Yet, at the beginning of the twenty-first century, these indicators represent 8 and 5 percent, respectively. Thus, it goes without saying that the transformation seen in the economy of Málaga during the second half of the twentieth century was rapid and radical. And tourism played an underlying role in this transformation.

Historical Background of Tourism in Málaga, 1880–1950

1880 to 1900

Málaga was a pioneer in Spain in the development of the tourism industry. During the last two decades of the nineteenth century, many citizens and some local associations envisaged tourism as a possible alternative to the economic crisis suffered by the province at the time. After being a rather prosperous business and industrial center with prospects of economic modernization, Málaga suffered a sharp recession during the last two decades of the nineteenth century. The steel industry was ruined, the textile industry and trading weakened, and the agricultural sector suffered a strong depression that affected stock farming and the main crops. Emigration became the only choice for most of the disadvantaged population.[1]

Málaga needed to boost its economy and many thought that tourism could be the best way to achieve this goal. Some prominent members of the community in Málaga were familiar with the fact that some French and Italian cities had been embellished, had seen their population increase, and had experienced the increased number of foreigners visiting due to their benign climate. Knowing that Málaga also offered a wonderful climate, they deemed that taking advantage of the natural wealth and turning the city into a winter resort could attract tourists, thus bringing profits. They figured that this could be the way to boost their wretched economy.[2]

All advocates of turning Málaga into a resort for tourists agreed that the most important asset of the province, or in other words, its main tourist attraction, was its climate. To this effect, they made an effort to promote the excellence of the climate in Málaga through studies, reports, and publications: around 320 sunny days per year, almost 3,000 hours of sun, and an average annual temperature of 18.7 degrees Celsius (an average of 13.8 degrees in the winter, and 24.4 degrees in the summer).

They also agreed that it did not suffice to broadcast the climate of Málaga. For Málaga to become a world-class tourist resort it was fundamental to improve dramatically the inadequate existing infrastructure. Urgent action was needed to facilitate access and stays in Málaga. In 1897, the Sociedad Propagandística del Clima y Embellecimiento de Málaga (Society for the promotion of the climate and embellishment of Málaga) was founded with the purpose of incorporating within a single project several initiatives and to try to manage in a rational and planned manner the exploitation of the tourism industry. Its main aim was to promote the climate, the urban surroundings and public hygiene, as well as cultural activities and festivities. Despite the difficult economic situation of the province and the lack of necessary and requested official support, the Society worked enthusiastically on their exciting project from the day of its foundation. This project aimed to provide Málaga not only with a reasonable exit to the end-of-the-century recession, but also with a solid economic alternative for the future through its tourist development.[3]

1900 to 1936

During the first decades of the twentieth century, and especially during the 1920s, Málaga became gradually more attractive to visitors. Although at the beginning of the century Málaga was marketed primarily as a winter resort, the city, and then many seaside towns, also became known for their appealing beaches. The Costa del Sol was also known as a summer destination. Málaga developed other worthwhile attractions for visitors, such as the Feria de Agosto (August Fair) and Semana Santa (Easter Week), which increased the complementary leisure offer. With this same aim, the Bathing Resort of Our Lady of Carmen was launched in 1918, which expanded the existing offer of the Bathing Resorts of La Estrella and Apolo. In addition to this, in 1928 the Golf Course of Torremolinos opened to the public.[4]

This increase in supply capacity, together with certain improvements in surface transportation and a significant one in air transportation, the opening of the first airport in Spain, contributed to raise the number of visitors. For instance, 1929 was a special year from the tourism industry's point of view due to the Ibero-American Exhibition in Seville and the International Exhibition in Barcelona. During that year Málaga received 12,313 visitors, which made it the fifth province in Spain according to the number of visitors after Barcelona, Madrid, Seville, and Granada, which received 82,462, 30,286, 18,022, and 14,411 visitors, respectively.[5]

The increase in demand was accompanied by qualitative and quantitative improvements in the hotel supply capacity of Málaga. The actual amount of accommodation available at any given moment during the first third of the twentieth century is unknown. However, we do know about the opening of a number of hotels during this period thanks to the publication of guidebooks. The capital city benefited the most in this sense. In 1930, the main twenty hotels in Málaga offered 1,505 beds in 1,051 rooms. Among the main hotels highlighted in this chapter are the Príncipe de Asturias, Caleta Palace, Regina, Reina Victoria, and Niza. In the rest of the province, especially on the coast, the number of hotel accommodations increased, being the most significant ones the Reina Victoria in Ronda, Colón in Antequera, Gaytán and Comercial in Marbella, and the Castillo de Santa Clara (Santa Clara Castle) and Parador de Montemar in Torremolinos.[6]

But hotels in Málaga not only improved in quantity but also attained a higher quality. During the first third of the twentieth century, the number of businesses concerned with supplying more and better services to their customers increased. These services included telephone access, electricity, bathrooms, reading lounges, garages, interpreting services, heating systems, and transportation to and from the station or port and the hotel.

1939 to 1950

The outbreak of the Spanish Civil War in 1936 brought a sharp decline to the tourism industry. Logically, the arrival of foreign visitors and the tourist activities of Spaniards came to a halt until the end of the war. Actually, there were virtually no tourists until the end of the 1940s. World War II and the consequent impoverishment of most European nations seriously affected the tourism industry worldwide. In addition, Spain in the 1940s was a poor country where food and fuel were rationed. The country was internationally isolated by the United Nations between 1946 and 1951, thus making it one of the least popular destinations for vacation. Finally, the recovery of tourism started in 1950, when economic improvements, together with transportation improvements, in most Western nations as a result of the Marshall Plan, allowed a growing number of citizens to take a leisure journey.

Naturally, tourists traveling to Málaga also declined during the Civil War and the post-war era. Overall, it must be pointed out that during this unfavorable period, both public and private sectors continued developing the tourism industry in Málaga. As an example we can find the opening of the hotels La Roca in Torremolinos and El Rodeo in Marbella, as well as two establishments on the state network: the Hostel on the Carretera de Antequera and the Gibralfaro Inn, located in Málaga, opened to the public in 1940, 1946, 1940, and 1948, respectively.

Growth and Consolidation of Tourism on the Costa del Sol: 1951–2000

As it occurred on the national level, and especially on the Mediterranean coast and on the two archipelagos of Spain, during the second half of the twentieth century the tourism industry on the Costa del Sol experienced an important boost and consolidation, both in terms of demand and supply. However, two separate periods can be identified during this long-term flourishing era. During the first period, from 1950 to 1975, the growth on the Costa del Sol was steady and very high. On the contrary, during the second period, which lasted until the end of the century, the growth was cyclical and rather moderate.[7]

This chapter provides a detailed analysis of this process, taking into account the constraints imposed by the official statistics available. For studying the evolution of the tourist demand, I have used statistics that show the number of visitors lodged in hotel establishments and the number of overnight stays registered. Note that by using this source of information, the travelers who do not stay in those establishments are ignored. However, the statistics used are the only information available over a long period of time, breaking information down by provinces. All of this is essential for the analysis of the Costa del Sol. In regards to the number of hotels available, this analysis is focused on the evolution of the number of registered tourist lodgings and the number of beds available. This chapter first analyzes the actual number of hotel establishments, which comprises both hotels and hostels. It then analyzes other establishments such as apartments and campsites.[8]

Evolution of the Demand

1950 to 1975. During the period analyzed, the number of visitors lodged in hotel establishments on the Costa del Sol increased by 513 percent, and the number of overnight stays by 447 percent. A slightly greater growth rate took place at the national level, where the cited indicators increased by 439 percent and 362 percent, respectively. However, within this same trend of growth some cyclical movements took place, both in Spain and on the Costa del Sol.

The growth was steady on the Costa del Sol until 1975. It had been steady at least since 1966, the first year for which data are available. In less than a decade, the number of visitors increased by 189 percent and the number of overnight stays increased by 138 percent. This spectacular rise of demand was highly influenced by the economic prosperity enjoyed in North America and most of Europe, the popularity of paid vacations, the increase of free time, low airfares, the increase of charter flights and, of course, the sun and beaches of the Costa del Sol. From 1966 to 1973, foreign customers, who represented between 64 and 74 percent of the total visitors, increased to 123 percent. Meanwhile, national customers represented just over 66 percent. Moreover, in 1974 and 1975 the scenario proved very different. As a result of the crisis caused by the increase on the price of raw materials, mainly fuel, recession period set in as well as a rise of unemployment in the Western economies. Thus, the number of foreign visitors lodged increased only by 18 percent and the number of overnight stays decreased by 7 percent. This loss of foreign market was replaced by national clientele. Tour

Figure 11.1 Number of travelers lodged in hotel establishments in Málaga (in thousands)

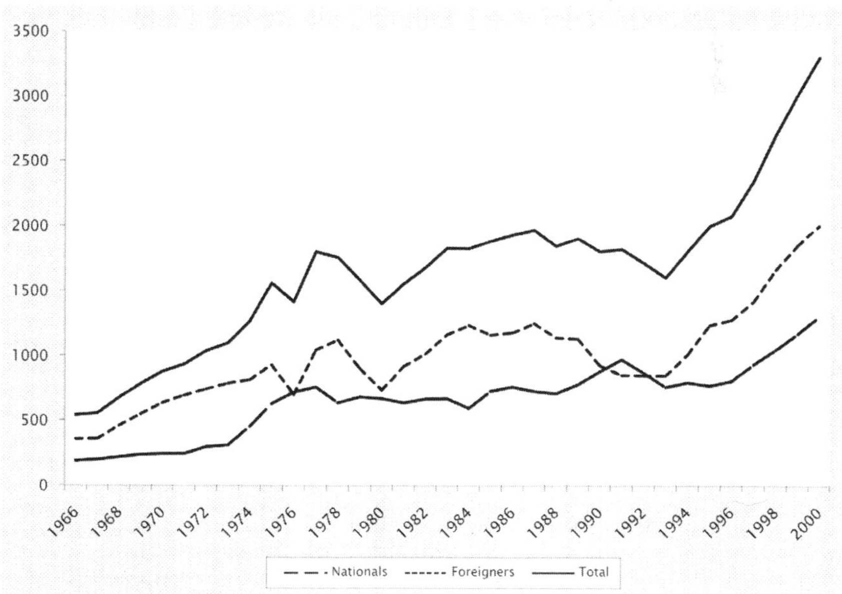

Sources: IEA (1991–99), INE (1965–70), INE (1971–72), INE (1973), INE (1974–77), INE (1978–90), SAETA (1996–2002), and SOPDE (1999–2001).

Figure 11.2 Number of overnight stays of travelers lodged in hotel establishments in Málaga (in thousands)

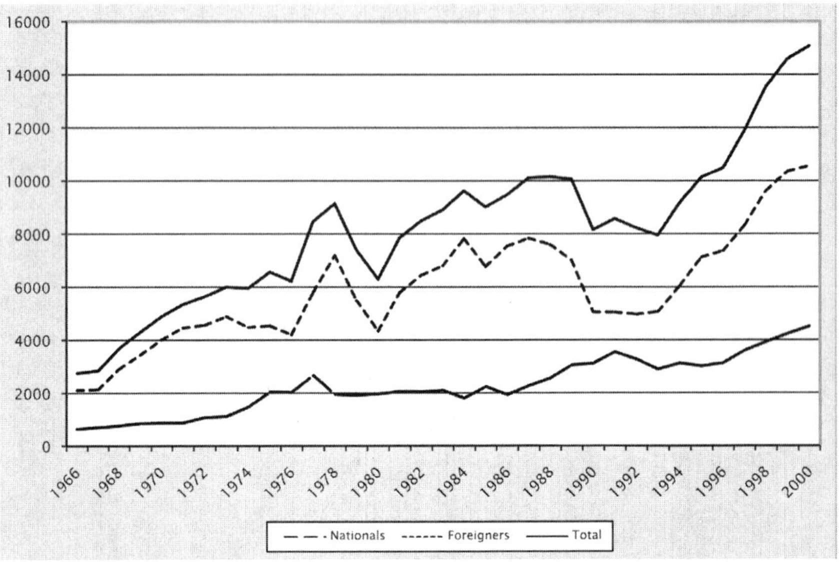

Sources: IEA (1991–99), INE (1965–70), INE (1971–72), INE (1973), INE (1974–77), INE (1978–90), SAETA (1996–2002), and SOPDE (1999–2001).

Table 11.1 Number of travelers lodged in hotel establishments (in thousands)

Year	MÁLAGA Nationals	%	Foreigners	%	Total (A)	SPAIN Total (B)	A/B %
1966	186	34.6	352	65.4	538	11,002	4.9
1970	241	27.6	633	72.4	874	15,472	5.6
1975	628	40.4	927	59.6	1,555	25,740	6.0
1976	715	50.6	697	49.4	1,412	24,193	5.8
1977	755	42.0	1,042	58.0	1,797	27,543	6.5
1980	666	47.7	731	52.3	1,397	23,078	6.0
1987	721	36.7	1,243	63.3	1,964	31,752	6.2
1990	876	48.7	922	51.3	1,798	33,237	5.4
1991	968	53.3	848	46.7	1,816	33,447	5.4
1993	754	47.2	844	52.8	1,598	32,052	5.0
1996	801	38.6	1,272	61.4	2,073	38,731	5.3
2000	1,299	39.4	2,000	60.6	3,299	59,283	5.5

Sources: AECIT (1995–2001), IEA (1991–99), INE (1965–70), INE (1971–72), INE (1973), INE (1974–77), INE (1978–90), SAETA (1996–2002), and SOPDE (1999–2001).

Table 11.2 Number of overnight stays in hotel establishments (in thousands)

Year	Nationals	%	MÁLAGA Foreigners	%	Total (A)	SPAIN Total (B)	A/B %
1966	644	23.4	2,112	76.6	2,756	49,147	5.6
1970	875	17.9	4,015	82.1	4,890	80,211	6.1
1975	2,037	31.0	4,532	69.0	6,569	103,171	6.4
1976	2,025	32.5	4,199	67.5	6,224	99,015	6.3
1977	2,667	31.5	5,799	68.5	8,466	118,602	7.1
1980	1,968	31.2	4,332	68.8	6,300	96,438	6.5
1987	2,272	22.5	7,836	77.5	10,108	138,721	7.3
1990	3,114	38.2	5,043	61.8	8,157	119,879	6.8
1991	3,539	41.3	5,036	58.7	8,575	134,499	6.4
1993	2,890	36.3	5,059	63.7	7,949	138,103	5.7
1996	3,129	29.8	7,365	70.2	10,494	158,259	6.6
2000	4,504	29.8	10,570	70.1	15,074	227,144	6.6

Sources: AECIT (1995–2001), IEA (1991–99), INE (1965–70), INE (1971–72), INE (1973), INE (1974–77), INE (1978–90), SAETA (1996–2002), and SOPDE (1999–2001).

Table 11.3 Main nationalities of foreign travelers lodged in hotel establishments in Málaga (average % for each period)

Travelers	Germany	Benelux	France	Great Britain	US/Canada
1966–1970	9.3	6.3	9.8	11.9	13.6
1971–1975	10.7	6.6	6.1	12.4	17.6
1976–1980	7.4	7.6	7.3	12.5	8.7
1981–1985	5.9	6.0	8.0	20.1	8.8
1986–1990	5.9	4.4	7.5	19.8	5.5
1991–1995	5.6	4.8	7.9	14.6	3.8
1996–2000	8.8	5.5	6.1	17.6	4.2

Overnight Stays	Germany	Benelux	France	Great Britain	US/Canada
1966–1970	17.9	10.0	6.8	13.9	13.3
1971–1975	15.3	9.3	6.3	18.1	14.7
1976–1980	11.3	13.0	7.8	19.1	7.5
1981–1985	8.3	10.3	8.2	30.8	6.7
1986–1990	7.5	7.3	7.5	33.6	3.7
1991–1995	5.8	8.3	7.8	24.7	2.5
1996–2000	10.3	8.0	5.6	27.5	3.0

Sources: AECIT (1995–2001), IEA (1991–99), INE (1965–70), INE (1971–72), INE (1973), INE (1974–77), INE (1978–90), SAETA (1996–2002), and SOPDE (1999–2001).

operators made important promotional campaigns to make up for the lack of foreign visitors. These campaigns reached the desired goal: domestic visitors increased by 103 percent and their overnight stays by 81 percent.

1976 to 1980. In 1976, a year still marked by the effects of the first fuel crisis, but also by the instability that followed Franco's death, the growth rate of lodged visitors was negative for the first time, both on the Costa del Sol and on the national level. However, the following year brought a clear recovery, due partly to the devaluation of the Spanish peseta. In 1977, the figures attained were the highest ever, both in the number of visitors and overnight stays. However, during the next three years, growth rates were again negative, and because of the second fuel crisis, which affected tourism and transport prices, the number of customers lodged in hotel establishments in Málaga decreased by 22.2 percent and overnight stays decreased by 25.6 percent. This recession affected both foreign and domestic markets, with the most affected being North American visitors. With regards to visitors lodged in hotels, the fall was 29.8 percent for foreigners and 11.8 percent for Spaniards. In the case of overnight stays, the negative rates were 25.3 and 26.2 percent, respectively.

1981 and 1987. Nineteen eighty-one was the start of a new cycle of sustained growth rate, which lasted until 1987. The number of visitors lodged increased by 40 percent and the number of overnight stays by 60 percent. This growth was due mainly to the recovery of foreign tourism, especially British, who became the main customers of the hotels on the Costa del Sol. The majority of other customers came from France, Germany, and the Benelux countries. Although domestic tourism, which represented between 32 and 40 percent of the total, increased 8 percent in terms of lodged visitors and 15 percent in terms of overnight stays, foreign tourism increased 70 percent and 81 percent, respectively. Moreover, a shift in customer motivation took place during these years. The passive tourist of the 1960s and 1970s, who claimed sun and sand as the sole tourist attractions, began to decline. It still holds true at the beginning of the twenty-first century that the main tourist attractions for tourists on the Costa del Sol are the climate and the sea. But it is also the case that in the 1980s the percentage of visitors demanded having other types of activities increased. In this sense, the Costa del Sol was one of the pioneers in adapting to such trends and started to develop proposals for active tourism: sports, incentives, circuit tourism, gastronomy, cultural, landscape, residential, among others, from which the rest of the region of Andalusia also benefited. However, we shall not forget that during these years of tourism boom very little was done to renew hotel facilities or to prevent the negative consequences of tourism over the environment and urbanism.

1988 and 1993. The growing trend, which was common during the 1980s stopped in 1988. Since that year until 1993, demand experienced a difficult period. The impact of the Gulf War, European economic problems, and the exchange rate of the Spanish peseta, overvalued until the devaluations of 1992 and 1993, all negatively affected the tourism industry. Other contributing negative factors were the environmental degradation, lack of safety for tourists, flaws in infrastructures, and lack of renewal of hotel establishments on the Costa del Sol. The consequences for the tourism sector were very important. According to the number of visitors lodged on the Costa del Sol, the growth rate was negative in 1988, 1990, 1992, and 1993. In terms of overnight stays, the rate was negative in 1989, 1990, 1992, and 1993. When comparing the data from 1987 with that from 1993, it can be concluded that the decrease on demand was around 20 percent.

As it happened during the second half of the 1970s, during this crisis foreign tourism again became essential, at least until 1991. In 1987 and 1991, the number of foreign visitors on the Costa del Sol decreased by 31.8 percent and the number of overnight stays by 53.7 percent, yielding all-time high negative growth rates. As a result, the quotas of foreign tourism in terms of visitors and overnight stays were reduced to 46.7 and 58.7 percent, respectively. These figures, corresponding to the year 1991, were the lowest recorded during the entire period analyzed in this study. On the contrary, domestic tourism demonstrated a different trend. On the Costa del Sol the number of Spanish visitors increased by 34.2 percent and the number of overnight stays increased by 55.8 percent. But during the years 1992 and 1993 this trend changed radically. While foreign demand stayed steady, domestic tourism fell 22 percent.

1994 to 2000. Since 1994 there had been a new wave of visitors to the Costa del Sol, both domestic and foreign. This was the beginning of a new boom phase, which lasted until the end of the century and enjoyed positive growth rates. During this period, visitors increased 106 percent in Málaga, and overnight stays went up by 89.6 percent. This occurred due to the devaluation of the peseta in 1992 and 1993, the difficulties experienced by some competitor destinations, and the competitive advantages of the Costa del Sol's tourist services. In this sense, it is worthwhile highlighting the huge effort made by the Costa del Sol to increase its standards through the improvement of quality and diversification. An effort was made to improve products, accommodations, promotion, the service dispensed to visitors, infrastructures, training of human force, environment and instruments to analyze the sector; in other words, everything related directly or indirectly to the tourism industry.

I conclude this analysis of the evolution of the demand on the Costa del Sol by highlighting the importance that this destination has had in the past and presently has on the national level. In terms of lodged visitors, Málaga ranks fifth nationwide after the Balearic Islands, Barcelona, the Canary Islands, and Madrid. Its share of the national total was 4.9 percent in 1966, growing until 1983 to 6.9 percent, and since then decreasing until 1993 to 5 percent. Since then there has been a new growing trend until 1998, to 5.9 percent. In terms of overnight stays, the Costa del Sol ranked sixth nationwide at the end of the 1960s. Presently it ranks fourth after the Balearic Islands, the Canary Islands,

Table 11.4 Spanish destinations with the highest number of travelers lodged in hotel establishments (in thousands)

Year	Alicante	Balearic Islands	Barcelona	Canary Islands	Gerona	Madrid	Málaga
1968	424	1,557	1,211	638	606	1,740	673
1970	586	2,209	1,272	926	679	1,970	874
1973	869	3,830	1,354	1,280	946	2,504	1,095
1976	1,380	3,240	1,775	1,736	1,073	2,806	1,412
1980	1,305	2,992	1,422	1,625	1,081	2,708	1,397
1983	1,434	3,499	1,961	1,905	1,281	2,952	1,825
1986	1,612	4,104	2,266	2,066	1,360	3,180	1,928
1989	1,656	3,299	2,511	2,342	1,667	3,850	1,898
1994	1,629	4,919	2,703	2,952	1,688	4,086	1,800
1998	1,966	5,648	3,979	3,048	2,046	5,045	2,704
2000	2,553	6,687	5,586	4,901	2,540	5,781	3,299

Sources: AECIT (1995–2001), IEA (1991–99), INE (1965–70), INE (1971–72), INE (1973), INE (1974–77), INE (1978–90), SAETA (1996–2002), and SOPDE (1999–2001).

Table 11.5 Spanish destinations with the highest number of overnight stays in hotel establishments (in thousands)

Year	Alicante	Balearic Islands	Barcelona	Canary Islands	Gerona	Madrid	Málaga
1968	2,136	13,729	6,157	4,845	3,808	6,617	3,683
1970	3,199	19,516	6,384	7,189	4,237	7,141	4,890
1973	5,263	31,493	6,699	9,210	6,332	8,612	6,001
1976	6,177	32,566	6,348	11,792	5,092	7,690	6,224
1980	7,155	30,556	4,451	12,694	4,696	7,214	6,300
1983	9,523	37,051	7,092	16,508	7,214	7,630	8,900
1986	10,603	38,760	7,648	18,145	7,910	7,815	9,471
1989	10,057	32,779	7,713	19,351	7,804	9,218	10,049
1994	10,367	47,030	8,406	24,749	9,014	8,057	9,170
1998	12,545	46,349	12,026	24,437	10,024	9,891	13,537
2000	14,500	53,427	16,933	37,750	11,489	12,655	15,074

Sources: AECIT (1995–2001), IEA (1991–99), INE (1965–70), INE (1971–72), INE (1973), INE (1974–77), INE (1978–90), SAETA (1996–2002), and SOPDE (1999–2001).

and Barcelona. In terms of its share, its highest value was in 1989 with 7.6 percent, and the lowest in 1972 with 5.4 percent. Presently its share is 6.6 percent.

Evolution of the Supply Capacity

Several periods can be distinguished in the evolution of the supply capacity on the Costa del Sol. The first period spans from the beginning of the 1950s until the mid-1970s. During this period, due to the steady growth in demand, there was a rapid increase on hotel capacity, mainly in seaside areas. These were years of hectic construction of hotels, hostels, campsites, and apartments. Also, during this period the typical small hotels of the 1950s, generally family-run, which offered room and board, were replaced by the first hotel chains run by foreign companies with new organizational techniques. These hotels increased the traditional capacity, including entertainment services. Logically, all this growth brought with it negative consequences. In this sense, it should be pointed out the limited concern for training and working qualification on this industry, as well as the environmental impact on the coastline of Málaga.

But this spectacular growth came to a halt during the second half of the 1970s. The high inflation recorded at that period, as a result mainly of the increase on energy costs and labor, together with the decrease in public investments and the failure of the idea of an endless tourist demand, all generated important changes on the supply capacity of hotel establishments on the Costa del Sol. The crisis brought also the closing of some establishments and a series of business adjustments in the industry; that is, the cut of additional costs, the appearance of the first labor regulations, and the use of new technologies.

These adjustments, which continued taking place during the 1980s, and the recovery on tourist demand helped the industry during most of this decade. Nonetheless, from 1989 on, hotel businesses suffered a sharp crisis that lasted until 1994. This period was affected by a fall in demand and the change of ownership of some establishments because of the infeasibility to keep the business. The causes were mainly the emergence of new destinations, the higher costs of tourist services due to a stronger peseta in relation to foreign currencies, and the growing competition among non-hotel accommodations as well as real estate construction developed on the coastline of Málaga.

After this difficult period, the industry enjoyed a strong recovery during the last five years of the twentieth century. It is clear that problems suffered by other competitor countries favored the situation on the Costa del Sol. But it is also a fact that the improvements carried out on the infrastructure of the area played an important role on the increase of the demand, as well as promotion in international fairs and, of course, the appropriate management of many hotels, which was greatly improved by the cultural change experienced during the last decade of the century. The cultural profile of the industry was marked at the turn of the century by a greater flexibility and the capability of responding to changes. Also more importance was placed on the training of workers, popular application of new technologies, mainly information technologies, and for keeping a better relation with the Public Administration and the Labor Union, for sharing a quality philosophy and by paying more attention to the sustained tourist development and the growth and internationalization of the tourist business.

However, the industry still had many challenges to face. Among others, to decrease their dependency on foreign companies, mainly tour operators, to develop an environment-friendly and cultural heritage–friendly tourism, to encourage research and development activities as well as training, and finally to promote the existence of small- and medium-size companies through the fostering of agreements and strategic alliances, as well as the existence of larger business groups.

Hotel Establishments' Capacity. During the period analyzed in this chapter, the number of hotel establishments on the Costa del Sol went from 36 to 281, that is an increase of 680 percent. This percentage was greatly above the national average, which was 367 percent. However, the expansion experienced by the Costa del Sol was not uniform throughout all hotel categories. This growth was more so for three- and four-star hotels, as they multiplied by 13.4 and 10.6, respectively. Also, there was no uniformity throughout this time. There were two clearly marked expansive periods. The first period ran until the mid-1970s, with the highest peak from 1955 to 1965 when the growth rate was 219 percent. The second expansive period ran from 1985 to 2000. During this period, the growth rate was 81 percent. In contrast, the period between 1979 and 1984 represented a clear halt because of the closing of certain hotels, the partial restorations made on others, and the spare construction of new facilities.

With regard to the number of beds, they experienced a much higher growth than hotels. While the number of hotels multiplied by 7.8, the number of beds multiplied by 30.2. This expansion experienced on the Costa del Sol clearly surpassed the national average, where bed-places multiplied by 11. It should be pointed out that three- and four-star hotels enjoyed the greatest growth. In the case of one-, five-, and two-star hotels, the figures multiplied by 2.6, 7.5, and 12.8, respectively, while beds in four- and three-star hotels multiplied by 81 and 71, respectively.

This evolution on the number of beds and hotels had important implications on the composition of the supply capacity according to category. The categories of five-, two-, and one-star hotels lost part of their share. While in 1955 their market shares were 21.8, 21.0, and 23.7 percent, respectively, in the year 2000, these figures were only 5.4, 8.9, and 2.1 percent, respectively. On

Figure 11.3 Number of hotel establishments in Málaga (in thousands)

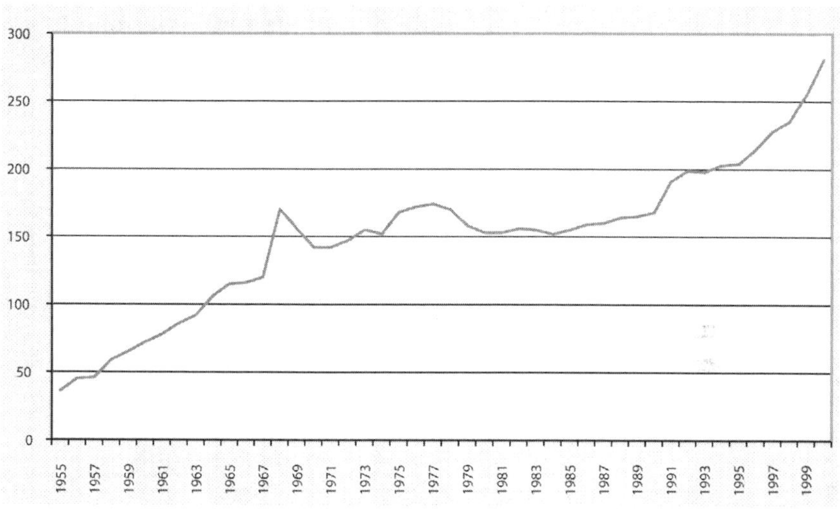

Sources: INE (1954–2001), MIT (1963–76), MCT (1977–78, 1992–93), MTTC (1979–89), MICT (1990–91), SAETA (1996–2002), and SOPDE (1999–2001).

Figure 11.4 Number of beds in hotel establishments in Málaga (in thousands)

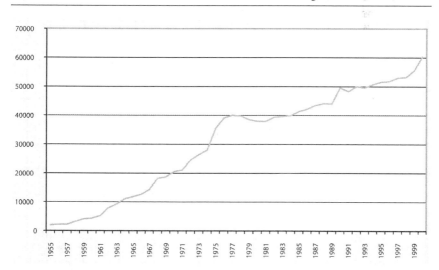

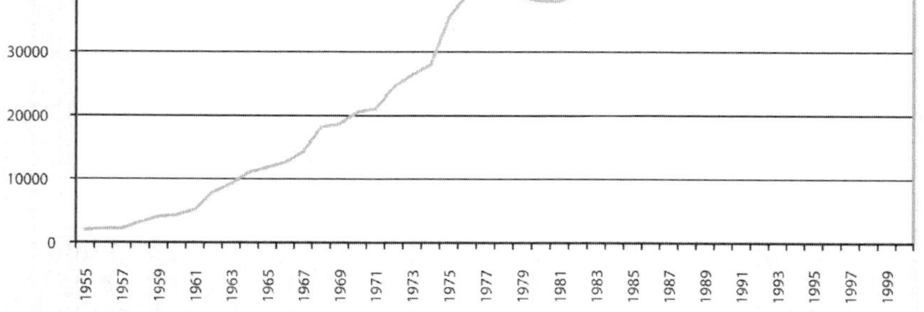

Sources: INE (1954–2001), MIT (1963–76), MCT (1977–78, 1992–93), MTTC (1979–89), MICT (1990–91), SAETA (1996–2002), and SOPDE (1999–2001).

Table 11.6 Number of hotel establishments according to category

Year	MÁLAGA 5-star	4-star	3-star	2-star	1-star	Total (A)	SPAIN Total (B)	A/B %
1955	2	5	9	10	10	36	1,330	2.7
1960	4	12	24	21	11	72	1,835	3.9
1965	11	24	48	22	10	115	2,866	4.0
1970	12	13	43	46	28	142	2,997	4.7
1975	12	18	65	47	26	168	3,504	4.8
1980	9	22	62	40	20	153	3,475	4.4
1985	9	22	68	37	19	155	3,528	4.4
1990	10	23	75	40	20	168	4,233	4.0
1995	7	36	87	47	27	204	5,290	3.9
2000	10	53	121	65	32	281	6,215	4.5

Sources: AECIT (1995–2001), IEA (1991–99), INE (1954–2001), MIT (1963–76), MCT (1977–78, 1992–93), MTTC (1979–89), MICT (1990–91), SAETA (1996–2002), and SOPDE (1999–2001).

Table 11.7 Number of beds in hotel establishments per category

Year	MÁLAGA 5-star	4-star	3-star	2-star	1-star	Total (A)	SPAIN Total (B)	A/B %
1955	434	283	386	419	474	1,996	96,200	2.1
1960	434	1,134	1,052	1,203	527	4,350	130,319	3.3
1965	3,306	3,202	3,610	1,373	343	11,834	230,327	5.1
1970	3,425	2,631	7,469	5,445	1,639	20,609	362,608	5.7
1975	3,933	6,924	15,566	6,898	2,173	35,494	571,006	6.2
1980	3,175	9,663	16,658	7,115	1,354	37,965	596,874	6.4
1985	3,201	9,407	21,012	6,367	1,361	41,348	622,428	6.6
1990	3,863	9,432	24,788	10,277	1,247	49,607	735,749	6.7
1995	2,735	14,895	27,327	5,248	1,390	51,595	876,810	5.9
2000	3,274	22,912	27,493	5,348	1,259	60,286	1,061,426	5.7

Sources: AECIT (1995–2001), IEA (1991–99), INE (1954–2001), MIT (1963–76), MCT (1977–78, 1992–93), MTTC (1979–89), MICT (1990–91), SAETA (1996–2002), and SOPDE (1999–2001).

the contrary, three- and four-star hotels increased their shares. While in 1950 these categories represented 33 percent of the total, at the turn of the century these figures put together had reached 83 percent.

The average size of hotel establishments was also increased as the number of beds was higher than the increase in hotels. During the second half of the twentieth century the average number of hotel beds in Málaga increased from 55 to 214 and in Spain from 72 to 171. This growth took place mainly from 1955 to 1990. During that period the average size of hotels in all categories increased. This was especially true for the three- and four-star hotels, mainly

Table 11.8 Average size of hotels (number of beds per hotel)

	MÁLAGA						SPAIN
Year	5-star	4-star	3-star	2-star	1-star	Average	Average
1955	217	57	43	42	48	55	72
1965	300	133	75	62	34	103	80
1975	328	385	239	147	84	211	163
1985	356	428	309	172	72	267	176
1995	391	414	314	112	52	253	166
2000	327	432	227	82	39	214	171

Sources: AECIT (1995–2001), IEA (1991–99), INE (1954–2001), MIT (1963–76), MCT (1977–78, 1992–93), MTTC (1979–89), MICT (1990–91), SAETA (1996–2002), and SOPDE (1999–2001).

Table 11.9 Number of hostels according to category

	MÁLAGA				SPAIN	A/B
Year	3-star	2-star	1-star	Total (A)	Total (B)	%
1965	16	16	54	86	3,383	2.5
1970	7	71	115	193	5,247	3.7
1975	10	70	130	210	6,013	3.5
1980	8	64	121	193	6,101	3.2
1985	7	65	128	200	6,140	3.2
1990	7	71	148	226	5,203	4.3
1995	0	80	147	227	4,712	4.8
1998	0	93	157	250	4,690	5.3

Sources: AECIT (1995–2001), IEA (1991–99), INE (1954–2001), MIT (1963–76), MCT (1977–78, 1992–93), MTTC (1979–89), MICT (1990–91), SAETA (1996–2002), and SOPDE (1999–2001).

Table 11.10 Number of beds in hostels according to category

	MÁLAGA				SPAIN	A/B
Year	3-star	2-star	1-star	Total (A)	Total (B)	%
1965	527	409	1,182	2,118	97,740	2.2
1970	450	3,503	2,794	6,747	183,190	3.7
1975	743	3,752	3,535	8,030	214,333	3.7
1980	665	3,419	3,386	7,470	216,920	3.4
1985	620	2,731	4,331	7,682	220,909	3.5
1990	620	2,651	4,087	7,358	193,784	3.8
1995	0	2,884	2,819	5,703	173,664	3.3
1998	0	2,832	3,252	6,084	165,809	3.7

Sources: AECIT (1995–2001), IEA (1991–99), INE (1954–2001), MIT (1963–76), MCT (1977–78, 1992–93), MTTC (1979–89), MICT (1990–91), SAETA (1996–2002), and SOPDE (1999–2001).

for the largest hotels and other five-star establishments. However, during the last decade of the century the average size of hotels decreased, mainly due to lower category hotels, that is, typically smaller establishments. This occurred to a certain extent due to the opening of small hotels within the two and one-star categories, which are intentionally small hotels, typical of rural tourism.

With regard to hostels, their number also increased during this period, although not by the same proportion: in Málaga they increased by 218.6 percent, while the national figure was 38.6 percent. As in the case of hotel establishments, this increase took place in cycles. Up to 1976 there was a significant increase – 197 percent. However, from then on, the industry suffered a recession, which lasted until the beginning of the 1990s. This trend changed again in 1994, when hostels started to appear on the Costa del Sol.

The evolution in the number of beds in hostels was also similar. First there was a period of growth until the 1970s, with an increase of 388 percent; then recession until 1990; sharp decrease during the next four years of approximately 23 percent; then a slight recovery starting in 1995. As a result of this evolution, very similar to the national situation, Málaga in 2000 had fewer beds in hostels than those offered at any time during the 1970s and 1980s.

With regard to the evolution of the average annual occupancy of the hotel capacity on the Costa del Sol, it must be pointed out that in times of tourism boom, for instance, in the 1980s and the second half of the 1990s, this figure oscillated between 64.9 percent and 73.7 percent. This figure stayed between 43.6 percent and 53.6 percent 1976, 1980, 1990, 1991, and 1992. However, by looking at the evolution of occupancy levels in monthly breakdowns, it can be found that there is a clear seasonal difference, which makes sense taking into

Table 11.11 Hotel cccupancy in Málaga by month (%)

Jan	Feb	Mar	Apr	May	Jun	Jul	Aug	Sep	Oct	Nov	Dec	Total
28.6	31.6	34.6	48.9	43.9	56.6	72.8	81.2	64.3	48.4	33.4	31.5	43.6
39.1	43.0	53.8	60.6	61.7	65.9	84.1	98.5	81.4	58.9	50.0	37.3	62.7
31.5	34.8	44.8	58.0	44.2	46.0	52.5	75.2	57.5	45.3	36.0	33.5	48.0
46.6	44.6	57.7	69.5	63.6	65.8	73.0	90.4	78.3	69.5	45.2	46.3	64.9
46.3	61.8	70.5	83.8	81.0	82.6	86.6	97.8	84.6	72.7	52.3	41.2	73.7
49.3	54.3	60.8	58.6	69.0	68.9	72.6	92.8	77.9	68.6	54.3	44.1	65.9
56.7	68.3	69.3	69.0	67.3	70.0	74.2	92.6	72.4	60.3	55.1	47.1	67.9
41.3	50.3	54.0	55.5	47.7	51.6	62.2	85.5	63.0	45.1	36.4	33.8	53.6
39.8	48.8	47.9	52.5	58.2	56.4	60.1	91.3	73.5	50.4	37.0	32.4	56.1
41.5	48.8	59.5	61.5	60.0	65.6	85.3	97.5	80.1	58.0	53.6	50.3	65.5
47.6	60.7	67.5	75.6	69.7	71.7	84.6	96.0	79.7	64.3	57.4	50.8	70.3
46.9	59.2	67.0	76.1	74.7	77.8	89.0	100.0	82.5	67.8	59.7	48.4	72.6
45.8	58.9	70.1	75.6	72.4	77.4	78.2	86.1	81.1	69.9	58.1	46.0	70.0

Source: SAETA (1996–2002).

Table 11.12 Spanish destinations with the highest number of hotels and hostels

Year	Alicante	Balearic Islands	Barcelona	Canary Islands	Gerona	Madrid	Málaga	Spain
1960	84	194	199	53	160	181	72	1,835
1970	337	1,498	775	434	928	747	335	8,244
1980	403	1,418	839	395	930	822	346	9,576
1990	362	1,400	697	312	849	747	394	9,436
1998	302	1,286	628	337	635	648	485	10,655

Sources: AECIT (1995–2001), IEA (1991–99), INE (1954–2001), MIT (1963–76), MCT (1977–78, 1992–93), MTTC (1979–89), MICT (1990–91), SAETA (1996–2002), and SOPDE (1999–2001).

Table 11.13 Spanish destinations with the highest number of beds in hotels and hostels

Year	Alicante	Balearic Islands	Barcelona	Canary Islands	Gerona	Madrid	Málaga	Spain
1960	4,371	13,859	14,125	38,026	8,657	19,457	4,350	130,319
1970	24,656	157,050	52,560	34,394	59,835	37,012	27,356	545,798
1980	49,098	226,525	63,425	68,668	74,109	47,774	45,435	813,794
1990	49,189	252,189	64,541	85,577	77,965	49,635	56,965	929,533
1998	51,053	283,290	79,707	113,496	74,070	55,238	59,309	1,121,217

Sources: AECIT (1995–2001), IEA (1991–99), INE (1954–2001), MIT (1963–76), MCT (1977–78, 1992–93), MTTC (1979–89), MICT (1990–91), SAETA (1996–2002), and SOPDE (1999–2001).

account the main product of the Costa del Sol: sun and sand. There is a high season that includes the months between July and September; a medium season between April and June; and a low season, from October to March.

To sum up, it should be noted that the accommodation capacity in Málaga, which is comprised of hotels and hostels, has always maintained a prominent position in the national ranking. By the number of hotels, its market share went from 2.7 percent in 1955 to 4.8 percent in the mid-1970s. From then on, this figure stayed around 4.4 percent value. With regard to the number of beds, the share of the Costa del Sol increased constantly since 1955, from 2.1 percent to 6.7 percent by the beginning of the 1990. From then on the importance of Málaga within the national average decreased slightly, until it reached 5.7 percent in 2000.

Compared with hotels, the market shares of hostels in Málaga were slightly lower, both according to establishments and to bed capacity, and their evolution was also different. Between 1965 and 1970, both shares went up from 2 percent to 3.7 percent. But in the following fifteen years the stagnation suffered by hostels in Málaga meant a slight loss of share on the national level. Exactly the opposite to what happened during the 1990s. Contrary to what happened on the national level, the number of hostels increased in Málaga. As a result of this fact, their share went from 3.2 in 1985 to 5.3 in 1998. The recovery of the number of beds was not as astonishing and the share of Málaga stayed stagnated. Still, Málaga ranked fifth or sixth among tourist destinations in Spain by the number of hotels and hostels throughout the second half of the twentieth century.

Other Lodging Establishments. There has been a clear increase in tourist campsites from 1965 to 2000, both in the number of establishments – 386 percent, and the number of places – 315 percent. This growth took place mainly during the last twenty years of the century. After a period of notable boom during the 1960s, similar to the national average of the time, a sharp stagnation period came in 1971, lasting until the end of the decade. Because of this, in 1980 there were 2 campsites and 521 places less than in 1970. The beginning of the 1980s brought a certain expansion in this field. From then on the trend went upward until the end of the century, although with some low peaks. During the last two decades of the century, the number of campsites and places increased 325 and 295 percent, respectively, mainly during the first half of the 1980s and the first half of the 1990s.

Málaga had a lower share of the national total in this type of lodging than in the case of hotel capacity. Taking into account the number of establishments, the lowest figure – 1.3 percent – occurred during the 1970s recession, and the highest value – 2.8 percent – in 2000. With regard to the number of places, the highest peaks were attained with 3.5 percent in 1965, and 3.1 percent in 1985. As can be expected, the lowest value occurred during the 1970s: 1.5 percent in

Table 11.14 Tourist campsites

	Málaga		Spain		Share of Málaga in national total	
Year	Number	Capacity	Number	Capacity	Number	Capacity
1965	7	4,270	333	120,820	2.1	3.5
1970	10	5,007	470	190,820	2.1	2.6
1975	7	3,416	529	224,049	1.3	1.5
1980	8	4,486	600	272,209	1.3	1.6
1985	15	11,976	767	385,378	1.9	3.1
1990	17	11,650	928	571,278	1.8	2.0
1995	30	15,852	1,130	622,400	2.6	2.5
2000	34	17,719	1,209	656,370	2.8	2.7

Sources: AECIT (1995–2001), IEA (1991–99), INE (1954–2001), MIT (1963–76), MCT (1977–78, 1992–93), MTTC (1979–89), MICT (1990–91), SAETA (1996–2002), and SOPDE (1999–2001

Table 11.15 Number of beds in tourist apartments

Year	Málaga	Spain	Share of Málaga in national total (%)
1981	33,193	270,922	12.2
1982	33,191	277,906	11.9
1983	33,229	292,655	11.3
1984	32,901	295,522	11.1
1985	29,921	298,008	10.0
1986	29,008	289,996	10.0
1987	25,106	303,992	8.3
1988	35,213	328,354	10.7
1989	34,976	335,803	10.4
1990	30,241	384,904	7.8
1991	32,842	402,724	8.1
1992	26,901	419,457	6.4
1993	22,359	438,800	5.1
1994	23,283	419,900	5.5
1995	24,240	402,900	6.0
1996	24,598	404,700	6.1
1997	25,668	413,420	6.2
1998	25,643	413,830	6.2
1999	25,497	404,210	6.3
2000	27,646	407,710	6.8

Sources: AECIT (1995–2001), IEA (1991–99), MTTC (1979–89), SAETA (1996–2001), and SOPDE (1999–2001).

1975. At present, the Costa del Sol holds 2.7 percent of the number of places of tourist campsites available in Spain.

The last type of lodging to be analyzed in this chapter are registered tourist apartments, that is, those present within the regulated offer, and in theory, controlled administratively. This represents only a small part of the number of apartments available in Spain, but this is the only part for which official statistics are available for the period analyzed here. This is a market whose clientele is mostly Spanish and has always shown a high degree of concentration. For example, in 1990, 88 percent of all places available in Spain were located within five tourist destinations: the Canary Islands, Balearic Islands, Tarragona, Málaga, and Gerona. Thus, it is clear that the regulated offer of tourist apartments takes place in those areas known for their sun and beaches. This is why the two archipelagos and the Mediterranean coastline reached the highest concentration.

During the last two decades of the twentieth century, the number of apartments on the Costa del Sol decreased by 16.7 percent. This is something that, as it has been pointed out earlier, only happened in the case of hostels. Actually, there are two clearly distinguished periods in the evolution of apartments on the Costa del Sol. The first period, from 1981 to 1993, had a downward trend. The number of places decreased by 32.6 percent and the share of the Costa del Sol on the national total went from 12.2 to 5.1 percent. The second period, from 1994 to 2000, was marked by a slight recovery of this field. The places available increased by 23.6 percent and its share on the national total reached 6.8 percent. Nevertheless, at the end of the century the Costa del Sol was offering 5,547 places less than twenty years earlier.

Socio-economic Impact of Tourism

The aim of the last part of this chapter is to analyze the possible impact of the tourist development experienced on the Costa del Sol during the second half of the twentieth century in terms of demographics and economic structure. In order to measure the impact on the population, I have used information compiled from different population censuses of the period. According to economic effects, an attempt has been made to achieve a picture as accurate as possible by analyzing the evolution of the specific share of the hotel and restaurant industry within the economy of Málaga and Spain, both in terms of GVA and employment rate. It is a fact that the tourism industry cannot be identified completely with the hotel and restaurant industry and vice versa. However, due to the lack of statistical data, it has been considered that the data regarding the said industry can be a useful indicator on the evolution of tourism.

Demographics

During the second half of the twentieth century, the islands and seaside provinces of Spain experienced a demographic dynamism much higher than the rest of the provinces, mainly due to their tourist development. Throughout the said period, the Spanish population increased by 45.3 percent. This indicator has been found to be much higher, for instance, in the provinces of Alicante, the Canary Islands, the Balearic Islands, Gerona, and Málaga.[9]

The impact of the tourism industry is clearly noticeable during the 1960s and 1970s. Tourism was then a factor that helped emphasize, to a certain extent, traditional center-periphery tensions, which have characterized the creation and development of the industrial society in Spain. This influx became flagrant during the 1980s, when demographic growth came to a halt. From 1981 to 1991, only the insular regions and the Mediterranean seaside of Spain presented growth rates above the stagnating national growth rate. This trend did not disappear during the last decade of the twentieth century.

Table 11.16 Growth of population according to census (in percentage)

Years	Spain	Alicante	Balearic Islands	Canary Islands	Gerona	Málaga
1950–1960	8.8	12.3	5.0	19.0	7.3	3.3
1960–1970	11.0	29.2	25.9	23.9	17.9	11.9
1970–1981	11.1	24.8	22.7	23.4	12.9	19.5
1981–1991	4.5	16.2	8.9	13.4	11.2	15.5
1991–2001	3.6	9.5	12.8	3.5	8.6	7.5
1950–2001	45.3	130.6	99.4	113.6	72.7	71.6

Source: INE (1950–2001).

Table 11.17 Evolution of the population in the province of Málaga

	Coastal areas of Málaga			Interior areas of Málaga			Provincial total
Year	Number of inhabitants	Share of provincial total (%)	Inter-census growth (%)	Number of inhabitants	Share of provincial total (%)	Inter-census growth (%)	Number of inhabitants
1950	373,063	49.7		377,052	50.3		750,115
1960	407,450	52.6	9.2	367,717	47.4	-2.5	775,167
1970	541,990	62.5	33.0	325,340	37.5	-11.5	867,330
1981	738,503	71.3	36.2	297,758	28.7	-8.5	1,036,261
1991	891,744	74.5	20.7	305,564	25.5	2.6	1,197,308
2001	964,583	74.9	8.2	322,434	25.1	5.5	1,287,017

Source: INE (1950–2001).

Table 11.18 Population density

Year	Coastal areas of Málaga	Interior areas of Málaga	Average of Málaga	Average of Spain
1950	311	62	103	56
1960	339	60	106	60
1970	452	53	119	67
1981	615	49	142	75
1991	743	50	164	78
2001	804	53	177	81

Source: INE (1950–2001).

In the case of the Costa del Sol, it is obvious that tourism was a relevant factor to explain demographic dynamics. During the second half of the twentieth century, the population in Málaga increased by 71.6 percent. This growth, much higher than the national average, occurred mainly from 1960 to 1991. During that period the population in Málaga increased by 54 percent while the national average was 29 percent.

The growth of the population of Málaga was not homogeneous throughout the whole province. During the analyzed period, the population of the seaside areas, that is the areas that received most tourists in Málaga, had a growth rate of 158.5 percent. On the contrary, the population in the inland areas decreased by 14.5 percent. While the population rates on the coast were always positive, especially from 1960 to 1991, the interior of the province had negative figures from 1950 to 1981. Because of this, the share of both areas notably changed over time. For example, the coast rate went from 49.7 to 74.9 percent.

These different demographic behaviors altered the density of the population. The province of Málaga always had a density higher than the national average and kept a growing trend. This indicator went from 103 inhabitants per square kilometers in 1950 to 177 kilometers in 2001. Moreover, population behavior was also different in different areas. The coast, that is, a region covering 1,200 square kilometers, went from a density of 311 inhabitants to 804. In the interior, that is, an area covering 6,000 square kilometers, the density went from 62 to 53, reaching its lowest number, 49, in 1981.

The Hotel and Restaurant Industry

From 1955 to 1993, the number of employees in the hotel and restaurant industry increased in Málaga by 418 percent and in Spain by 131 percent. Consequently, the share of Málaga in the national total also increased in that time from 2.6 to 5.8 percent. A similar pattern occurred with the GVA to the cost of the factors provided by the industry in question. In Málaga, it multiplied by 836 percent while in Spain it multiplied by 431 percent. Overall, it is obvious that both in terms of employment and production, the hotel and restaurant industry became increasingly important in Málaga and also in Spain as a whole.[10]

It is a fact that the tourism industry contributed to a large extent to the transformation experienced by the economic structure in Málaga and Spain during the second half of the twentieth century. By analyzing the evolution of employment and the GVA at cost of relevant factors in different fields of the economy both in Málaga and Spain, a significant change toward the third sector can be identified. This process was more so in Málaga due to its special tourist development: the share in services sector went from 30.1 percent to 72.4 percent, and in the case of employment, it went from 53.1 percent to 76.6 percent in terms of added value. Logically, the global transformation experienced by the productive structure played an important role in the hotel and restaurant industry. This contribution was especially significant in tourist locations as important in the industry as Málaga. In 1955, this industry represented 3.7 percent and 3.8 percent of all employment and the GVA of the whole province, respectively. In 1993, those indicators were already 15.9 percent and 15.4 percent, respectively

Table 11.19 Hotel and restaurant industry

	Málaga		Spain		Málaga/Spain (%)	
Year	Employment	Gross added value (in mill. of pesetas)	Employment	Gross added value (in mill. of pesetas)	Employment	Gross added value (in mill. of pesetas)
1955	9,562	276	366,787	10,049	2.6	2.7
1965	17,551	1,531	509,699	46,908	3.4	3.3
1975	30,541	10,112	644,874	242,174	4.7	4.2
1985	41,396	80,617	726,713	1,606,739	5.7	5.0
1993	49,528	230,804	848,526	4,329,252	5.8	5.3

Source: Fundación BBV (1999).

Table 11.20 Total employment according to activity segments (%)

Málaga	Agriculture & fishery	Industry	Construction	Services	Hotel & restaurant
1955	56.9	9.5	3.5	30.1	3.7
1965	39.6	11.5	10.8	38.1	6.4
1975	24.9	13.4	11.1	50.6	10.5
1985	14.1	11.5	9.8	64.6	14.3
1993	9.5	9.5	8.6	72.4	15.9

Spain	Agriculture & fishery	Industry	Construction	Services	Hotel & restaurant
1955	46.1	18.0	6.5	29.4	3.1
1965	33.9	22.8	8.0	35.3	4.0
1975	23.2	24.4	9.8	42.6	4.8
1985	15.7	23.4	7.5	53.4	5.8
1993	9.9	20.9	8.8	60.4	6.5

Source: Fundación BBV (1999).

Table 11.21 Gross added value according to activity segments (%)

Málaga	Agriculture & fishery	Industry	Construction	Services	Hotel & restaurant
1955	23.7	18.9	4.3	53.1	3.8
1965	19.6	15.8	11.2	53.4	5.3
1975	9.6	15.1	13.9	61.4	7.9
1985	7.7	12.3	9.3	70.7	12.3
1993	5.6	9.2	8.5	76.7	15.4
Spain	Agriculture & fishery	Industry	Construction	Services	Hotel & restaurant
1955	20.4	30.7	6.3	42.6	2.3
1965	16.2	31.3	7.6	44.9	3.1
1975	9.4	30.2	10.3	50.1	3.7
1985	6.5	27.8	6.7	59.0	5.5
1993	5.0	21.8	7.6	65.6	6.8

Source: Fundación BBV (1999).

Conclusions

This chapter presented a picture of how tourism experienced an important boom on the Costa del Sol during the second half of the twentieth century. Up until 1975, the tourist growth was spectacular, both in terms of demand and supply capacity. After envisaging the huge possibilities offered by the booming industry of tourism for the economy in Málaga, every effort was made to increase the number of foreign and national visitors choosing to the Costa del Sol as a destination for their vacations. It should be pointed out that some environmental and urban considerations were left out of this aim. The result of this work was the rapid conversion of Málaga into a world-class tourist destination.

During the last quarter of the twentieth century, except from 1976 to 1980 and from 1989 to 1993, the tourism industry continued its boom on the Costa del Sol, albeit with lower growth rates than those achieved between 1950 and 1975. Also, during the last two decades of the century, important changes have occurred in Málaga from a qualitative point of view. The sole product of sun and sand have been extended to wider range of offerings to include cultural tourism, sports tourism, incentive tourism, conference tourism, rural and residential tourism. By the beginning of the twenty-first century, there was a fully professional industry, which divides the market by nationality and tourist typology. This sector enjoys global and strategic planning and more and better analysis tools.

Finally, it should be pointed out that the tourism boom clearly influenced the evolution of Málaga's population, both in terms of growth and territorial distribution, and in the global transformation experienced by the productive structure during the second half of the twentieth century.

Notes

1. J.A. Lacomba, *Crecimiento y crisis de la economía malagueña* (Málaga: Diputación Provincial, 1987); E. Mateo Avilés, *La emigración andaluza a América (1850–1936)* (Málaga: Arguval, 1993); A. Parejo Barranco, *Málaga y los Larios. Capitalismo industrial y atraso económico (1875–1914)* (Málaga: Arguval, 1990); C. Pellejero Martínez, *La filoxera en Málaga. Una crisis del capitalismo agrario andaluz* (Málaga: Arguval, 1990).
2. L. León, *Málaga, estación de invierno* (Málaga: Tipografía de Las Noticias, 1894n. Díaz de Escovar (s.a.), El clima de Málaga, Archivo Díaz de Escovar, Caja 103, Manuscrito, Málaga; V. Martínez y Montes, *Del clima de Málaga* (Málaga: Imprenta de R. Giral, 1880); P. Marcolains San Juan, *Medios prácticos de convertir a Málaga en la mejor estación de invierno de Europa* (Málaga: Tipografía de la Viuda e Hijos de J. Giral, 1893); J. Ramos Power, *Málaga, estación de invierno. Por y para ella* (Málaga: Tipografía de Poch y Creixell, 1895).
3. F. Arcas Cubero and A. García Sánchez, "Los orígenes del turismo malagueño: la Sociedad propagandística del Clima y Embellecimiento de Málaga," *Jábega* 32 (1980): 42–50; C. Pellejero Martínez, "El turismo como alternativa económica en la Málaga de principios de siglo," *Revista de Estudios Regionales* 42 (1995): 297–312.
4. M.P. Lara García, *La cultura del agua: los baños públicos en Málaga* (Málaga: Sarriá, 1997); R. Bejarano Pérez and M.P. Lara García, *Los orígenes y evolución de la Feria de Málaga* (Málaga: Archivo Histórico de Málaga, 2001); E. Mateo Avilés, *Historia de la Feria de Málaga* (Málaga: Arguval, 2002); R. Esteve Secall, *El turismo, la hacienda municipal y la Semana Santa en Málaga durante el primer tercio del siglo XX* (Málaga: Universidad de Málaga, 2005); J. Jiménez Guerrero, *Breve historia de la Semana Santa de Málaga* (Málaga: Sarriá, 2005).
5. Patronato Nacional de Turismo, *Memoria de los trabajos realizados por el Patronato Nacional del Turismo desde julio de 1928 a 31 de diciembre de 1929* (Madrid: 1930).
6. Patronato Nacional del Turismo, *Guía de Hoteles* (Madrid, 1929); V.M. Heredia Flores, "La arquitectura del turismo. Los orígenes de la oferta hotelera en Málaga (siglos XIX–XX)," *Jábega* 86 (2000): 3–20; N. Bravo Ruiz, "El Hotel Caleta Palace: arquitectura de vacaciones y lujo para una Málaga moderna," *Boletín de Arte* 18 (1997): 307–28.

7. F. Bayón, ed., *50 años del turismo español* (Madrid: Centro de Estudios Ramón Areces, 1999); R. Esteve Secall, *Ocio, turismo y hoteles en la Costa del Sol* (Málaga: Diputación Provincial, 1982); R. Esteve Secall and R. Fuentes, *Economía, historia e instituciones del turismo en España* (Madrid: Pirámide, 2000); R. Fuente, ed., *La calle de Europa* (Málaga: SOPDE, 2001); M. Marchena, *Territorio y turismo en Andalucía* (Seville: Junta de Andalucía, 1987); I. Martín Rojo, *La cultura empresarial de los hoteles de la Costa del Sol* (Seville: Junta de Andalucía, Consejería de Industria, Comercio y Turismo, Dirección General de Turismo, 1995); Junta de Andalucía, *El cambio en la cultura empresarial del sector turístico de la Costa del Sol (1992–2001)* (Málaga: Cámara de Comercio, 2002); V.M. Mellado and V. Granados, eds., *Historia de la Costa del Sol* (Málaga: Diario Sur, 1997); C. Pellejero Martínez, ed., *Historia de la economía del turismo en España* (Madrid: Civitas, 1999); idem, "El turismo, factor decisivo en el desarrollo económico de Málaga," *Péndulo* 13 (2001): 51–59; E. Uriel, ed., *El sector turístico en España* (Alicante: Caja de Ahorros del Mediterráneo, 2001).
8. Asociación Española de Expertos Científicos en Turismo (AECIT) (1995–2001), *La actividad turística española*, Madrid; Instituto de Estadística de Andalucía (IEA) (1991–2000), *Anuario estadístico de Andalucía,* Seville; Instituto Nacional de Estadística (INE) (1954–2001), *Anuario Estadístico de España*, Madrid; INE (1965–1970), *Estadística del movimiento de viajeros en alojamientos hoteleros y acampamentos turísticos*, Madrid; INE (1971–1972), *Estadística del movimiento de viajeros en establecimientos hoteleros y acampamentos*, Madrid; INE (1973), *Estadística de turismo. Viajeros en hoteles y acampamentos. Resumen anual*, Madrid; INE (1974–1977), *Viajeros en hoteles y acampamentos. Resumen anual*, Madrid; INE (1978–1990), *Movimiento de viajeros en establecimientos turísticos. Resumen anual*, Madrid; Ministerio de Información y Turismo (MIT) (1963–1976), *Anuario de Estadísticas de Turismo,* Madrid; Ministerio de Comercio y Turismo (MCT) (1977–1978 and 1992–1993), *Anuario de Estadísticas de Turismo*, Madrid; Ministerio de Transporte, Turismo y Comunicaciones (MTTC) (1979–1989), *Anuario de Estadísticas de Turismo*, Madrid; Ministerio de Industria, Comercio y Turismo (MICT) (1990–1991), *Anuario de Estadísticas de Turismo*; Sistema de Análisis y Estadística del Turismo de Andalucía (SAETA) (1996–2002), *Boletín de Indicadores Turísticos de Andalucía*, Seville, Junta de Andalucía; Sociedad de Planificación y Desarrollo (SOPDE) (1999–2001), *Observatorio turístico de la Costa del Sol*, Málaga, Patronato de Turismo de la Costa del Sol.
9. Instituto Nacional de Estadística (INE) (1950–2001), *Censos de población,* Madrid.
10. *Renta Nacional de España y su distribución provincial* (Bilbao: Fundación BBV 1999); J. Alcalde Inchausti, *Evolución económica de las regiones y provincias españolas en el siglo XX* (Bilbao: Fundación BBVA).

Contributors

Patrizia Battilani is Professor of Economic History at the University of Bologna. She has written extensively on business history and on the history of tourism. Her publications include, among others, "Rimini and Costa Smeralda: How Social Values Shape Recreational Sites," *Water Leisure and Culture*, ed. Susan C. Anderson and B. Tabb (Berg, 2002) and "How to Beat Competition without Losing Co-Operative Identity: The Case of the Italian Consumer Co-Operatives," in *Consumerism versus Capitalism?* (Amsab-Institute of Social History, 2005).

Hubert Bonin is Professor of Modern Economic History at Bordeaux Political Sciences Institute. His specialties include services companies' history and French banking history, with several publications in this area. He is a member of the GREThA research unit in theoretical and applied economics at Bordeaux 4 University, the Association française des historiens economistes, is on the board of the Société française d'histoire moderne et contemporaine. He is also a member of the Council of the European Business History Association, the academic advisory council of the European Association for Banking and Financial History, and the scientific committee of *Enterprise & Society* journal.

Benedita Câmara is Associate Professor in the Department of Management and Economy at the University of Madeira, Portugal. Her areas of interest and research include institutional history: agricultural contract, business history of the nineteenth and twentieth centuries, and history of tourism.

Margarita Dritsas is Professor of European Economic and Social History at the School of Humanities, Hellenic Open University, Greece. Her recent publications include the tourism and culture in Europe.

Ellen Furlough is Associate Professor of History at the University of Kentucky, United States. Her work currently focuses on tourism, vacations, and consumer cultures in France from the 1930s to the 1970s.

Jaume Garau-Taberner is a Lecturer in the Department of Applied Economics at the University of the Balearic Islands. He studied applied economics and is at present completing a PhD on tourism destination competitiveness and economic growth in the Mediterranean area. He has published various articles in this field. He has also worked for the European Parliament and the European Commission as an expert on EU regional policy.

Peter Lyth is a Teaching Fellow at the Christel DeHaan Tourism and Travel Research Institute at the Nottingham University Business School. He is a past editor of the internationally recognized *Journal of Transport History* and has research interests that cover a wide range of subjects from the history of air transport to the growth of heritage tourism.

Carles Manera is Doctor of History (University of the Balearic Islands, 1987) and Doctor of Economics (University of Barcelona, 2000). He has received several prizes for his research, including the Prize of Economics in Catalonia (2003). He held the post of Vice Chancellor at the University of the Balearic Islands (1996–2003). Currently, he is Director of the Research Group on Economic History at the University of the Balearic Islands and is a researcher in charge of the project "Economic History of Mass Tourism in Spain, 1940–2000: The Balearic Islands and the Mediterranean contrasts," financed by the Ministry of Science and Education of Spain.

Philippe Mioche is Professor of Contemporary History at the University of Provence (Aix Marseille I) and Director of the European Studies Master's Degree Program at the University of Provence. He holds the Jean Monnet chair in European Integration History and is also Director of the journal *Industries en Provence.*

Carmelo Pellejero Martínez holds a PhD in Economics from Málaga University (Spain). He is currently Associate Professor of Economic History at Málaga University, where he regularly teaches on the History of Tourism. He has specialized in the Economic History of Tourism in Europe, a field in which he has published several books and articles in leading journals. He is currently engaged in the research project *Historia económica del turismo de masas en España, 1940–2000: Las Islas Baleares y los contrastes mediterráneos*, sponsored by the Spanish Ministry of Education.

Manfred Pohl received his PhD in history from the University of Saarbrücken, Germany. He is Founder and Chairman of the International Centre for Corporate Culture and History (ICCCH), which consists of the European Association for Banking and Financial History (EABH), the Institute for Corporate Culture Affairs (ICCA), as well as the Frankfurter Kultur Komitee. He is also Founder of the Gesellschaft für Unternehmensgeschichte. After forty years with Deutsche Bank he officially retired in May 2007. Since 1997 he has been Honorary Professor at the University of Frankfurt. In October 2001 he received the European Award for Culture at the European Parliament in Strasbourg.

Luciano Segreto is Professor of Economic History and the History of International Economic Relations at the University of Florence. His main research interests are in post–World War II international business and financial history. Chairman of the Cultural Memory Council of the ICCA, he is a member of the Scientific Committee of the Maison des Sciences de l'Homme d'Aquitaine, and on the board of many international journals. He is the author of numerous articles and books on business history and culture.

Antoni Serra is Professor in Marketing Management and Tourism Marketing at the Department of Economics and Management at the University of the Balearic Islands. He is teaching undergraduate and postgraduate courses in tourism and tourism marketing.

Bibliography

Abufalia, D. 2003. *The Mediterranean in History*, Cambridge: Cambridge University Press.

Alcaide, J., ed. 1999. *Renta Nacional de España y su distribución provincial. Serie homogénea.* Bilbao: Fundación BBV.

Alegre, J., and L.L. Pou. 2002. "The Determinants of Probability of Tourism Consumption: An Analysis with a Family Expenditure Survey." Universitat de les Illes Balears Departament d'Economia Aplicada Working Paper no. 39.

Alenyà, M, ed. 1999. *Informe econòmic i social de les Illes Balears* 1998, Palma de Mallorca: Sa Nostra Caixa de Balears.

Allegrucci, L. 1999. "Alpitour si allarga con Viaggidea s.r.l.," *Italia Oggi*, 11 November.

Amatori, F., and G. Jones, eds. 2003. *Business History Around the World*, Cambridge: Cambridge University Press.

Anderson, S., and B. Tabb. 2002. *Water Leisure and Culture*, Oxford: Berg.

Apostolopoulos, Y., P. Loukissas, and L. Leontidou. 2001. *Mediterranean Tourism. Facets in Socioeconomic Development and Cultural Change*, London: Routledge.

Arcas Cubero, F., and A. Garcia Sanchez. 1980. *Los orígenes del turismo malagueño: la Sociedad propagandística del Clima y Embellecimiento de Málaga*, Jábega.

Archer, F. 1985. *Tourism: Transnational Corporations and Cultural Identities*, Paris: UNESCO.

Arnoux, R. 1989. *Les 40 ans qui ont changé la Provence*. Ed. J. Michel Garçon.

Aron, C.S. 1999. *Working at Play: A History of the Vacations in the United States*, New York: Oxford University Press.

Babel, R., and W. Paravicini. 2005. *Grand Tour: adeliges Reisen und europäische Kultur vom 14. bis zum 18. Jahrhundert*, Akten der internationalen Kolloquien in der Villa Vigoni 1999 und im Deutschen Historischen Institut Paris 2000, Ostfildern: Thorbecke.

Baranowski, S., and E. Furlough. 2001. *Being Elsewhere: Tourism, Consumer Culture, and Identity in Modern Europe and North America*, Ann Arbor: University of Michigan Press.

Barbier, B. 1966. "Tourisme et emploi en Provence Côte d'Azur," *Méditerranée*, no. 3 (July-September).

Baron-Yelles, N. 1999. *Le tourisme en France. Territoires et stratégies*, Paris: Armand Colin.

Bartlett, C., and S. Ghoshal. 1989. *Managing Across Borders: The Transnational Solution*, Cambridge: Harvard Business School Press.

Battilani, P. 2001. *Vacanze di pochi, vacanze di tutti. L'evoluzione del turismo europeo*, Bologna: il Mulino.

Baumol, W., R. Nelson, and E. Wolff, eds. 1994. *Convergence of Productivity. Cross-National Studies and Historical Evidence*, New York: Oxford University Press.

Biella, A. 1996. *L'industria del viaggio organizzato*, Milan: Angeli.

Blàzquez, M., I. Murray, and J.M. Garau. 2002. *El tercer boom. Indicadors de sostenibilitat del turisme de les Illes Balears 1989–1999*, Centre d'Investigacions Turístiques de les Illes Balears (CITTIB): Palma (Mallorca).

Blednick, P. 1988. *Another Day in Paradise? The Real Club Med Story*, Toronto: Macmillan of Canada.

Blitz, G. 1990. *La Vacance*, Croissy-Beauborug: Dervy.

Boissonas, F. 1921. *Ancient Athens*, Geneva.

______. 1930. *Le Tourisme en Grece*, Geneva.

Bonin, H. 1987. *Suez, du canal à la finance, 1858–1987*, Paris: Economica.

Bonniot, O. 1982. *La ligne de chemin de fer de Gardanne à Carnoules*, Mémoire de maîtrise, Université de Paris I.

Bosio, R. 1984. "Positivi i risultati Alpitour. Verso quota 180 mila clienti," *Il Sole-24 Ore*, 9 August.

______. 1990. "Alpitour, la vacanza è business," *Il Sole-24 Ore*, 23 November.

Boyer, M. 1997. *Il turismo: dai gran tour ai viaggi organizzati*, Trieste: Editoriale Libraria.

______. 2000. *Histoire de l'invention du tourisme, XVIe –XIXe siècles*, La Tour d'Aigues: Editions de l'Aube.

Braudel, F. 1966. *La Méditerranée et le monde méditerranéen à l'époque de Philippe 2*, Paris: Colin.

Briglia, F. 1999. "Vacanze culturali, arriva Alpitour," *Italia Oggi*, 1 July.

Brilli, A. 2006. *Il viaggio in Italia: storia di una grande tradizione culturale*, Bologna: il Mulino.

Bryant, W.K. 1996. "A Comparison of the Household Work of Married females: The Mid-1920s and Late 1960s," *Family and Consumer Sciences Research Journal* 24, no. 4, June.

Buisán, A. 1997. *Exportaciones de turismo y competitividad, Revista de Economía Aplicada*, num. 13, Zaragoza.

Cals, J. 2000. *La recepción turística y la política de turismo de la democracia en España 1977–1998: entre la descentralización y los cambios en los mercados, Papers de Turisme*, núm. 27, Valencia.

Caron, F., and F. Cardot. 1991. *Histoire de l'électricité en France*, vol. 1: *1881–1918*, Paris: Fayard.

Castronovo, V. 1999. *Fiat 1899–1999. Un secolo di storia italiana*, Milan: Rizzoli.

Chandler Jr., A.D. 1962. *Strategy and Structure: Chapters in the History of the American Industrial Enterprise*. Cambridge: MIT Press.

Charitakis. 1934. *Economic Yearbook of Greece, 1933*, Athens.

Clarke, T., and J.F. Chanlat. 2006. *European Corporate Governance*, London: Routledge.

Codeluppi, V. 2000. *Iperpubblicità. Come cambia la pubblicità italiana*, Milan: F. Angeli.

Colli, A. 1999. *Impresa e industria in Italia dall'Unità a oggi*, Venice: Marsilio.

______. 2003. *The History of Family Business 1850–2000*, Cambridge: Cambridge University Press.

Constant, E.W. 1980. *The Origins of the Turbojet Revolution*, Baltimore: Johns Hopkins University Press.

Cooper, C.P., ed. 1990. *Progress in Tourism, Recreation and Hospitality Management*, vol. 2, Chichester, UK: Belhaven.

Coutty, M. 2001. "Au Club Med jeunes, Si tu dors, t'es mort," *Le Monde*, 2 March.

Crafts, N., and G. Toniolo, eds. 1996. *Economic Growth in Europe since 1945*, Cambridge: Cambridge University Press.

Culbreth, J. 1991. *Club Med Magic*, Working Mother.

Cunha, L. 2001. *Introdução ao Turismo*, Lisbon: Verbo.
Cuthbert, G. 1988. *Flying to the Sun. Quarter Century of Britannia Airways, Europe's Leading Leisure Airline.*
Cyert, R.M., and J.G. March. 1965. *Teoría de las Decisiones Económicas de la Empresa*, Mexico: Prentice-Hall.
Daurat, C. 1999. "Paradise Regained," *Forbes*, 22 March.
De Feo, M. 2001. "Ifil, allanza nel turismo con la Preussag," *Corriere della Sera*, 19 May.
De Keyse, R., and N. Vanhove. 1997. "Tourism Quality Plan: An Effective Tourism Policy," *Revue du Tourisme* 3.
Del Piano, A. 1911. "I bagni di Rimini," *L'Ausa*, 5 August.
Diaz De Escovar, N. s.a. *El clima de Málaga*, Archivo Díaz de Escovar Caja 103, Manuscrito, Málaga.
Doganis, R. 1991. *Flying off Course. The Economics of International Airlines*. London: HarperCollins Academic.
Dritsas, M. 1995. *To Chroma tes Epitychias: The Colour of Success, ThePaint and Varnish Industry 1830-1990*, Athens: Trochalia.
Duchêne, R. 1986. *Naissance d'une région: 1945–1985 Histoire de Provence-Alpes-Côte d'Azur.* Paris: Fayard.
Dunning, J., and M. Mcqueen. 1982. "Multinational Corporations in the International Hotel Industry," *Annals of Tourism Research* 9.
Edgerton, D. 1991. *England and the Aeroplane: An Essay on a Militant and Technological Nation*, Basingstoke: Macmillan.
El-Agraa, A.M., ed. 1994. *The Economics of the European Community*, London: Harvester Wheatsheaf.
Ellis, J., and Williams, D. 1995. *International Business Strategy*, London: Pitman.
Escartín, J.M., C. Manera, and J.M. Petrus. 1995. "Le Role de l'ile de Majorque dans la formation des réseaux de transports européens 1945–1973)," in *Les réseaux européens transnationaux XIXème–XXème siècles. Quels enjeux?* ed. M. Merger, A. Carreras, and A. Giuntini. Nantes: Ouest Editions Nantes.
Faché, W. 2000. "Methodologies for Innovation and Improvement of Services in Tourism," *Managing Service Quality* 10, no. 6.
Farrant, S. 1987. "London by the Sea: Resort Development on the South Coast of England, 1880–1939," *Journal of Contemporary History* 22.
Fayos-Solá, E. 1994. "Competitividad y Calidad en la nueva era del turismo," *Estudios Turísticos*, no. 123.
Ferraino, G. 1997. "Turismo, maxipolo di Francorosso e Alpitour," *Corriere della Sera*, 18 December.
______. 2006. "Isoardi investe sugli hotel tramite la halley Partecipazioni," *Plus24* 2 December.
Ferrier, J.-P. 1983. *Leçons du territoire. Nouvelle géographie de la région Provence-Alpes-Côte d'Azur*, Aix-en-Provence: Edisud.
Frances, P. 1998. "Les habits neufs du Club Med," *Le Monde*, 24 September.
Fridenson, P., and A. Strauss. 1987. *Le capitalisme français 19e-20e siècle. Blocages et dynamismes d'une croissance*, Paris: Fayard.
Fourniau, J.-M. 1989. *Des grandes vitesses au TGV. Les transformations de la politique commerciale de la SNCF*, in Association pour l'Histoire des Chemins de fer en France, *Les chemins de fer l'Espace et la Société en France*, Actes du colloque mai 1988, Paris.
Furlough, E. 1993. "Packaging Pleasures: Club Méditerranée and Consumer Culture in France, 1950–1968," *French Historical Studies* 18, no. 1.

Furlough, E., and R. Wakeman. 1997. "Composing a Landscape: Coastal Mass Tourism and Regional Development in the Languedoc, 1960s–1980s," *International Journal of Maritime History* 9, no. 1, June.

Gay, J-C. 1996. "Monaco, station touristique prestigieuse," *Méditerranée,* no. 3.

Gibson, H. D., ed. 2001. *Economic Transformation and Integration in the European Union, Southern Europe in Comparative Perspective*, New York: Palgrave.

Ginard, D. 1999. *L'economia balear 1929–1959.* Palma de Mallorca: Documenta balera.

Go, F., and R. Pine. 1995. *Globalization Strategy in the Hotel Industry,* London: Routledge.

Go, F., S.S. Pyo, M. Uysal, and B.J. Mihalik. 1990. "Decision Criteria for Transnational Hotel Expansion," *Tourism Management* 114.

Gordon, B. 2004. "The Mediterranean as a Tourist Destination from Classical Antiquity to Club Med," *Mediterranean Studies,* 12 March.

Gregoretti, M. 1992. "Vacanze con l'Avvocato," *Panorama,* 23 February.

Gueron, L. 1985. "Le tourisme à Menton," *Méditerranée,* no.1, 1966.*Guide bleu Provence Alpes Côte d'Azur,* Paris, Hachette, édition 1985.

Guiral, P., ed. 1978. *La Provence de 1900 à nos jours,* Toulouse: Privat.

Hanlon, P. 1996. *Global Airlines. Competition in a Trans-National Industry,* Oxford: Butterworth-Heinemann.

Harvey, D. 1989. *The Condition of Postmodernity,* Oxford: Blackwell.

Hayward, K. 1989. *The British Aircraft Industry,* Manchester: Manchester University Press.

Held, J.-F. 1966. *Le Bonheur en Confection–II: Des filles, du soleil, des garçons,* Le Nouvel Observateur.

Hibbert, C. 1987. *The Grand Tour,* London: Metheun.

Hill, H. 1939. *The Economy of Greece,* New York.

Humphreys, B.K. 1976. "Nationalisation and Independent Airlines in the United Kingdom, 1945–51," *Journal of Transport History,* second series 3, no. 4.

______. 1979. "Trooping and the Development of the British Independent airlines," *Journal of Transport History,* second series 5, no. 1.

Inglis, F. 2000. *The Delicious Story of the Holiday,* London: Routledge.

Issa, J.J., and C. Jayewardene. 2003. "The 'All Inclusive' Concept in the Caribbean," *International Journal of Contemporary Hospitality Management* 15, no. 3.

Jasor, M. 2005. "Succession chez Accor: une série de faux pas," *Le Monde,* 14–15 October 2005.

Kanigel, R. 2004. *High Season: How One French Rivera Town Has Seduced Travelers for Two Thousand Years,* New York.

Kapferer, J.-N. 1998. "Le Club Med: Déclin vieillissement et revitalisation d'une marque," *Cahiers Espace* 59.

Keller, P. 1996. *Globalization and Tourism,* St. Gallen, Switzerland: Editions AIEST.

Knafou, R., ed., and MIT Team 2002. *Tourismes. Lieux communs,* vol. 1, Paris: Belin.

Koehn, N. F. 2001. *Brand New: How Entrepreneurs Earned Consumers' Trust from Wedgwood to Dell,* Boston: Harvard Business School Press.

La Ferla, M. 1998. "Tutti in ferie con gli Agnelli," L'Espresso, 15 January 1998.

Lacomba, J. 1987. *Crecimiento y crisis de la economía malagueña,* Málaga: Servio de Publicaciones.

Lafond, P. 2004. "La France et le miracle économique italien, 1945–1963," PhD diss., Université de Paris XII.

Laker, F. 1966. "Private Enterprise in British Air Transport," *Journal of the Royal Aeronautical Society,* February.

Lambert, O. 1995. *Marseille entre tradition et modernité. Les espérances déçues 1919–1939. Histoire du commerce et de l'industrie de Marseille, XIXe-XXe siècles,* vol. 10, Marseille: Chambre de Commerce et d'Industrie Marseille Provence.

Langevin, P. 1981. *L'économie provençale: I-Les structures économiques*, Aix-en-Provence: Edisud.
______. 1983. *L'économie provençale: II-L'aménagement du territoire*, Aix-en-Provence: Edisud.
Langevin, P., and B. Morel. 2002. *L'économie: dynamique de la région Provence-Alpes-Côte d'Azur*. La Tour d'Aigues: Editions de l'Aube.
Leon, L. 1894. *Málaga, estación de invierno*, Málaga: Tipografía de Las Noticias.
Levitt, T. 1983. "The Globalization of Markets," *Harvard Business Review*, May/June.
Lévy-Leboyer, M., and H. Morsel, eds. 1994. *Histoire de l'électricité en France*, vol. 2: *1919–1946*, Paris: Fayard.
Livet, R. 1978. *Atlas et géographie de Provence Côte d'Azur et Corse*, Paris: Flammarion.
Logothetis, M.I. 1961. *Tourism in Rhodes*, Athens: NBG.
______. 1962. *Tourism and the Economy of the Island of Nisyros*, Athens.
______. 1963. *Tourist Studies*, Athens.
Lozato-Giotart, J.P. 1990. *Méditerranée et tourisme*, Paris: Masson.
Luc, V. 1998. *Impossible n'est pas français. L'histoire inconnue d'Accor, leader mondial de l'hôtellerie*, Paris: Albin Michel.
Lyth, P.J. 1996. *Air Transport*, Aldershot: Scolar Press.
Lyth, P.J., and M.L. Dierikx. 1994. "From Privilege to Popularity: The Growth of Leisure Air Travel," *Journal of Transport History* 15, no. 2.
Mak, J. 2004. *Tourism and the Economy: Understanding the Economics of Tourism*, Honolulu: University of Hawaii Press.
Manera, C., ed. 1990. *La indústria a Mallorca: una perspectiva històrica*, Palma de Mallorca: *Estudis d'Història Econòmica*.
______. 1999. *Exploracions en Història Econòmica contemporània Randa*, nos. 42 and 43.
______. 2000a. "El coll d'ampolla ecològic del creixement econòmic balear, 1985–2000. Una perspectiva des de la historia econòmica," paper presented at the Seminario de Historia Económica, Universitat de les Illes Baleares.
______. 2000b. "L'endarreriment econòmic de les illes Balears fins el turisme de masses: la construcció d'un mite," unpublished.
______. 2001a. *Història del creixement econòmic a Mallorca, 1700-1930*, Palma: Lleonard Muntaner.
______. 2001b. *Història ecològica a les Illes Balears. Estudis sobre energia, economia i medi ambient*, Lleonard Muntaner, ed., Palma.
Manera, C., and J. Garau. 2006. "Il turismo di massa nel Mediterraneo 1987–2002: un'opportunità di crescita," *Economia Marche*, 1.
March, J.G., and J.P. Olsen. 1979. *Ambiguity and Choice in Organizations*, 2nd ed., Bergen: Universitetsforlaget.
March, J.G., and H.A. Simon. 1969. *Teoría de la Organización*, 2nd ed., Barcelona: Ariel.
Marcolains San Juan, P. 1893. *Medios prácticos de convertir a Málaga en la mejor estación de invierno de Europa*, Málaga: Tipografía de la Viuda e Hijos de J. Giral.
Martinez, Y., and V. Montes. 1880. *Del clima de Málaga*, Málaga: Imprenta de R. Giral.
Martorell Cunill, O. 2002. *Cadenas Hoteleras. Análisis del Top 10*. Barcelona: Ariel.
Mateo Aviles, E. 1993. *La emigración andaluza a América 1850-1936*. Málaga: Arguval.
Mateus, A. 2001. *Economia portuguesa*, Lisbon: Verbo.
Mclaren, D. 2003. *Rethinking Tourism and Ecotravel*, 2nd ed. Bloomfield, CT, Kumarian Press.
Mellado, V.Y., and V. Granados, eds. 1997. *Historia de la Costa del Sol*, Málaga: Diario Sur.
Merger, M., A. Carreras, and A. Giuntini, eds. 1995. *Les réseaux européens transnationaux XIXème-XXème siècles. Quels enjeux?* Nantes: Ouest Editions.
Millward, R., and J. Singleton. 1995. *The Political Economy of Nationalisation in Britain, 1920–1950*, Cambridge: Cambridge University Press.

Mioche, P. 1994. *L'alumine à Gardanne de 1893 à nos jours. Une traversée industrielle en Provence*. Grenoble: Presses Universitaires de Grenoble.

______, ed. 1998. *Histoire industrielle de la Provence*, Aix-en-Provence: Publications de l'Université de Provence.

______. 1999. *EELM: succès ou boulet pour l'économie régionale?* in XIIe colloque de l'AHEF, Paris les 3, 4, 5 February "Stratégies, gestion, management. Les compagnies électriques et leurs patrons 1895–1945."

Mioche, P., and X. Daumalin. 2002. *Provence, terre de chimie. Cent ans de l'Union des Industries Chimiques en région Provence-Alpes-Côte d'Azur*, Marseille: UIC.

Mokyr, J. 2000. Why Was There More Work for Mother? Knowledge and Household Behaviour, 1870–1945," *Journal of Economic History* 60, no. 1, March.

Mons, S., and M.A. Pipito. 1986. *La société d'énergie électrique du littoral méditerranéen EELM*. Maîtrise: Université de Montpellier III.

Morck, R., A. Shleifer, and R.W. Vishny. 1990. "Do Managerial Objectives Drive Bad Acquisitions?" *Journal of Finance* 46, no. 1.

Murphy, P.E. 1985. *Tourism: A Community Approach*, New York: Methuen.

Naud, R. 1992. *Les flux migratoires intra communautaires dans la région Provence Alpes Côte d'Azur des années 1959 à nos jours*, Maîtrise d'histoire contemporaine de l'Université de Provence, Aix Marseille I.

Navinés, F. 1995. *Turisme i territori*, Revista Econòmica núm. 107, Barcelona: Banca Catalana.

______. 1998. *Economia, turisme i territori a les Illes Balears*, Serra d´Or, núm. 468, Barcelona.

Neubauer, F., and A.G. Lank. 1998. *The Family Business: Its Governance for Sustainability*. London: McMillan.

Nye, D.E. 1997. *Narratives and Spaces, Technology and the Construction of American Culture*, Exeter: University of Exeter Press.

Olivier, L. 1992. *Le Club Méditerranée: De l'Utopie à l'Internationalisation, 1950–1990*, master thesis, Université Paris I.

Ouvry-Vial, B. 1990. *Les Vacances*, Paris: Edition Autrement.

Palmieri, G. 1984. "I grandi del turismo vanno alla conquista dell'Europa," *Il Sole-24 Ore*, 3 November.

Parejo Barranco, A. 1990. *Málaga y los Larios. Capitalismo industrial y atraso económico 1875–1914*. Málaga: Arguval.

Pearce, D.G. 1987. *Tourism Today: A Geographical Analysis*, New York: Wiley.

______. 1989. *Tourist Development*, Longman, London and New York: Longman.

Pellejero Martinez, C. 1990. *La filoxera en Málaga. Una crisis del capitalismo agrario andaluz*, Málaga: Arguval.

______. 1995. *El turismo como alternativa económica en la Málaga de principios de siglo*, Revista de Estudios Regionales, nº 42, Málaga, Málga, Imprenta de R. Giral.

Pensabene, S. 1993. "L'altra Fiat esce dal guscio," *Mondo economico*, 1 May.

Peyre, C., and Y. Raynouard. 1971. *Histoire et Légendes du Club Méditerranée*, Paris: Edition du Seuil.

Phalon, R. 1988. "Trouble in Paradise," *Forbes*, 19 September.

Pimlott, J. 1947. *The Englishman's Holiday*, London: Faber and Faber.

Pitteri, D. 2002. *La pubblicità in Italia. Dal dopoguerra a oggi*, Roma and Bari: La Terza.

Poon, A. 1998. "All-Inclusive Resorts," *Travel and Tourism Analyst* 6.

Porter, M.E. 1980. *Competitive Strategy: Techniques for Analyzing Industries and Competitors*, New York: Free Press.

______. 1985. *Competitive Advantage*, New York: Free Press.

______. 1986. *Competition in Global Business*, Cambridge: Harvard University Press.

Ramos Power, J. 1895. *Málaga, estación de invierno. Por y para ella*, Málaga: Tipografía de Poch y Creixell.
Raymond, H. 1960. "L'Utopie concrète: Recherches sur un village de vacances," *Revue française de sociologie* 1.
Reig, E., and A.J. Picazo. 1998. *Capitalización y crecimiento de la economía balear, 1955–1996*, Bilbao: Fundación BBV.
Rhode, P., and G. Toniolo, eds. 2006. *The Global Economy in the 1990s. A Long-Run Perspective*, Cambridge: Cambridge University Press.
Ritichie, W.K. 1972. *The Eighteenth Century Grand Tour*, London: Longman.
Rugman, A.M., ed. 1982. *New Theories of Multinational Enterprise*, London: Croom Helm.
Salgado De Matos, L. 1973. *Investimentos Estrangeiros em Portugal*, Lisbon: Seara Nova.
Silva, J.S. 1990. "Receitas e Despesas atribuídas ao Turismo," *Turismo* 2, nos. 22/23.
Silva, M., ed. 1986. *Portugal Contemporâneo. Problemas e Perspectivas*, Oeiras: Instituto Nacional de Administração (INA).
Sinclair, M.T., and M. Stabler. 1997. *The Economics of Tourism*, London and New York: Routledge.
Snudden, A. 1990. "Success in a Package," *Journal of the Institute of Transport*, January/February.
Soula, C. 1993. "Club Med: le bonheur n'est plus ce qu'il était," *Le Nouvel Observateur Economie*, 9–15 September.
Stonehouse, G.H., J. Hamill, D. Campbell, and A. Purdue. 1999. *Global and Transnational Business- Strategy and Management*, London: John Wiley.
Sunseri, N. 1996. "Club Med e Valtur, destini incrociati all'ombra della Mole," *il Lunedì della Repubblica*, 16 December 1996.
Teare, R., M.D. Olsen, and J.J. West, eds. 1992. *International Hospitality Management: Corporate Strategy in Practice*, London and New York: Pitman and John Wiley.
Teich, M., and R. Porter. 1996. *The Industrial Revolution in National Context, Europe and the USA*, Cambridge: Cambridge University Press.
Tissot, L. 2001. *Development of a Tourist Industry in the 19th and 20th Centuries. International persPECTIves*, Neuchâtel: Editions Alphil.
Toivonen, T. 2004. "Changes in the Propensity to Take Holiday Trips Abroad in EU Countries between 1985 and 1997," *Tourism Economics* 10, no. 4.
Toulier, B. *L'influence des guides touristiques dans la représentation et la construction de l'espace balnéaire 1850–1950*. CNRS, UMR 22, on line paper.
Trigano, G. 1980. *Consommation de loisir et nouvelle convivialité*, Temps Libre.
______. 1996. "Les conditions pour un second soufflé," *Espaces*, no. 140.
Trigano, G., and S. Trigano. 1998. *La Saga du Club*, Paris: Grasset.
Tsartas, P. 1989. *Social and Economic impact of tourist development in the Cyclades region 1950-1980*, EKKE, Athens.
Urry, J. 1990. *The Tourist Gaze: Leisure and Travel in Contemporary Societies*, Sage, London.
______. 1995. *Consuming Places*, Routledge, London.
Vieira, J. M., *A Economia do Turismo*, Lisbon: Publicações Dom Quixote.
Vella, F. 1985. *Economie Poilitique du Tourisme International*, Paris: Economica.
Vogel, H. 2001. *Travel Industry Economics. A Guide for Financial Analysis*, Cambridge: Cambridge University Press.
Wahab, S., and C. Cooper. 2001. *Tourism in the Age of Globalization*, London: Routledge.
Walton, J.K. 1983. *The English Seaside Resort: A Social History 1750–1914*, Leicester: Leicester University Press.
______. 2000. *The British Seaside: Holidays and Resorts in the Twentieth Century*, Manchester: Manchester University Press.

Waxman, S. 1994. "Club Med Resorts to Tough Measures," *Washington Post*, 6 January 1994.

Whittington, R., and M. Mayer. 2000. *The European Corporation: Strategy, Structure and Social Science*, Oxford: Oxford University Press.

Williams, J.E.D. 1967. "The Role of Private Enterprise in British Air Transportation," *Journal of the Royal Aeronautical Society*, June.

Williams, M., and G. Shaw, eds. 1988. *Tourism and Economic Development, Western European Experiences*, London and New York: Belhaven Press.

Wolkowitsch, M. 2000. *La construction du réseau ferré en Provence*, Provence historique.

Wyatt, M.D.N. 1963. "British Independent Aviation–Past and Present," *Journal of Institute of Transport*, May.

Yip, G.S. 1992. *Total Global Strategy–Managing for Worldwide Competitive Advantage*, Englewood Cliffs, NJ: Prentice Hall.

Ziegfeld, S. 1994. *Noi americani non ci avevamo pensato*, in La Classe non è acqua, Aquafan.

Index